Funny Money: Stablecoins, CBDCs and the Tokenization of the Global Economy

Jonny Fry and James Tylee

Contents

Foreword

There is a particular kind of trust that develops between two people who have both learned, in their own ways, that the world was not designed with them in mind. James Tylee has been in a wheelchair since the age of ten. I am dyslexic. Neither of us has had a straightforward ride. But the most interesting work rarely comes from straightforward rides, and what James and I have built together is proof of exactly that.

James spent more than twenty years on Wall Street as a programmer, helping integrate machine-readable code into Bloomberg's platform. When he left to build Cyber.FM, now reaching 5.1 million listeners in 170 countries, he brought that same precision to conversations about the future of money. Pierre Bourque, a Canadian broadcaster, introduced us through Blockchain Radio. We recorded one podcast; it became a weekly ritual. Then Pierre died suddenly. In his memory we kept Digital Bytes alive, turning my weekly written analysis into a global conversation.

This first volume is the result. It is not a cheerleader's manifesto or a regulator's warning. It is an honest examination of why money itself is being reinvented: the creditor problem nobody talks about, the gig economy's hidden friction, the rise of stablecoins, the Terra/Luna collapse that exposed algorithmic fragility, and the central banks now racing to respond with CBDCs. We examine the collateral question, the Big Bang thesis, the Eurodollar parallel, MiCA's unintended leverage trap and the Bank of England's two-speed problem. We look at tokenized deposits as banks' countermove and the cross-border payments revolution already underway.

The analysis is independent, commercially grounded and shaped by years of conversations with the people building, regulating and challenging this new monetary architecture. If this volume succeeds, it will do so by helping readers see more clearly why 2025 marked a turning point in the evolution of money.

Jonny Fry and James Tylee

co-authors, *Funny Money: Stablecoins, CBDCs and the Tokenization of the Global Economy*

TeamBlockchain Ltd · Publisher, Digital Bytes

London, 2026

Preface

TeamBlockchain was founded on a simple observation: the most consequential changes in money were being widely misunderstood. Digital assets were either presented as inevitable salvation by those with capital at stake, or dismissed as passing speculation by institutions with incentives to delay adaptation. Neither perspective helped practitioners make decisions.

Digital Bytes was launched to provide something different: independent analysis grounded in market reality, regulatory evolution, and technological capability. Over time, that effort developed into a global community of readers including policymakers, investors, treasury professionals, and financial infrastructure builders seeking clarity rather than advocacy.

This book is a synthesis of that work. It draws on years of reporting, research and direct engagement with central banks, fintech founders, legal experts, and capital markets participants at the early stages of monetary transition. Our objective has been to explain not only what stablecoins and CBDCs are, but why they emerged, how they interact with existing financial systems, and what their adoption implies for sovereignty, liquidity, and global trade.

The shift in how money moves is not abstract. It affects real decisions made daily by migrant workers sending remittances, corporate treasurers managing working capital, and regulators balancing innovation with systemic stability. This volume therefore focuses on foundations: the evolution of digital currency models, regulatory responses, and the architecture of tokenized finance now taking shape across institutions and economies.

The analysis is ours. The lessons are shared. The errors remain our responsibility.

Acknowledgments

Jonny Fry and James Tylee would like to begin by acknowledging SFSF, known to most simply as Scotty, whose proofreading and encouragement have helped shape Digital Bytes over the past eight years.

This book draws together those weekly publications with the guest contributions and podcast conversations that have enriched the Digital Bytes community over time. We are deeply grateful to the individuals, companies, and experts who shared their time, articles, insights, and experience so generously. Their willingness to engage difficult questions openly has helped make this work more grounded, useful, and relevant.

Since its inception, Digital Bytes has aimed to track the real-world application of blockchain technology and digital assets: who is using them, how they are being deployed, why they matter, and where meaningful structural change is beginning to take hold.

By bringing together research, commentary, interviews and source-linked reporting, we have tried to create something useful to busy professionals without flattening the subject. To everyone who has read, contributed, appeared on the podcast, or supported the work, thank you.

Introduction: The Year Money Changed

There are moments when a financial transition that has been building quietly for years becomes impossible to mistake for a side story. By 2025, that moment had arrived. Stablecoins were no longer a fringe experiment, central banks were no longer observing from a distance, and tokenization had moved from white papers and pilot programs into live institutional infrastructure.

Money was becoming programmable. Settlement was moving closer to real time. Questions that once belonged to specialist corners of fintech and capital markets, about custody, collateral, sovereignty, interoperability and legal form, were becoming central questions of economic power. The pace varied by jurisdiction and institution, but the direction was unmistakable.

This volume begins with the foundations of that transition. It examines how digital currency models evolved, why stablecoins gained traction, how authorities responded, and why digital money now matters far beyond crypto markets alone. Its purpose is simple: to help readers see the structure beneath the headlines and understand why money changed this year.

How This Book Was Created

This book draws on more than three years of continuous analysis published through the Digital Bytes research series and its companion podcast. From the outset, the intention was not to produce a conventional newsletter, but to build a structured record of how blockchain technology, digital assets and programmable finance are being deployed across jurisdictions, industries and financial institutions. Each weekly edition examined practical questions: who is adopting new financial infrastructure, how it is being implemented and why regulatory responses differ. To support credibility, Digital Bytes relied on independent hyperlinks and primary sources, allowing readers to verify statistics, quotations and policy claims directly.

A defining feature of the research process has been the integration of practitioner insight. Guest contributions from commercial leaders, legal specialists and regulatory professionals have provided firsthand perspectives on market realities. These written analyses have frequently formed the basis for recorded conversations on The Digital Bytes Podcast, broadcast via Cyber.FM and distributed globally across major podcast platforms. This interplay created a layered understanding that combines analytical rigor with lived experience.

The material in this volume synthesizes that blend of written research and spoken insight. It brings together edited commentary, referenced notes and observations drawn from hundreds of hours of discussion with market participants. Throughout, the emphasis has been on producing work that is thoughtful, educational and commercially useful, while remaining deliberately free from advertising, promotion or institutional advocacy.

The aim has been clarity over noise, and analysis over enthusiasm.

Chapter 1: Why Reinvent Money?

There is a phrase that keeps coming up in conversations about the global financial system, one that sounds like a minor quibble but, on reflection, points at something fundamental. Our current payment infrastructure, Charles McManus observed on The Digital Bytes Podcast in 2025, is "electrified, not digitized." McManus is well-placed to make that distinction. He co-founded ClearBank, the first new clearing bank established in the United Kingdom in over 250 years, and is co-chair of Innovate Finance's Unicorn Fintech Council, a lobbying body that spent much of 2025 working directly with HM Treasury, the DTI and Number 10 on what would become the UK's new financial services industrial strategy. He knows the payments system from the inside. And his point is not semantic: we have built faster wires. We have not built digital money.

When you make a payment today, through your banking app, via a debit card, across a wire transfer, you are using the digital layer wrapped around an analog system. Your money sits in a commercial bank. The moment you deposit it, you become a creditor to that institution. The bank can lend it out, move it around, leverage it up. What you hold on your phone is not money in any native digital sense. It is a claim on a bank's promise, processed through rails designed for a world of paper ledgers, clearing houses and correspondent relationships that can span multiple time zones and institutions before your payment arrives.

McKinsey captures the scale of the inefficiency with precision: global cash usage now stands at 80% of its 2019 levels and continues declining at 4% a year. The $26 trillion in payments still made in physical cash represents a "massive opportunity for digitization", but cash is not the only problem. The global payments industry processed 3.4 trillion transactions totaling $1.8 quadrillion in 2023, generating $2.4 trillion in revenue. That revenue is largely a measure of friction: every correspondent bank that touches a cross-border transfer extracting its share. McKinsey projects that pool will grow to $3.1 trillion by 2028. A meaningful fraction of it represents costs that digital money could eliminate.

The Bank for International Settlements has modeled what eliminating some of that friction would mean at the macro level. In an analysis that McManus cites readily, the BIS estimated that a 10% adoption of digital money within an economy over a two-year period could produce a 1% increase in GDP. "Phenomenal," McManus called it, without irony, given the anemic growth rates currently haunting the G7. "If we could save just a percentage of the frictional cost of moving money around the world: how that could be used in terms of GDP growth." The money that currently hemorrhages through correspondent banking fees, delayed settlement windows and foreign exchange spreads is money that could be doing something productive instead.

The creditor problem nobody talks about

This is a thread we return to regularly on the podcast, but the retail dimension bears repeating. The experience of the ordinary consumer illustrates it clearly: you make a payment of $300 to your credit card, it leaves your current account immediately and visibly, but it does not credit your card for three to five business days. The money has moved, but the ledgers disagree. Add a public holiday and you are into the following week. "I'm not going to know it's a smart contract or a blockchain," James noted when the topic came up, "but I do know that I want my money to settle immediately. Fed Now is not doing it."

That is the consumer side of a systemic problem. At the wholesale level, the stakes are proportionally larger. Jonny put it plainly on air: "If you want to spend more than a million pounds as a business today, a Friday before a public holiday, the chances are they're not getting paid till Wednesday, possibly Thursday. Whereas digitally, they could get paid today." Charles McManus, who spent his career in institutional banking before founding ClearBank, framed the institutional version: "The banks have been allowed to get away with such poor service to SMEs. The world lives in instantaneous: you do your search engine and it comes back immediately. Why is it when you make a payment that it doesn't settle immediately?" The answer is not technical. The infrastructure for instant settlement exists. The answer is inertia, and the profitable extraction model that depends on it.

The risk architecture underneath this system runs deeper still. When your deposits sit in a commercial bank, you are an unsecured creditor to that institution. Retail depositors in most jurisdictions are protected up to a ceiling: £85,000 in the UK, €100,000 in the EU. Above that threshold, there is no protection. Organizations with material working capital held at a bank that fails lose it, as the SVB depositors discovered in March 2023, until an emergency intervention restored confidence. Digital money backed by assets held at a central bank, or by short-term government securities in bankruptcy-remote custody, changes that risk profile entirely. ClearBank built its model around exactly this: a narrow bank that holds all deposits at the Bank of England rather than lending them out. It is not a coincidence that the same logic underpins the best-designed stablecoin reserve models.

The moment this risk became concrete for central banks came not from a bank failure but from a technology company. In 2019, Facebook announced Diem, then called Libra, a digital currency that would serve its 2 billion users and enable direct transfers of value between them. The reaction from central banks and regulators was, as McManus put it, "a massive panic attack." An understandable one. If the underlying movement of funds began to occur outside the central banking system, on a proprietary ledger controlled by a private company, the traditional levers of fiscal and monetary policy, interest rates, reserve requirements, money supply management, would apply to a shrinking portion of the economy. Diem never launched. But the panic it triggered did more to accelerate central bank research into digital currencies than any academic paper or policy consultation. The question it posed has not gone away: if you cannot stop private digital money, you had better design public digital money that people actually want to use.

The gig economy is already feeling it

The payments system fails most visibly at the margins of the formal economy, where the timing and cost of settlement have the most direct impact on people's financial lives day to day. The gig economy is where this shows most clearly.

Platforms like Fiverr and Upwork have enabled millions of workers globally to earn through short-term, remotely-delivered contracts. These workers are paid across borders, across currencies and across time zones: frequently by clients who are entirely indifferent to the settlement mechanics, but whose payment timing determines whether the worker can cover rent. Remittance flows from migrant workers showed the same pattern at scale: the United Nations estimated the average cost of sending $200 internationally at around 6.25%. On a $200 remittance, that is $12.50 extracted by correspondent banking infrastructure before a worker's family sees the money, and it routinely takes three to five days to arrive. A digital payment mechanism could bring that cost to 1% or below and settle in minutes.

Globally, approximately 35 million people now describe themselves as gig workers or digital nomads, a figure growing faster than most governments can service through conventional banking channels. The most useful example here is not theoretical: the research contributors for this book, spread across Latin America, Asia and Africa, are paid using stablecoins. “It’s very quick, very cheap, very transparent,” Jonny noted, “and that’s how they like being paid.” No correspondent bank. No 3–5 business day delay. No 6% fee deducted before the money reaches the person who earned it. This is not a future state. It is how part of the knowledge economy already works today.

There is a useful historical parallel. Visa was originally set up and owned by the banks themselves, with a single stated aim: to reduce the use of cash, which was expensive to handle and created risk for its carriers. Its playbook was not technological evangelism but consumer normalization: make cards feel safer and more convenient than notes until the behavior shifted. “I think we’re going to see a very similar thing when it comes to digital money,” Jonny observed. “You’re not going to necessarily be told this is a smart contract or a blockchain or a whatever. You’re just going to be given the option: do you want to use this version, or do you want to use that version?” The infrastructure already exists. The question is whether the regulatory frameworks arrive in time for the institutions that want to roll it out.

The Bank of England's own modeling acknowledges this potential. CBDCs, central bank digital currencies, were initially conceived in part as a mechanism to enable financial inclusion, delivering fast and cheap payments to those currently underserved by the formal banking system. Sarah Breeden, Deputy Governor for Financial Stability, has pointed to the $290 trillion in cross-border payment flows expected by 2030 as the scale of the prize. But as McManus observed, the shift is moving faster than most central bank timelines anticipated: driven not by governments but by the private sector, and specifically by stablecoins.

Electrified or digitized: it matters which

The distinction McManus draws, electrified versus digitized, is worth unpacking carefully, because it reveals exactly what the stablecoin movement is trying to accomplish.

An electrified payment is a traditional instrument transmitted electronically. A card payment, a wire transfer, an ACH batch: these route instructions through intermediaries, often netting and reconciling at day's end, with actual settlement occurring hours or days later. The instruction is digital. The money is not.

A digitized payment involves money that is itself a digital instrument: native to a ledger, programmable, transferable without an intermediary, settling in real time. Tokenized deposits, stablecoins and CBDCs are digital money in this sense. They do not just carry instructions about money. They are the money.

To understand why this distinction matters, it helps to take a short detour through monetary history. For much of human economic life, commerce operated through barter: wheat for fish, labor for goods, physical assets for services. The Lydian kings introduced coined money around 600 BC as a standardizing mechanism, reducing the inefficiency of direct exchange. For more than two thousand years, coins remained the dominant form of money because they were portable, tradeable, and verifiable. Then, in the 11th century, China introduced paper money, solving the portability and weight problem without sacrificing liquidity. By the 1860s, governments were issuing paper currencies at scale. By the 1950s, fractional reserve banking had turned money itself into a claim on future assets rather than a simple store of value. Digital money does not break that arc so much as extend it. It returns to a version of the earliest principle: direct transfer of value with far less intermediation. As we noted on The Digital Bytes Podcast, "In an interesting historical sense, we're potentially going to see digital money do a full cycle: going back from barter through all those other iterations and back to swapping real value rather than money being based on debt." The stablecoin, the CBDC, and the tokenized security are the 21st-century equivalents of the Florentine florin or the Dutch guilder: instruments designed to be portable, verifiable, and immediately transferable.

The practical consequence is programmability. Smart contracts can release payment automatically on delivery of a good, on the filing of a trade document, on the completion of a milestone in a complex project. The coupons on a tokenized gilt can be distributed algorithmically to every bondholder the moment they fall due. The payroll of a gig economy platform can settle to hundreds of workers in different currencies simultaneously, at the close of each completed task rather than at the end of a calendar month. Larry Fink, CEO of BlackRock, framed this vision at the institutional end: the future lies in the tokenization of every financial asset, with Bitcoin ETFs, then the most visible blockchain use case, merely the "first step in the technological revolution of finance."

None of this requires the elimination of cash or the abolition of commercial banks. McManus was careful to say so, and Jonny echoed it: "We're not saying get rid of cash, get rid of physical money, don't use the banking system. We're simply saying that in certain circumstances, digital money is just faster and cheaper. So why wouldn't you use it?" The answer, in a rational market, is that you would. The obstacle has never been the technology. As McManus summarized the regulatory landscape in 2025: "Central banks, regulators and policymakers, those that are forward-thinking and those that are very risk-averse, will get left behind in this space."

That shift is already well underway in the parts of the world that are not waiting for G7 regulators to catch up. At a conference in 2025 attended by 36 central bankers from across the global south, the entire agenda had shifted. The question was no longer whether to issue central bank digital currencies. It was how to respond to digital money that was already being adopted: billions of dollars a day moving through stablecoin rails, particularly in economies outside the G7. "They've got to go with it," Jonny noted, "otherwise they really will lose control." The regulatory question, in other words, is not whether to permit digital money. It is whether to shape it, or be overtaken by it.

The geopolitical dimension runs deeper still. The BRICS nations, Brazil, Russia, India, China and South Africa, have begun exploring alternative monetary arrangements, a response both to sanctions and to the structural asymmetry of a global financial system dominated by the US dollar and the institutions that operate it. The dollar's position as the world's reserve currency has held since the Bretton Woods era, a dominance interrupted only briefly by sterling in the 19th century and before that by the Dutch guilder, the French livre, and the Florentine florin dating back to 1250. But that dominance rests on confidence, and confidence is eroding. As we discussed on the podcast, "if Brazil, Russia, India, China, and South Africa say we're going to create our own BRICS unit, and we're all going to put reserves into a pot, we can trade between ourselves without needing to buy dollars. That means the use of dollars becomes lower and lower." A reserve currency is not a permanent fixture. It is a market consensus that can shift. The moment a significantly large bloc of the global economy stops denominating trade in dollars, the mathematics of US fiscal dynamics become sharply harder. That moment, while not imminent, is now within the range of plausible scenarios. And when it arrives, the form that replaces the dollar will almost certainly be digital: because any system attempting to manage trillions in daily cross-border settlement without digital infrastructure will be stillborn before it launches.

This book is not asking whether money will become digital. That is already happening, visible in trillions of dollars of stablecoin activity, billions in tokenized money-market funds, and the White House executive order of January 2025 explicitly directing the United States government to promote lawful dollar-backed stablecoins worldwide. The real questions are whose digital money will dominate, who will write the rules, what assets will stand behind it, and what all of that will mean for the billion-plus people who still lack access to formal financial services.

The Rails That Time Forgot

Lewis McLellan, a researcher at the Digital Monetary Institute who spent 2024 working with banks and regulators on public blockchain integration, made a point on The Digital Bytes Podcast about why the incumbent financial architecture had been so slow to adapt. The Society for Worldwide Interbank Financial Telecommunication, SWIFT, was established in 1973. Its messaging standards are essentially unchanged from those designed for a world of paper confirmations, settlement windows that closed on Friday and reopened on Monday, and trust derived from the restricted membership of institutions that could afford to participate. The infrastructure, McLellan observed, had not been built for a world in which assets could be moved, verified, and settled in seconds on a network accessible to any participant with a digital wallet.

The structural obstacle was regulatory as well as architectural. The Basel Committee on Banking Supervision had stipulated that banks holding any asset on a public blockchain were required to maintain 1,250% capital against it, a requirement so severe that it made institutional participation in public blockchain infrastructure economically impossible. The rule drew no distinction between a Bitcoin held speculatively and a tokenized government bond issued on a public network and fully verified at the token level; both attracted the same draconian capital treatment. The market, McLellan noted, had been unable to determine which blockchain infrastructure was appropriate for which purpose because the regulator had placed its thumb decisively on one side of the scale.

By late 2024, the Basel Committee had acknowledged that the rules needed to be redrafted. The Office of the Comptroller of the Currency in the United States had issued guidance permitting national banks to custody digital assets and participate in stablecoin issuance on public blockchain infrastructure without requiring prior regulatory approval for individual activities. McLellan observed that the political change following the November 2024 US election had been the single most significant accelerant. "After Trump's victory," he said, "public blockchain became a much more palatable thing, and a lot more banks are working on it now than was the case even quite a short time ago." The rails that time had left largely unchanged, the messaging standards, the settlement windows, and the correspondent relationships, were, for the first time in half a century, being rebuilt rather than merely patched.

Those questions lead directly into the next chapter, with the instrument that did more than anything else to make digital money real: the stablecoin.

Chapter 2: The Rise of Stablecoins

For most of its first decade, blockchain technology was a solution looking for a problem. The ICO boom of 2017 and 2018 promised to tokenize everything, private equity, real estate, art, commodities, and largely failed, not because the technology was unworkable but because a critical piece was missing. You could tokenize the asset easily enough. But when the time came to settle, to pay for it, to move value across the ledger, you were back to writing a check. The payment leg was still analog. Stablecoins changed that. And in so doing, they became the first genuinely transformative use case that blockchain had produced in fifteen years of trying.

Bridge Tilley, Head of Market Development at Archax, the UK's first FCA-regulated digital broker, exchange and custodian, is direct about it: "The largest part of tokenization today is actually the tokenization of cash in the form of stablecoins. Looking back, it's obvious that a digital payment function would be the killer app for the tech, but that wasn't clear at the time because the building blocks simply weren't in place." Back in the ICO era, crypto-to-crypto volatility made any stablecoin equivalent unreliable. USDT existed but hadn't achieved critical mass. Fiat on-ramps were clunky, custodians were scarce and institutional buyers weren't there. The ecosystem needed to mature around the payment rail before that rail could matter. By 2023 it had. By 2025 it was irreversible.

What stablecoins actually are

The word "stablecoin" covers a broader taxonomy than most people realize, and understanding the differences matters enormously when assessing stability, risk and regulatory posture.

The dominant category is fiat-backed: digital tokens pegged one-to-one to a traditional currency, with the backing held as cash, short-term government securities or other liquid instruments in regulated financial institutions. Tether's USDT is the largest, sitting at around $140 billion in circulation. Circle's USDC, at over $40 billion, is its closest rival, and the one that institutional counterparties generally prefer, given its Deloitte-audited reserves and its early compliance with the EU's MiCA regulations, including an e-money license in France. Together, USDT and USDC command roughly 73% of the entire stablecoin market.

The second category is crypto-backed: decentralized stablecoins such as MakerDAO's DAI that use volatile cryptocurrencies as collateral, typically at an over-collateralization ratio designed to absorb price swings. They offer the philosophical elegance of having no centralized issuer and no traditional reserve manager. They also carry a structural vulnerability: if the collateral falls sharply enough in a single session, the peg can fail under pressure. That weakness proved fatal to the algorithmic variant, which attempts to maintain its peg through programmatic supply adjustments rather than any backing at all. The clearest lesson of the 2022 Terra/Luna implosion, covered in the next chapter, is that algorithmic stability without collateral is not stability at all.

Then there are commodity-backed stablecoins, tokens pegged to physical gold, such as Paxos Gold (PAXG) and Tether Gold (XAUT), and the newer category of yield-bearing stablecoins, effectively tokenized money-market funds. Ondo's USDY and Hashnote's USYC (the latter recently acquired by Circle) function less as transactional rails and more as on-chain treasury instruments. They hold US Treasuries, pass yield to holders and can be pledged as collateral in digital asset markets. BlackRock's BUIDL fund, a tokenized money-market fund broadly equivalent, passed $1 billion in assets in under a year from launch. As Bridge Tilley observed, the institutional appetite for these instruments isn't purely about yield: "Being able to use that fund as collateral is absolutely key. You see issuers of stablecoins come into the Archax platform not only to park reserves in treasuries but to place those reserves into money-market funds, earn yield, and then benefit from the improved collateral mobility."

The result is a rapidly differentiating market where the word "stablecoin" encompasses everything from Tether's opaque mountain of reserves to a fully-audited, MiCA-compliant euro token to a tokenized slice of a money-market fund. These are not variations on a theme; they are fundamentally different instruments with different risk profiles, regulatory treatments and use cases.

The numbers that explain the urgency

By early 2025, the aggregate stablecoin market capitalization exceeded $220 billion, a figure that, if it belonged to a bank's deposit book, would rank among the largest in the world. McKinsey's analysis of the global payments market provides context for why that number is significant rather than merely large: in 2023 alone, the global payments industry processed 3.4 trillion transactions representing $1.8 quadrillion in value, generating $2.4 trillion in revenue. That pool is projected to reach $3.1 trillion by 2028: roughly 35% of total banking revenue globally. Stablecoins are positioning themselves to capture a share of that.

Visa's on-chain analytics captured $5.4 trillion in stablecoin transaction volume in 2024, a 33% increase on the prior year. Standard Chartered and Zodia Markets, in a joint analysis, estimated that stablecoins could ultimately represent up to 10% of US M2 and FX transactions globally: up from a current base of roughly 1%. Most of that growth, in their assessment, would be driven by regulatory clarity in the United States.

The cross-border payments opportunity is vast, and stablecoins only need to capture a small fraction of it to reshape the competitive dynamics of international finance. The largest near-term applications are already visible: remittances to regions where correspondent banking is slow and expensive; payroll for remote workers in emerging markets; collateral in institutional DeFi; and settlement for tokenized securities, the very gap that Archax was built to fill.

The collateral question

Whether a stablecoin's backing is trustworthy enough to hold, trade and rely on in a moment of market stress is not a technicality. It is, as we have consistently argued on the podcast, "the cornerstone of their stability and credibility."

Tether's history illustrates both the scale of the opportunity and the cost of opacity. As of mid-2024, USDT held approximately \$90 billion in US Treasuries, \$4.7 billion in Bitcoin and \$3.8 billion in gold. The company generated \$5.2 billion in profit in the first half of 2024 alone: extraordinary economics for a firm that employs roughly 125 people. Yet its past caught up with it: in 2021 Tether paid \$18.5 million to the New York Attorney General following findings that it had made misleading representations about its dollar reserves. It has since moved to quarterly attestations by BDO Italia rather than full audits by a Big Four firm, a disclosure standard the market continues to view with a measure of skepticism.

USDC has taken a deliberately different path. Circle's decision to submit to full Deloitte audits, comply with MiCA ahead of its 2024 deadline and maintain a reserve structure that meets the Bank of

England's criteria for oversight aligns it more naturally with the expectations of institutional counterparties. PayPal, which launched its own stablecoin PYUSD in August 2023 via Paxos and grew it to over $1 billion in assets within eighteen months, similarly uses independent attestation by WithumSmith+Brown.

The Bank of England and the Bank for International Settlements have formalized this concern through Project Pyxtrial: named deliberately after the Trial of the Pyx, the ceremony dating to 1282 in which the Royal Mint's coins were tested for weight, composition and legal standard by independent assay. Pyxtrial applies the same logic to stablecoins: advanced data tools designed to confirm that the assets backing each token consistently exceed its liabilities. The historical parallel is apt. Trust in money has always required demonstration, not declaration. As Andrew Bailey, the Governor of the Bank of England, has emphasized, the way money is used is evolving rapidly and policymakers must remain humble: predictions made today may be outdated tomorrow. But two criteria must hold regardless: the singleness of money, meaning different forms remain exchangeable at par; and the finality of settlement, meaning a payment, once made, cannot be unwound. Any stablecoin that cannot sustain both is not, in the Bank's assessment, adequate for widespread use in payments.

The Big Bang thesis

In mid-2025, David Parsons, an entrepreneur working on a property-backed stablecoin called USDP, came on The Digital Bytes Podcast to sketch a more sweeping thesis about where this was heading, and we tested the argument hard.

Parsons's case began with the GENIUS Act, the US legislation that passed the Senate in 2025 and established the first federal framework for stablecoin issuance. The historical precedent it invokes is closer than it might appear. Abraham Lincoln signed the National Banking Act into law in 1863–64, authorizing thousands of institutions, banks, regional lenders and eventually a stagecoach company called Wells Fargo, to issue their own dollar-denominated banknotes, each backed by US Treasury bonds held in federal custody. At the system's peak, over eight thousand distinct dollar notes were in circulation, each redeemable at par. The GENIUS Act completes the same architecture, but opens the franchise globally. In the 1860s, only US banks could issue the dollar. Under the new framework, any institution anywhere that holds eligible US Treasury securities may do so. Scott Bessent, the US Treasury Secretary, estimated that as much as $3 trillion could ultimately flow into stablecoin reserves, buying American short-term government debt in the process, a financing arrangement that suits an administration carrying a deficit above 6% of GDP with few palatable options for reducing it. "What's happening in the States," Parsons explained, "is that the

Trump administration has identified this as one of their tools to expand dollar dominance globally, and this is now forcing all of the legacy banking infrastructure to deploy their own stablecoins." The top-five US banks, in his reading, are not choosing to enter this market so much as being compelled to: if stablecoin-settled transactions become the norm for cross-border commerce, any institution that cannot offer them is operating without a competitive payments product.

The parallels Parsons drew, with the petrodollar of the 1970s, with the eurodollar market that allowed offshore dollar balances to circulate independently of the Federal Reserve, were ones we had been tracking with intent. "Stablecoins are going to give the US dollar another sort of lifespan," Jonny observed during their exchange. "In countries with high inflation, having access to US dollars is quite an attractive proposition. Now you can have that digitally, instantly, at low cost, without a bank." For the Venezuelan holding bolivars worth 40% less than 12 months ago, the arrival of USDC on a smartphone is not a financial technology story. It is an escape hatch. A central banker from a major Latin American economy, speaking at a conference we attended, said it plainly: "Have you ever had 100% inflation? I'm talking about per month."

The mechanics Parsons described for USDP, a stablecoin backed not by Treasuries but by tokenized UK residential property, redeemable against Land Registry title, were immediately legible to anyone with hands-on experience of the same structure. "If I wanted to get out of a property, I would just sell the tokens that equal the weight of the amount of the title deed I own in the DAO." What USDP proposed was to turn that familiar structure into a monetary instrument: not an IOU from the federal government, but an asset backed by something physical, local-law-governed and independently verifiable. Given that UK residential property represents roughly £7 trillion in unencumbered real estate, the theoretical ceiling for such an instrument is not trivial. Issuing USDP tokens only where Land Registry title exists means a stablecoin that is always fully covered by a real asset, in a property system backed by nearly a thousand years of English common law.

The deeper point in Parsons's Big Bang analogy was not just scale but irreversibility. The stablecoin ecosystem, in his reading, is at the initial point of cosmic inflation: before anyone fully understands how large it will become or how permanently it will reshape the territory it expands into. The question for central banks and finance ministries is whether monetary policy still works in a world where a significant proportion of transactions settle in a programmable, dollar-denominated token that requires no bank account, no SWIFT correspondent and no central bank reserve. If more transactions happen in stablecoins, central banks lose the ability to steer economies through interest rates. Tax collection falters. Capital controls erode. The policymaking toolkit begins to rust. Governments face a stark choice: either embrace the stablecoin ecosystem and regulate it into a public utility, or risk monetary disintermediation as citizens opt out.

The banking sector wakes up

What makes this transition urgent for traditional banks is an economic reality that arrived with rising interest rates. For a decade, near-zero central bank rates meant that a bank's profit margin on deposits was razor-thin. Holding deposits was a cost, not a revenue stream. Stablecoins did not offer a compelling alternative because they paid no yield. That changed as soon as inflation returned and central banks began raising rates.

In early 2022, the largest bank in Australia, ANZ, announced that it would become the first bank to mint its own CBDC-grade stablecoin, backed 100% by Australian dollars. The announcement was notable not for its technological sophistication but for what it signaled about banking economics. "Banks are realizing," we noted on air, "that they need an alternative to just having fiat because they can then start using those things, smart contracts, to do everything they really want." As interest rates returned to the 3–5% range, well above the near-zero norm of the previous decade, the economics of stablecoin issuance became materially attractive. A bank issuing a stablecoin backed 100% by reserves earning 3–4% in short-term government securities could credibly offer 2–3% to stablecoin holders and retain the spread as profit. More importantly, that structure actually increased safety: unlike a traditional bank deposit, where the bank lends out those funds and builds leverage, the stablecoin holder had direct claims on the underlying securities. "A stablecoin that is 100% backed by cash is safer than a bank deposit because it's backed by actual assets, not backed by a promise to pay by a commercial bank," Jonny observed. "And if the bank goes bust, unlike a normal deposit, the cash is at risk." That safety advantage, combined with yield, transformed the stablecoin from a fringe experiment into something mainstream banks needed to offer or be left behind.

The infrastructure layer

The Big Bang thesis is dramatic, but it rests on a set of more prosaic questions about market infrastructure: settlement, custody, compliance and the unglamorous plumbing that makes financial systems trustworthy. This is where Archax's work becomes directly relevant.

Bridge Tilley's firm operates as custodian, broker, exchange and, through its Montes subsidiary, regulated out of Luxembourg, the first global digital central securities depository. A CSD is a deliberately unsexy concept: a centralized registry that gives legal certainty to ownership transfer. But it matters because many jurisdictions do not yet recognize on-chain transfer as legally sufficient for securities settlement. Even where the technology is adequate, the law hasn't caught up. Montes bridges that gap and its role in the UK's Digital Securities Sandbox is helping to establish what natively-digital settlement looks like under a common-law framework. Broadridge is already processing $1.5 trillion in tokenized repo transactions per month, exploring integration of USDC and tokenized money-market fund units as the cash leg. This is the stablecoin economy becoming invisible: embedded in institutional back-offices, processing transactions that never appear in press releases. That invisibility is, arguably, the mark of genuine arrival.

One of the least-discussed obstacles to mass institutional adoption has received almost no public policy attention: accounting treatment. Tony McLaughlin, a payments strategist and long-time Digital Bytes contributor who moved into stablecoin settlement infrastructure after the November 2024 US election, identified it with clinical precision. Under IAS 32 international accounting standards, stablecoins are classified as financial instruments, not cash equivalents. Every corporate treasury policy on the planet specifies that short-term operational liquidity must be held in cash and cash equivalents. A corporate treasurer who receives a stablecoin payment is holding, in McLaughlin's formulation, "a hot potato": counterparty risk against the issuer, counterparty risk against the off-ramp, and the wrong accounting classification. Until stablecoins achieve cash-equivalent status in the accounting standards that govern every major corporation's treasury, every large institution has a structural incentive to convert out as fast as possible. That reclassification, McLaughlin argued on Digital

Bytes, is "the unlock that turns stablecoins from a payments curiosity into the dominant form of payment on the planet." He then staked his career on it: he left a highly compensated role to prove it.

The UK's pace remains a persistent frustration. As we have put it more than once: "We've put the cart before the horse. We have a digital securities sandbox encouraging tokenization of debt, equities, commodities and real estate, but the sandbox does not yet include the payment leg: stablecoins. If you've got digital assets, you've got to be able to buy and sell them digitally." The US GENIUS Act, the EU's MiCA framework and Asia's advancing regulatory structures are creating competitive pressure that the Bank of England, for all its methodical consultation, will struggle to absorb indefinitely. HM Treasury disbanded its CBDC policy team in early 2025, even as the Chancellor was committing to a digital gilt. The mixed signals are real, and the ground is moving.

The asset on the public chain

One of the significant technical discoveries of the early 2020s, Lewis McLellan of the Digital Monetary Institute told The Digital Bytes Podcast, was that it was possible to issue regulated financial instruments on public, permissionless blockchain infrastructure without abandoning the compliance controls that regulators required. The earlier assumption had been categorical: public blockchains were accessible to anyone, and regulated instruments could not be held by just anyone.

The conclusion drawn was that regulated instruments must therefore require permissioned, private chains. The discovery that invalidated this assumption was simpler than expected. The permissioning did not need to be applied at the protocol level. It could be applied at the level of the token itself.

A tokenized stablecoin, under the model that the Office of the Comptroller of the Currency guidance was beginning to enable, could sit on a public and permissionless blockchain while carrying embedded rules about who could hold it: rules that required Know Your Customer verification to be completed before any transfer was accepted, that restricted holdings to residents of non-sanctioned jurisdictions, and that permitted immobilization or clawback in the event of a court order. "You're not banning the infrastructure," McLellan said. "What you're doing is putting control mechanisms on the actual products that are running through and using the blockchain." A tokenized bond operating under these constraints moved around the public Ethereum network as freely as any other token; what it could not do was move into a wallet whose holder had not been verified.

The practical implication for stablecoins was direct. A dollar-backed stablecoin issued by a licensed trust bank under the GENIUS Act framework, with KYC embedded at the token level, monthly reserve disclosures published to a public ledger, and seize-and-freeze capabilities meeting OFAC requirements, was qualitatively different from the unaudited dollar-denominated tokens that had precipitated the crises of 2022. The compliance layer was being built into the instrument rather than applied retrospectively by the issuer. Whether that was sufficient to prevent the next crisis depended on whether the compliance layer was designed, audited, and maintained to the standard that regulators and institutional counterparties were beginning to demand.

The stablecoin market that exists today was not inevitable. It emerged from a technology looking for a use case, a regulatory vacuum waiting to be filled, and a series of crises that clarified what was real and what was not. What survived was a durable insight: the world needs digital money that is programmable, portable, accessible without a bank account and stable enough for actual transactions. For now, fiat-backed stablecoins meet that test best.

The next questions, who issues them, who backs them, who regulates them, and who gains power when code moves faster than law, run through the rest of this book. Right now the strongest early answer runs through the United States Treasury, by proxy, via the sovereign debt sitting behind USDT and USDC. As the GENIUS Act industrializes stablecoin issuance and major banks launch dollar tokens, the reach of the American monetary system is set to expand.

Who controls the code controls the value. Right now, that is predominantly Washington, whether Washington has fully understood that yet or not.

Chapter 3: The Terra/Luna Collapse

On the evening of 7 May 2022, a single large holder of TerraUSD, the algorithmic stablecoin that had grown to an $18 billion market capitalization on the promise that it had solved the fundamental problem of digital money, began to sell aggressively. By morning, the peg had slipped. By the following Monday, it had broken. Within two weeks, TerraUSD was worth fractions of a cent. Its sister token LUNA, which had traded at over $80 in April, was essentially worthless. Together, in one of the fastest and most complete destructions of financial value in modern financial history, the Terra ecosystem erased approximately $60 billion. No algorithm saved it. No reserve was there to redeem. The code, which its creator Do Kwon had publicly declared impervious to failure, had failed completely.

What happened in those two weeks matters not just as a story of spectacular loss, but as the clearest demonstration of a single proposition: that trust in code is not a substitute for trust in assets. And that when you build a financial instrument on an elegant theory rather than a real reserve, you are not reducing risk. You are hiding it.

The twenty percent promise

To understand why Terra collapsed, you first need to understand why it grew. TerraUSD was an *algorithmic* stablecoin: meaning it maintained its dollar peg not by holding actual dollars in reserve, but through a software mechanism linking it to a second token, LUNA. The theory was ingenious in its simplicity: if UST traded above a dollar, holders could burn one dollar's worth of LUNA to mint one UST, pocketing the arbitrage and expanding supply. If UST fell below a dollar, they could burn one UST to receive one dollar's worth of LUNA, reducing supply and restoring the peg. The mechanism was self-regulating. It required no custodian, no central bank, no counterparty. It was governed entirely by code and market incentives.

What it required was that people continued to want UST. And for a remarkable period, they did, in part because of Anchor Protocol, a lending platform built on Terra that offered depositors a yield of 20% per annum on UST holdings. In a world of near-zero interest rates, that proposition was striking. Retail investors in the United States, Europe and Asia poured money in. Institutional funds followed. At its peak, Anchor held over $17 billion in deposits. The 20% yield was not organic; it was substantially subsidized by the Luna Foundation Guard, a reserve fund established by Terraform Labs to prop up demand. But the marketing rarely foregrounded that detail. What the marketing said was: 20%, stable, no custodian, no bank. For anyone living in a high-inflation economy, the kind of country where, as a Latin American central banker put it at one Digital Bytes event, monthly inflation could reach 100%, the appeal was not irrational. It was desperate.

The death spiral

The mechanism that was supposed to guarantee stability became, under stress, the instrument of destruction.

The initiating event is still debated. What is clear is that in the first days of May 2022, large volumes of UST were sold, and the peg slipped below a dollar. Under normal conditions, arbitrageurs would step in: burn UST, mint LUNA, restore equilibrium. But the selling pressure was too large, and too fast, and it exposed a flaw that had always been present in the design. As UST lost confidence and holders rushed to exit, the arbitrage mechanism required minting ever-larger quantities of LUNA to absorb the redemptions. More LUNA in circulation meant LUNA's price fell. A falling LUNA price meant each new UST redemption required even more LUNA to be minted. The system fed on itself.

We had written about this category of risk directly: "Algorithmic stablecoins have demonstrated a susceptibility to significant de-pegging events," we noted in our analysis, citing the systemic consequences that follow when the incentive mechanisms on which they depend are "gamed or may fail under extreme market conditions, particularly when driven by speculation rather than genuine utility." The Terra collapse was not a black swan in the sense of being unforeseeable. It was a black swan in the sense that the founders had chosen to act as though it were unforeseeable. Do Kwon, whose public posture throughout the growth period had been one of near-messianic confidence, had dismissed prior warnings. "I don't debate the poor," he said on Twitter to critics raising questions about structural vulnerabilities. Within weeks of the collapse, he was in hiding from Interpol.

By 13 May, LUNA had gone from $80 to less than one cent. The Terra blockchain was halted twice in an attempt to stop the hemorrhage. It made no difference. The Luna Foundation Guard, which had accumulated $3.5 billion in Bitcoin as a reserve backstop, spent almost all of it in failed attempts to defend the peg, and failed anyway. The Bitcoin reserve, which had been presented as an additional layer of security, turned out to be too small, too slow and too correlated with the general crypto market sell-off to provide meaningful protection.

The contagion

Sixty billion dollars of paper wealth disappearing would be serious enough. What made Terra's collapse a systemic event was what it triggered downstream.

Three Arrows Capital (3AC) was one of the most prominent crypto hedge funds in the world, with over $18 billion under management at its peak. It had material exposure to LUNA, to UST, and to funds that held both. As the Terra ecosystem imploded, 3AC's positions collapsed simultaneously. The fund could not meet margin calls across multiple counterparties. By June 2022 it had defaulted on loans from nearly every major crypto lender, including Voyager Digital, BlockFi and Genesis. Within weeks, all three had suspended withdrawals or filed for bankruptcy. Celsius Network, a lending platform with over $12 billion in client assets, froze withdrawals on 12 June, citing "extreme market conditions," before its own insolvency became clear. The creditors were not abstractions. They were individuals who had been told their money was earning yield, and who discovered it was gone.

The human record of those weeks is preserved in the forums and community boards where retail investors had gathered to celebrate the 20% returns they had been certain were real. A retired teacher in South Korea who had moved the equivalent of her pension savings into Anchor Protocol to protect them from local inflation. A freelance developer in the United States who had converted his emergency fund on the advice of a YouTube channel with 200,000 subscribers. A family in Turkey whose UST holdings had represented the closest thing to dollar stability they could access without a bank account. None of them had understood the mechanism. Most of them had not needed to, because the product had been sold to them as a savings account, not a speculative instrument. When Celsius froze withdrawals on 12 June, its support lines stopped responding within hours. Hundreds of thousands of people learned simultaneously that the money they thought was parked safely was locked inside a system that was failing, and that there was no regulator, no compensation scheme, and no recourse of any kind.

This is exactly what earlier critics of algorithmic stablecoins had warned: that the interconnectedness of the cryptocurrency ecosystem meant that the failure of a significant algorithmic stablecoin could have cascading effects, potentially destabilizing other protocols and assets. The systemic risk was not theoretical. May and June 2022 were the proof.

What the code gets wrong about trust

The Terra/Luna collapse was, at its root, a failure of a particular idea: that you could replace institutional trust with mathematical trust, and that formalizing guarantees in code was categorically superior to formalizing them in law, regulation or collateral.

What cuts to the heart of the matter is this: algorithmic stablecoins fundamentally shift the basis of trust from institutions or tangible assets to the perceived reliability and immutability of code. The proponents of this shift argued that code was superior, it could not be corrupted, could not be overridden by a bad actor, was auditable by anyone. What this argument missed was that code is written by humans, that humans have incentives, that complex systems behave unexpectedly under extreme conditions, and that "auditable by anyone" is meaningless when the people whose money is at stake cannot read the code. Transparency that only experts can interpret is not transparency in any meaningful sense. It is an alibi.

There is also the governance problem. When TerraUSD began to fail, there was no mechanism that could intervene with sufficient speed. Decentralized governance, which distributes decision-making across token holders, is incompatible with crisis management, which requires rapid unilateral action. The very features that made Terra attractive, no central authority, no custodian, no intermediary, made it impossible to arrest the collapse. It had no Andrew Bailey to call a press conference. It had no Federal Reserve to backstop the system. It had only the code. And the code, given the conditions it was operating in, destroyed everything it was supposed to protect.

What no safety net looks like

Reed Winthrop, founder of the Winthrop Law Group, spent the months following the 2022 collapses working with clients who had confronted a version of loss that the legal system had no adequate framework to address. Unlike a failed bank, there was no deposit protection scheme standing behind a failed crypto lender. Unlike a stolen security, there was no transfer agent who could declare the theft and reissue. Unlike a fraudulent investment, there was no Financial Services Compensation Scheme or Federal Deposit Insurance Corporation with the mandate and resources to compensate ordinary holders.

3AC's exposure to LUNA meant that when the algorithmic mechanism failed, it triggered cascading defaults across every institution that had extended credit to 3AC. Those institutions, Voyager Digital, BlockFi, Genesis, then became unable to meet their own margin calls, which froze the customer deposits they held. A single flaw in one system had propagated through the entire interconnected network, touching retail savers whose only connection to Terra was that their lending platform happened to have counterparty exposure to a fund exposed to LUNA. Speaking on The Digital Bytes Podcast, Winthrop described the position bluntly: "FDIC is protecting your bank accounts. Right now, there is no protection really for these tokens."

The absence of a safety net was not an oversight or an administrative gap. It was structural. The algorithmic stablecoins and centralized lenders that collapsed in 2022 had operated outside the regulatory perimeters that existed precisely to create the backstops Winthrop's clients needed. TerraUST was not a bank. Celsius was not a deposit-taker within the meaning of applicable law. Three Arrows Capital was not a fund regulated under the frameworks that would have required it to publish accurate disclosures of its leverage and liquidity position. The instruments that described themselves using financial vocabulary, "yield", "savings", "reserves", had not been issued within the legal structures that gave those words legal force.

Winthrop anticipated that the market would, over time, develop compensating mechanisms. Insurance products were beginning to emerge that could protect holders against the specific risks of crypto custody: key loss, exchange insolvency, smart contract vulnerability. Services offering structured key escrow and emergency access procedures addressed, in part, the inheritance and incapacity risks that traditional financial instruments handled through beneficiary designations and probate. "Insurance companies are going to build products that are going to buttress the traditional risks of ownership," he said. What the 2022 collapse had demonstrated, at enormous cost to ordinary savers, was the distance between the financial vocabulary that the industry had borrowed and the legal substance that vocabulary required to be reliable.

The regulatory reckoning begins

What Terra's collapse achieved, unintentionally, was to do the work that years of lobbying had failed to do: it forced regulators to act.

Within months of the collapse, the European Union accelerated the finalization of MiCA, the Markets in Crypto-Assets Regulation, which, when it came into force, explicitly prohibited the issuance of algorithmic stablecoins in the EU. The UK's financial services bill was amended to include stablecoin provisions with specific requirements for reserve adequacy. In the United States, the Senate Banking Committee held hearings, and the Treasury Secretary publicly called for stablecoin legislation. The GENIUS Act, which passed the Senate in 2025 and moved to the House, included language specifically prohibiting "endogenously collateralized" stablecoins, the regulatory term for instruments whose collateral is itself a token created by the same issuer.

The practical consequence was to draw a bright line that the industry had resisted drawing itself: between stablecoins backed by real assets held in verifiable reserve, and stablecoins backed by nothing but an algorithm and the confidence of the market. After Terra, the latter were increasingly unacceptable, not merely as a matter of regulatory preference, but as a matter of market reality. USDT saw brief outflows in the immediate aftermath of the collapse as confidence in all stablecoins faltered, but recovered strongly as Tether's quarterly attestations of Treasury holdings held up. USDC, already MiCA-compliant in structure, gained institutional users who had previously avoided stablecoins entirely. The collapse that was supposed to demonstrate the fragility of digital money had, perversely, strengthened the hand of those who had been arguing for well-collateralized stablecoins all along.

Do Kwon was arrested in Montenegro in March 2023, carrying a forged passport. He was subsequently extradited to the United States to face fraud charges. The case against him alleged that he had misled investors about the stability of UST, and that he had been aware of fundamental vulnerabilities in the system far earlier than his public statements suggested. The algorithm had not been neutral. It had been a sales pitch.

The lesson of Terra is not that stablecoins are inherently dangerous. It is that the word "stablecoin" carries very different meanings depending on what is actually behind it. A stablecoin backed by short-duration US Treasuries held in bankruptcy-remote custody and audited by a Big Four firm is a fundamentally different instrument from one maintained by an arbitrage loop between two tokens on the same blockchain. Calling both of them stablecoins is a category error that cost ordinary people tens of billions of dollars. Regulators, having watched that happen, were no longer willing to let the market self-regulate the distinction.

The question that followed, for governments from Westminster to Washington, was not merely how to police bad stablecoins, but whether the answer lay in letting the private sector issue good ones, or in the state issuing its own. The central banks were already working on an answer. Their designs would consume much of the next three years.

Chapter 4: Central Banks Enter the Race

The Terra/Luna collapse of May 2022 had barely settled when, across the world, central bank governors who had spent years cautiously monitoring the digital money space began moving with unusual speed. The pressure had been building for longer than Terra. The real catalyst was Diem, Facebook's ill-fated stablecoin that had briefly threatened to hand money creation to a company with two billion users and no regulatory mandate. But after Terra, the theoretical risks became undeniable. If private digital money could vaporize $60 billion in a fortnight, the argument ran, then the state needed to be building something better. Not as an experiment. As infrastructure.

By 2025, the Atlantic Council's CBDC tracker counted 134 countries and currency unions, representing ninety-eight percent of global GDP, actively exploring central bank digital currencies. The number had been thirty-five in May 2020. Every G20 nation was at some stage of development, with sixty-six in the advanced phases. OMFIF, in its annual outlook, reported that eighty-one percent of central banks were now formally exploring CBDCs and forty-seven percent expected to launch one within five years. The question was no longer whether. It was in what form.

The case the numbers make

The underlying economic argument for digital money is not subtle. McKinsey estimated, in research dating back to 2016, that broad adoption of digital finance could increase the GDP of all emerging economies by six percent, equivalent to $3.7 trillion, and generate up to ninety-five million new jobs. The Bank for International Settlements put the cross-border payments opportunity more precisely: CBDCs could reduce the cost of international transfers by up to fifty percent, by eliminating the correspondent bank intermediaries who currently extract their fee at each hop. The FSB set itself a concrete target: seventy-five percent of cross-border retail payments settled within one hour by 2027. With the World Bank's data showing an average cost of 6.25 percent on a $200 remittance, that ambition is not a marginal improvement. It is a structural redesign.

The macroeconomic lever is significant. A BIS working paper found that a one percentage point increase in digital payments use was associated with a 0.10 percentage point increase in GDP per capita growth over a two-year period, alongside a 0.06 percentage point decline in informal sector employment. The remittance market alone reached $730 billion globally in 2023 and is projected to exceed $1 trillion by 2029. As we noted on the podcast: "The only way to get out of the current situation of massive debts is that we either default, which no one wants to talk about, or we grow our way out." At growth rates that have barely exceeded three percent in major Western economies for a decade, any mechanism that demonstrably accelerates economic activity commands urgent attention from governments that have spent fifteen years expanding debt. Digital money, in this reading, is not primarily a payments story. It is a fiscal imperative.

The global south goes first

The most important thing about the CBDC race is who is winning it. It is not the G7.

Kenya's M-Pesa transformed mobile payments across sub-Saharan Africa, demonstrating that a population without bank branches could build a functionally cashless economy through mobile phones. Brazil's PIX instant payment system, launched in 2020, processed more than a third of all banking transactions within its first two years, advancing financial inclusion to levels the country's banks had never achieved. India's Unified Payments Interface handled billions of transactions a month, with a market share cap deliberately kept in place to prevent any single player from dominating. These were not CBDCs in the technical sense, they were government-sponsored or government-regulated instant payment networks, but they established the proof of concept that Sheila M'Mbijjewe, former Deputy Governor of the Central Bank of Kenya, drew on when she observed: "Being scared of having your business model interrupted is not the way to go." The banks that resisted disruption in these markets found themselves circumvented. The banks that adapted gained customers they had never been able to reach before.

China's digital yuan, the e-CNY, is the most advanced state-sponsored CBDC program in the world. By the mid-2020s, the People's Bank of China had expanded the e-CNY pilot to dozens of cities, distributing the currency directly to random citizens as spending vouchers, with restrictions on category and geography that physically could not be imposed on cash. In 2024 it was introduced to Hong Kong for use in local shops, a significant step toward internationalization. Brazil's DREX program reported three successful transactions in its pilot phase and targeted a 2025 rollout. The Bahamas had already launched the Sand Dollar. The Eastern Caribbean Central Bank had its DCash. Across the global south, the CBDC was not a future technology. It was a present one.

Beyond the policy and geopolitical dimensions of this rollout lay a more fundamental question about how enterprises would operate in a world of state-backed digital currencies. When Hayden Jones, a digital transformation advisor at PwC, spoke to us about the institutional implications of CBDCs, he articulated something that most official discussions of central bank digital currencies had left implicit: these systems were not merely payment networks. They were platforms for transforming how organizations managed the integration of three critical operations, the ledger that recorded transactions, the payment rails that moved value, and the verification layer that confirmed what could settle. "The real opportunity for enterprises," Jones noted, "is when the ledger, the payment mechanism, and the value transfer become one integrated system." In traditional finance, these operations required separate infrastructure: a general ledger system, a SWIFT message network, a settlement institution, and a custodian. A properly designed CBDC offered the possibility of consolidating these into a unified layer where the central bank's digital money carried not just value but the conditions under which that value could move. For a multinational corporation managing cash across twelve jurisdictions, a supply chain requiring conditional payment upon delivery verification, or a financial institution needing programmable settlement, that integration was not a marginal efficiency gain. It was a reimagining of how capital moved through the enterprise.

Notably, China's digital yuan does not use blockchain. This matters more than it might appear. MIT's work on "Project Hamilton," its CBDC research program with the Federal Reserve Bank of Boston, found that a distributed ledger operating under multiple actors was not actually necessary to achieve the goals of a CBDC: "We found that separating a transaction processor into modular components improves system scalability and flexibility... Despite using ideas from blockchain technology, we found that a distributed ledger operating under the jurisdiction of different actors was not needed to achieve our goals." The question of technology architecture is secondary to the question of what the currency is designed to do.

What CBDCs can do that cash cannot

The capabilities that distinguish a CBDC from a banknote are the same capabilities that make the private sector nervous about them.

Programmability is the most significant. A CBDC can be conditional: it can expire, it can be restricted to certain categories of spending, it can be released automatically on the completion of a verified condition. JP Morgan's institutional digital currency platform Onyx demonstrated what this means in practice. Umar Farooq, who headed the Onyx division, reported that since adding programmability features, the platform had seen transactions "explode by factors of ten, if not hundreds." Some days, transaction volumes reached "the high single-digit billions of dollars." Notably, JP Morgan found that the demand was not primarily for 24/7 availability: clients were not particularly exercised about making payments at 3am. The demand was for programmable execution: the automated, conditional, instant release of funds when a defined event occurred. That is not something a banknote or a wire transfer can offer.

Beyond payments, CBDC infrastructure opens a range of policy applications that have barely begun to be explored. Welfare payments can be programmed to release automatically at verified life events. Subsidies can be targeted to specific goods rather than granted as general cash, which often flows to unintended uses. Programmable universal basic income becomes technically trivial to administer. In jurisdictions where tax collection is weak or informal employment is high, programmable CBDCs allow governments to embed taxation directly into transactions, reducing evasion without increasing enforcement costs. Financial inclusion is perhaps the most frequently cited advantage: a citizen who has no bank account, no credit history and no proximity to a branch can hold and spend a CBDC via a mobile phone. The IMF argued that "if properly designed to address the barriers to financial inclusion, CBDCs have the opportunity to gain acceptance by the financially excluded for digital payments: CBDC can then serve as an entry point to the broader formal financial system."

The surveillance problem

The capabilities that make CBDCs attractive to policymakers are precisely the capabilities that make civil liberties advocates alarmed. They are not wrong to be.

In February 2022, the Canadian government invoked emergency powers to freeze the bank accounts of truckers who had organized a convoy blockade. No criminal conviction was required. No judicial order was served in advance. The accounts were frozen by administrative instruction to the banks, and the banks complied. The episode was a demonstration, in a functioning Western democracy with an independent judiciary and press freedom, of what programmable financial infrastructure can enable at the stroke of a pen. Now imagine that capability built into a CBDC architecture, where the central bank, not the commercial bank, is the direct counterparty, and where programmable restrictions can be applied algorithmically, in real time, to every transaction in the economy.

China's digital yuan, officials have repeatedly stated, is not linked to the social credit system. The infrastructure, however, enables that integration trivially. A score falls below a threshold: a travel restriction is applied. A keyword appears in a monitored communication: a spending category is blocked. The mechanism need not be activated for its existence to alter behavior. This is the defining ethical question of the CBDC era: are we building the infrastructure for financial innovation, or the rails for digital authoritarianism? Russia's digital ruble program, advancing toward full implementation, draws similar concerns: given the government's track record of using financial tools against political opponents, a programmable digital currency with state custody is not a neutral instrument. The question is not hypothetical. It is architectural.

The key distinction lies in design choices that are not technical but political. Zero-knowledge proofs can enable transaction verification without disclosing identity. Offline capability preserves a fallback channel that is not surveillance-enabled. Independent oversight bodies, separated from both government and central bank, can audit access to transaction data. These are not default features of CBDC systems: they require explicit design decisions that some governments are making and others are deliberately avoiding.

Retail versus wholesale: two different debates

The central bank community has largely settled on a distinction that the public debate often conflates: wholesale CBDCs and retail CBDCs are different instruments, serving different purposes, raising different risks.

Wholesale CBDCs, designed for institutional settlement between banks and financial market infrastructure, have attracted broad enthusiasm. Projects like Hong Kong's mBridge, which tested multi-currency wholesale CBDC settlement across multiple central banks, demonstrated clear advantages in efficiency and finality. Deutsche Bank summarized the wholesale case: faster settlement speeds, enhanced security for securities transactions and improved cross-border liquidity, all without disrupting existing financial intermediaries. The wholesale CBDC shores up the plumbing of the financial system without changing who the plumbers are.

Retail CBDCs are more contested. The economic literature is genuinely divided. Copenhagen Economics, in a rigorous assessment of the proposed digital euro, found that it "could lead to a permanent reduction in GDP of 0.12–0.34 percent," driven primarily by costs imposed on commercial banks, which would need to rebuild customer-facing infrastructure and would face potential deposit flight if citizens moved savings from bank accounts to CBDC wallets. The implementation cost alone was estimated at €6.5 billion to €19.5 billion per annum across EU banks. The banking lobby's resistance is not purely self-interest; it reflects a genuine structural risk: if depositors can hold central bank money directly, outside the commercial banking system, the fractional reserve model that underwrites most lending in the economy is weakened. A retail CBDC, poorly designed, is a mechanism for bank runs in slow motion.

Meanwhile, Copenhagen Economics found that the digital euro would have "very little impact" on financial inclusion in Europe, where the thirteen million unbanked adults are typically excluded not by lack of access to digital systems but by lack of legal status, credit history and social complexity that a wallet cannot resolve. Where retail CBDCs have demonstrably worked, M-Pesa, PIX, UPI, the operating context was a large underserved population, rudimentary existing payment infrastructure and a strong government mandate. Critics who argue that retail CBDCs in developed economies are "a solution searching for a problem" have a reasonable point.

The race is not over. But by 2025 its shape is clear. The global south has already demonstrated that state-backed digital money can work at scale, and the economic case for broader adoption is strong. The wholesale tier is converging toward implementation. The retail tier remains contested, not primarily as a technical question but as a political one: what kind of relationship between citizen, state and money do we want to build into the architecture?

Those questions are most acute in the three jurisdictions that matter most for global finance. The European Union, the United Kingdom and the United States are each approaching this moment from different angles, with different answers, and their decisions will set the template for most of the countries that follow.

When the regulators began to listen

Lewis McLellan, speaking to The Digital Bytes Podcast in December 2024, described the change in the US regulatory posture toward public blockchain as more rapid than most practitioners working in the field had anticipated. The Digital Monetary Institute had spent several years in conversation with bank supervisors on both sides of the Atlantic about the Basel Committee's rules on bank holdings of public blockchain assets. The 1,250 percent capital requirement that effectively prohibited banks from holding any asset on a public network had been the subject of sustained industry feedback. "Very few of the countries have actually gone very far toward implementing them," McLellan noted. "The US, among others, had just said they weren't going to do that. And Basel has now come out and said they acknowledge the rules need to be redrafted."

The Digital Monetary Institute's position, as McLellan explained it, was not that public blockchains were superior to private ones but that the market should be free to determine which infrastructure was appropriate for which purpose. The regulator, in drawing a blanket red line around public blockchain assets, had made a categorical judgment that the evidence no longer supported. Permissioned tokens on public chains — tokens that required KYC verification before transfer, that embedded compliance controls at the instrument level, that could be immobilized by court order — were not the same risk as an anonymous cryptocurrency transfer. The Basel rules had treated them identically.

The November 2024 US election accelerated the process. The Office of the Comptroller of the Currency issued interpretive letters permitting national banks to provide custody services for digital assets, participate in stablecoin networks, and engage with public blockchain infrastructure as part of their permissible business activities. McLellan observed that the volume and pace of bank engagement with public blockchain had increased sharply in the following weeks. The central banks that had been developing CBDC architectures were now doing so in an environment where the private sector had been invited to help build the payment infrastructure of the next financial era, rather than waiting for regulators to act first.

Chapter 5: The Digital Currency Race

Take a USDT token, or a USDC, or any of the hundred-and-counting dollar-backed stablecoins now in circulation, and consider where it lands differently depending on which jurisdiction you happen to inhabit. In the United States, the GENIUS Act signed by President Trump on 18 July 2025 has given it a legal framework, a reserve requirement and a pathway to the mainstream financial system. In the European Union, MiCA has regulated it into compliance but inadvertently created structural conditions that may make any euro equivalent less stable than its dollar counterpart. In the United Kingdom, it is met by consultation papers that industry participants have called "unworkable," proposed holding caps that drew sharp rebukes from UK crypto groups, and a central bank whose response to each piece of new stablecoin legislation has been to retreat and reconsider. One instrument. Four rulebooks. An increasingly divergent set of outcomes.

The contest over which currencies, and which jurisdictions, remain relevant in a world of programmable money is already underway. Beneath the legislation runs a deeper shift: stablecoins are beginning to look less like an extension of crypto and more like what we have called the new Eurodollar, a dollar-denominated credit system operating largely outside any single sovereign's control.

The Eurodollar parallel

To understand why the stablecoin regulatory race matters at sovereign level, it helps to understand what it threatens to replicate at scale.

The Eurodollar market, US dollar deposits held outside the United States, primarily in offshore banks and international accounts, has underpinned global finance since the 1950s. By 2023, it had grown to approximately $13 trillion in offshore dollar liabilities, more than double its size at the time of the 2008 financial crisis. Roughly 60–70 percent of global trade financing flows through it. It has, on at least two occasions, nearly broken the world: in 2008, when confidence in counterparties collapsed and the Federal Reserve deployed $580 billion in emergency swap lines to prevent the Eurodollar system from seizing; and in 2019, when a dollar shortage spiked overnight repo rates from 2 percent to 10 percent in hours, exposing the system's continued fragility.

The parallels with stablecoins are structural rather than incidental. Both involve dollar-denominated liabilities created by private institutions operating outside direct Federal Reserve oversight. Both provide liquidity for global trade. Both distribute dollars into parts of the world that cannot easily access them through conventional banking. And both have a habit of becoming more significant than anyone anticipated at inception. According to the Bank for International Settlements, ninety-nine percent of stablecoin volume is denominated in dollars, the same dollar dominance that characterizes the Eurodollar system, reproduced on a public blockchain with twenty-four-hour settlement and near-zero transaction fees.

The stablecoin market capitalization reached $300 billion in September 2025: trivial relative to the $13 trillion Eurodollar pool, but the Eurodollar market was also dismissed as inconsequential before it became integral to global finance. As David Parsons, a digital assets specialist writing on the GENIUS Act for Digital Bytes in June 2025, observed: "It is a little bit like what we saw with the petrodollar and the Eurodollar: stablecoins are going to give the US dollar another sort of lifespan." The petrodollar anchored dollar dominance through the oil trade from the 1970s; the Eurodollar extended it through offshore banking from the 1950s. Stablecoins may become the third chapter in that expansion, not because the US intended it, but because the market dynamics are structurally identical.

The medium-term picture is already visible. Stablecoins are disintermediating foreign exchange brokers, remittance providers and specific shadow banking liquidity functions. In the long term, if they secure central bank backing, regulatory clarity and widespread institutional adoption, they could become the dominant form in which dollar-denominated value moves worldwide: programmable, borderless, integrated across traditional and decentralized financial systems.

The dollar's advantage is that it got there first on public blockchains. Whether it stays there, as competitors scale their own infrastructure, remains unresolved.

The GENIUS Act: America's dollar bet

The United States has decided not to wait for any of that to play out by itself. The GENIUS Act, signed into law on 18 July 2025, is one of the most significant pieces of monetary legislation enacted in generations. Any institution anywhere in the world that holds eligible short-duration US Treasury securities can now issue a dollar stablecoin and access US markets through a licensed digital asset service provider.

The law's mechanics are precise: reserves must be 100 percent backed by cash or Treasury securities maturing within ninety-three days; monthly attestations are required; bank-issued stablecoins must operate through separate entities; stablecoins cannot pay interest to holders, a provision inserted at commercial bank lobbying to prevent deposit flight from the fractional reserve system. Foreign issuers are explicitly accommodated. The implication, as Lewis McLellan of the Digital Monetary Institute observed, is that if the US can channel even a portion of global dollar-denominated commerce into stablecoin rails that require the purchase of short-duration American government debt, it has found an elegant way to finance a fiscal deficit running above six percent of GDP. US Treasury Secretary Scott Bessent described the outcome as the "golden age of crypto" in July 2025. Estimates from JP Morgan and Reuters project the framework will expand the stablecoin market to $2 trillion by 2030.

Dollar stablecoins already account for ninety-nine percent of the $300 billion market, and they are still growing. Tether's supply rose from $89 billion to $181 billion during the same period MiCA was attempting to constrain it in Europe. Circle's USDC grew from $24 billion to $76 billion. Together, Tether and Circle became the third-largest purchasers of US Treasury bills in 2024. The US had acquired a new class of sovereign debt buyer: one that requires no yield subsidy and actively promotes dollar adoption in markets the Federal Reserve has never directly served.

But the assumption that dollar dominance through stablecoins was inevitable was being tested simultaneously elsewhere. The BRICS nations had spent five years building alternatives to the dollar-settlement infrastructure that the West had long taken for granted. Russia was developing its own digital settlement rail outside SWIFT. China had internationalized the digital yuan into Hong Kong and Southeast Asia. India's Unified Payments Interface had reached 13 billion monthly transactions by 2024. Brazil's PIX was processing more payments annually than Visa and Mastercard combined. These systems were not hostile replacements for the dollar. They were parallel infrastructure, built on the sovereign capacity to denominate transactions in local currency without requiring access to dollar-settlement rails.

The national security dimension cuts both ways. The same infrastructure that extends dollar reach also provides channels for sanctions evasion: recent Treasury reports cited Russian arms smugglers using Tether to acquire billions in weaponry outside the conventional banking system. Decentralized stablecoin networks operating on permissionless blockchains are structurally harder to surveil than correspondent banking chains. As volumes grow, whether the US can maintain both the reach advantage and the enforcement capacity of the Eurodollar system is a question the GENIUS Act's drafting committee has not resolved.

MiCA's unintended consequence: the leverage trap

The European Union's response to the same challenge was regulation first, market development second. MiCA, the Markets in Crypto-Assets Regulation, came into force in 2024, establishing the most comprehensive crypto framework anywhere in the world and creating, in Circle's French e-money license, the first stablecoin issuer operating under full regulatory clarity in a major jurisdiction. The achievement was real. The unintended consequence was structural and damaging.

Under MiCA, e-money institution stablecoin issuers must hold a minimum of thirty percent of their reserves in regulated bank deposits. That sounds sensible. The problem lies in what happens next. In the United States and the United Kingdom, central bank reserves are excluded from leverage ratio calculations. When a US bank receives stablecoin deposits and places them at the Federal Reserve, there is no impact on its leverage metrics. The same applies at the Bank of England. In the European Union, no such exemption exists. Stablecoin deposits held at the central bank are included in the leverage ratio calculation, generating capital constraints that US and UK competitors simply do not face.

The consequence is as perverse as it is predictable. EU banks wishing to issue stablecoins cannot hold their reserves in the safest possible place, central bank deposits, without straining their capital ratios. They are structurally incentivized to hold reserves in higher-yielding, riskier assets instead. A regulation designed to make stablecoins safer has created the conditions under which EU-issued stablecoins may be the least safe of all. The ECB and BIS had both modeled cybersecurity and anti-money laundering risks. Neither had modeled the risk that their own capital rules would push EU bank stablecoin reserves up the risk curve.

The figures tell the story. By mid-2025, euro-denominated stablecoins had a combined market capitalization of approximately €350 million. Dollar stablecoins stood at $280 billion. The ratio is approximately 450 to one. MiCA reduced Tether's European market share. It did not create European alternatives. It redistributed dollar-stablecoin market share between Tether and Circle rather than building any euro-stablecoin competitor. The ECB's digital euro may eventually change this dynamic, but the ECB increasingly looks, in OMFIF's assessment, "more like an outlier than a leading charge" among central banks that have moderated their retail CBDC ambitions.

The Bank of England's two-speed problem

The United Kingdom sits between a US that has decided and a European Union whose structural disadvantage is now visible. It has done neither, and is running out of time in which neither is viable.

The UK's regulatory ambivalence has a particular character worth stating directly. On one side: BoE Governor Andrew Bailey, a career central banker with more than four decades of service, whose instincts are shaped by the post-2008 stability framework and who has presided over speeches extolling "trust and innovation in the multi-moneyverse" while the Bank's proposals have consistently prioritized incumbent protection over competitive market entry. On the other: a US regulatory process shaped, in part, by Brian Armstrong of Coinbase, whose industry testimony helped form the GENIUS Act's interoperability standards. The generational asymmetry is not merely cosmetic. It reflects a difference in what each institution believes it is primarily trying to protect.

The BoE's 2025 conduct on stablecoins is instructive. In July, Sasha Mills signaled that the Bank was open to stablecoins playing a role in wholesale payments, hinting at potential integration into high-value settlement through the Digital Securities Sandbox. Within weeks, the Bank proposed holding caps, £10,000 to £20,000 for individuals, up to £10 million for firms, framed as protection against runs on uninsured digital dollars. UK crypto industry groups reacted with documented alarm; critics described the caps as more likely to drive business offshore than to manage systemic risk. The FCA's parallel consultation paper, CP25/14, published in May 2025, was described as "unworkable," with enforcement mechanisms that smaller players cannot absorb. By August 2025, the UK had spent three years describing itself as a "global cryptoasset hub", a commitment made publicly in 2022, without producing a framework that would allow a GBP-pegged stablecoin to operate under that aspiration.

The risk is not theoretical. BIS data establishes London's position clearly: the most foreign banking institutions of any financial center; the largest cross-border bank lending operation; daily foreign exchange turnover six times that of Frankfurt. Those leading positions were built on London's ability to pioneer and host new financial instruments. Ninety-nine percent of current global stablecoin value is denominated in dollars. UK market participants, without sterling-stablecoin alternatives, are increasingly defaulting to

USD-pegged tokens for digital transactions. The Imperial College Business School's "Mind the Gap" report put it plainly: "Delay is not a passive choice, it is an active risk. The real question isn't whether the UK should regulate stablecoins, but whether it wants to shape the future of money or be shaped by it."

Meanwhile, EY Parthenon surveys show the institutional window is open now, not at some future point: 13 percent of financial institutions globally already use stablecoins, and 54 percent of non-users expect to adopt them within six to twelve months. Industry projections from multiple sources converge on the same estimate: 5–10 percent of cross-border payments will be denominated in stablecoins by 2030, equivalent to $2.1–$4.2 trillion per annum. The firms and institutions making those payments will denominate them in whatever currency is most accessible, most liquid and most clearly regulated. At present, that is not sterling.

Four rulebooks, one winner

The global stablecoin regulatory contest now has four active frameworks: GENIUS, MiCA, Singapore's Monetary Authority framework and Dubai's VARA. They diverge on reserve requirements, interest payments, custodial arrangements and the treatment of foreign issuers. Singapore and VARA permit interest payments to stablecoin holders in some circumstances; GENIUS and MiCA do not. GENIUS requires sub-93-day Treasuries; VARA mandates 100 percent cash equivalents or 90-day sovereign debt; MiCA requires 30 percent bank deposits. Singapore demands strict custodian arrangements with monthly attestations.

The structural differences matter less than the network effect that already defines the outcome. Dollar stablecoins account for ninety-nine percent of global market capitalization. The GENIUS Act's global entry provisions mean that any issuer in any jurisdiction that wants to access dollar-denomination at scale is operating within, or adjacent to, the American regulatory framework. Singapore and Dubai are building clean, business-friendly regimes, but they are building elegant frameworks for distributing US monetary dominance, not challenging it. The contest over which currency will anchor the programmable money era is already resolved. What remains is the question of which institutions, in which jurisdictions, will participate in that dollar infrastructure on the most competitive terms.

The UK's challenge is distinct from the EU's. MiCA has failed to build euro-stablecoin mass, but MiCA exists, is comprehensive and creates a regulated market within which European firms can operate. The Global South has bypassed the question by adopting dollar stablecoins directly: Nigeria leads global stablecoin adoption, and stablecoin-powered remittance corridors already reduce fees by thirty to sixty percent relative to traditional correspondent banking.

The dynamic is easiest to understand at street level. At a conference organized by OMFIF in 2025, a central bank governor from a major Latin American economy was asked whether dollarization via stablecoins represented a threat to monetary sovereignty. His response was direct: "Have you ever had a hundred percent inflation? And I am talking about per month." The people most enthusiastically adopting US dollar stablecoins are, in many cases, the same people whose governments have spoken most loudly against dollar dominance — because the alternative, in real terms, is watching savings disappear. The UK sits in an unusual position: a major financial center with world-class payments infrastructure, a credible regulatory reputation, and a declared intention to be a digital asset hub, that has produced none of the three instruments needed to make that intention real: no GBP stablecoin framework, no clear reserve requirements, no competitive licensing pathway for foreign issuers.

Whether that changes in time to matter is one of the central questions running through this book. What changes first, in the chapter that follows, is the infrastructure underneath all three regimes: the payment rails themselves, which are being rebuilt faster than most policymakers anticipated. The regulatory debates described here are unfolding while cross-border payments are already shifting, corridor by corridor, toward digital settlement. In programmable money, the law still matters. But it is increasingly reacting to code that is already in motion.

The digital dollar that was not built

Jason Myers, chief executive of Auto Chain Labs, attended all five of the crypto task force roundtables that the US Securities and Exchange Commission ran in the spring of 2025: structured working sessions designed, for the first time, to develop disclosure, compliance and investor protection standards in consultation with the industry rather than through adversarial enforcement. Appearing on The Digital Bytes Podcast, he described a political context that had turned the digital dollar question in an unexpected direction: Donald Trump had signed an executive order on 23 January 2025 explicitly prohibiting the United States from developing a central bank digital currency. The government expected to lead the field in official digital money had chosen to champion private-sector stablecoins and a Strategic Bitcoin Reserve instead.

The contrast with European monetary policy was stark. The ECB's digital euro project proceeded on the explicit basis that European monetary sovereignty required a state alternative to private digital money. The ECB framed private stablecoins, predominantly dollar-denominated, as a threat to euro-area monetary autonomy: a form of currency substitution without any of the protections of an official monetary arrangement. Washington's position treated those same private stablecoins as an extension of dollar hegemony, a mechanism through which the dollar's global reach would be deepened without requiring government-issued infrastructure or the surveillance concerns that CBDCs inevitably attracted.

Myers had watched this divergence from the vantage point of someone who had spent his earlier career building compliance infrastructure for US regulators. MiCA's machine-readable disclosure requirements, white papers filed in a standard data format that regulators could parse automatically, represented one model of how official oversight would function in a world of digital money at scale. The United States, having banned its own CBDC and embraced private stablecoins, was constructing a different answer. The code was moving in both jurisdictions simultaneously. Which model would prove more durable was, in Myers's view, far from settled.

Chapter 6: Payments Transformed

In 2010, JP Morgan observed, a transfer of funds from New York to London could be reliably accelerated by one method above all others: buying a plane ticket from JFK to Heathrow and delivering the money yourself. The same-day movement of significant sums across borders was, at best, an act of expensive intermediation through a chain of correspondent banks. At worst, it simply could not be done.

Fifteen years later, that same transfer takes seconds, costs fractions of a cent, and can be executed from a mobile phone at two o'clock in the morning on a Sunday. Yet the institutions at the heart of global cross-border payments, correspondent banks, SWIFT messaging, nostro and vostro accounts holding trillions locked in pre-funding, have barely changed. The rails are old. The freight is new. And the gap between them is where the most significant financial transformation of this decade is now taking place.

The numbers illustrate both the opportunity and the urgency. Cross-border B2B payments are projected to reach $43 trillion by 2025 and $56 trillion by 2030, driven by the expansion of global trade and the growth of B2B e-commerce, a market set to reach $66.9 trillion by 2029. Payments overall now cost more than $2.2 trillion annually to process, a figure McKinsey expects to surpass $3.2 trillion by 2027. And $26 trillion in payments are still made in cash every year, declining at only 4 percent annually — what McKinsey calls "a massive opportunity for digitization." When remittances cross borders through the traditional correspondent banking system, they typically cost the sender around 6.25 percent of the transaction value. The same transfer routed through stablecoins costs approximately 1 percent. For the hundreds of millions of people who depend on remittances from family members working abroad, that difference is not merely an inconvenience. It is the difference between a family receiving support and a bank taking a tithe.

A system built for another century

The architecture of cross-border payments was not designed for the world it is now asked to serve. Correspondent banking relies on a web of bilateral relationships, each bank maintaining accounts, nostro and vostro accounts, named after the Latin for "ours" and "yours", at every bank with which it needs to transact. These accounts must be pre-funded, locking up working capital for days at a time simply to ensure liquidity is available when a payment arrives. The process is slow, opaque and expensive, and structurally biased toward wealthy, well-connected financial institutions in advanced economies.

SWIFT, the Society for Worldwide Interbank Financial Telecommunication, provides the messaging layer that connects this system. Founded in 1973 and headquartered in Belgium, it carries approximately 44 million messages per day between over 11,000 financial institutions in more than 200 countries. But SWIFT is a messaging network, not a settlement mechanism. It tells banks what to do; it does not do it. Dan Feaheny, a Chicago-born payments entrepreneur who moved to London to work at the center of cross-border infrastructure, was direct on The Digital Bytes Podcast in April 2025: "SWIFT has become quite an expensive email system. $25 a pop to tell one bank that it owes another bank some money." SWIFT itself acknowledged the scale of that system: every third day, the network moves the equivalent of the entire global GDP through its messaging rails. Settlement remains dependent on the correspondent banking relationships underneath, with all the delays, costs and opacity those entail.

Then came the morning of 31 May 2022. G10 nations announced that major Russian banks would be disconnected from SWIFT in response to Russia's invasion of Ukraine. The decision was deliberate, but its consequences extended far beyond Russia. Governments in Asia, the Middle East and Latin America watched as a critical piece of global financial infrastructure was weaponized by a small group of Western nations. The concentration of power in entities such as SWIFT, DTCC, CREST and Euroclear had always represented a structural vulnerability for non-Western participants in the global economy. After the Russia decision, many nations began looking for alternatives with new urgency.

Cross-border transactions that had previously been automatic became subject to financial warfare: frictionless transfer could be converted into impossibility through a single decision by Western authorities. For nations outside the dollar-dominated settlement sphere, this was not merely an inconvenience. Settlement infrastructure, in that moment, became visible as what it had always been: the foundation of monetary sovereignty itself. Blockchain-based settlement, immutable, decentralized, requiring no permission from any government or banking consortium, acquired not merely technical appeal but geopolitical necessity for nations seeking genuine financial autonomy.

China was already moving. Cross-border yuan payments hit a record in March 2025 as Beijing continued to accelerate the internationalization of the renminbi amid rising US tariffs and global trade disruption. China UnionPay expanded its QR-code-based payment network across Vietnam and Cambodia. Russia itself was developing alternatives to SWIFT. The global enthusiasm for a unified, Western-controlled payments infrastructure was eroding, not because the technology had failed, but because the geopolitics surrounding it had changed.

Stablecoins as infrastructure

Into this fragmented and urgent market came stablecoins, not as speculative instruments, but as settlement plumbing. In 2024, stablecoin transfer volumes reached $27.6 trillion, surpassing the combined transaction volumes of Visa and Mastercard by 7.7 percent. Between January 2023 and February 2025, $94.2 billion in stablecoin payments were executed on a business-to-business basis, marking a shift from niche trading tool to genuine commercial infrastructure. The global stablecoin market exceeded $170 billion in outstanding value. Coinbase reported that stablecoin settlements reached $30 trillion in the year prior, representing three times year-on-year growth.

These were not fringe numbers. Walmart and Amazon were separately exploring the launch of their own US dollar-backed stablecoins. The implications were profound. A Walmart Coin or Amazon Dollar would not merely be a payment method, it would be the creation of a closed-loop financial ecosystem in which a global retailer internalized its payment infrastructure entirely, reducing dependence on Visa, Mastercard, SWIFT and the correspondent banking network. Suppliers could be paid conditionally upon delivery confirmation. Shoppers could receive instant refunds. Microcredit lines could be issued at checkout. Cross-border payments to overseas suppliers could settle instantly at near-zero cost.

There was also a monetary dimension. Every USD-backed stablecoin issued by a private corporation requires US Treasury securities as reserves. The more stablecoins proliferate globally, the greater the demand for Treasuries, and the lower the cost at which the United States government can borrow. When Treasury

Secretary Scott Bessent described stablecoins as a potential $3 trillion additional source of demand for US government debt, he was describing a mechanism the GENIUS Act was designed to deliberately activate.

Japan's Project Pax offered a different model, one that wove blockchain infrastructure into existing banking relationships rather than replacing them. Backed by MUFG, SMBC and Mizuho, Japan's three largest financial institutions, Project Pax integrated SWIFT messaging with Progmat's stablecoin-based settlement system. The result was a framework allowing banks to offer 24/7 cross-border payments while shielding customers from the complexity of wallets and private keys. Progmat's use of Datachain's interoperability tools connected private blockchains, including Corda, to public chains such as Ethereum and Polygon, creating cross-chain stablecoin payment pathways designed to meet G20 standards for faster, cheaper and more transparent international settlement.

JP Morgan's Kinexys platform, the renamed JPM Coin, was processing over $1 billion daily in institutional payments. DBS Bank's Partior project, developed with JPMorgan and Temasek, was advancing multi-currency wholesale settlement. Siemens became the first corporate client to use JPMorgan's programmable payment functionality, establishing "if-this-then-that" architecture for treasury operations — automatic account top-ups, margin calls and real-time securities settlement triggered by defined conditions. In Singapore, DBS Bank launched Token Services, using blockchain and smart contracts to allow clients to manage multi-currency settlements without the friction of traditional treasury processes.

The practical stakes of programmability are clearest in trade finance. Consider a scenario from the Minima-Mercury programmable bank account collaboration in 2025: a vessel docking in port to load a high-value commodity. Three parties, a commodity provider, a ship operator and a harbor authority, need to align on fees and delivery confirmation before any payment can be released. Under SWIFT, that settlement typically arrives the following day, sometimes 48 hours later, by which point the commodity price may have moved and the port's fee schedule updated. The result is a cascade of top-up payments, disputed invoices and administrative delay that adds cost at every stage. With IoT sensors tracking physical goods delivery onto the vessel, and programmable conditional settlement embedded in the bank accounts of each party, the entire chain settles simultaneously and instantly the moment all parties confirm: no intermediary, no lag, no renegotiation.

For a corporate treasurer managing a supply chain across twelve countries, these were not incremental improvements. They were a different way of thinking about what money does when it moves.

PIX, UPI, and the proof that scale is possible

Before stablecoins and blockchain could make the case for rebuilding cross-border payments architecture, two national-scale projects in emerging markets had already demonstrated something crucial: that instant, zero-friction payment systems could achieve mass adoption, practically overnight, and transform the economic behavior of entire nations.

In Brazil, the Central Bank's PIX system launched in November 2020. By 2024, PIX accounted for 76.4 percent of all payment transactions in the country. Monthly transaction volumes exceeded six billion. Cash, which had accounted for 76.6 percent of payments in 2019, had fallen to 40.5 percent by 2023. E-commerce previously dominated by credit cards saw PIX seize a third of online retail transactions before the end of its third year. The system was available twenty-four hours a day, seven days a week. It was free for individuals. It used phone numbers, QR codes and email addresses as payment identifiers, eliminating the friction of bank account numbers and sort codes. For merchants, transaction fees fell close to zero.

In India, the Unified Payments Interface had reached 13 billion transactions per month by the first quarter of 2024, accounting for 81.8 percent of India's total digital payments. UPI had launched in 2016. Its growth accelerated dramatically after the COVID-19 pandemic, and its open infrastructure, allowing third-party developers to build UPI-integrated apps, created a dynamic ecosystem with no single point of failure or control. Unlike PIX, which was centralized under the Central Bank of Brazil, UPI was decentralized, with user data stored across individual providers. Both systems shared the same outcome: mass financial inclusion, dramatically lower transaction costs, and proof that real-time payment infrastructure could displace cash at scale.

The rest of the world noticed. Australia's New Payment Platform launched in 2018. The US Federal Reserve's FedNow went live in July 2023. The ECB's TARGET Instant Payment Settlement system operated across the eurozone. Thailand's PromptPay was estimated to contribute 2.08 percent to national GDP by 2026, an extraordinary figure that illustrated the macroeconomic multiplier effect of reducing payment friction. The BIS found that a one percentage point increase in digital payments use was associated with a 0.10 percentage point increase in GDP per capita growth over a two-year period, largely through reduced payment costs and the formalization of the informal economy.

The lesson these systems offered for stablecoins and tokenized deposits was not merely technical. It was institutional. PIX and UPI succeeded because they were backed by credible authorities, operated within clear rules, and were designed around the needs of the people using them rather than the intermediaries positioned to extract rents from them. For private stablecoin issuers seeking mass adoption in cross-border payments, the implication was straightforward. Scale would require regulatory legitimacy, interoperability, and the kind of trust that comes only from transparent governance.

The SME dividend

For small and medium-sized enterprises, 400 million companies globally, representing more than 95 percent of all firms and 60–70 percent of global employment, the existing cross-border payments system had always been designed by large banks for large banks. SMEs paid higher fees, had less visibility into their positions, waited longer for settlement and were offered fewer options.

Digital payment infrastructure was beginning to change that arithmetic. India's UPI had allowed SMEs to receive payments instantly, enabling them to manage working capital without the delays of traditional banking. In Kenya, over 60 percent of micro and small enterprises were already using mobile money for business transactions by 2021. DBS Bank's Token Services in Singapore gave companies treasury tools previously available only to institutions with dedicated foreign exchange desks.

The volume of embedded B2B payments, solutions built directly into the operational software businesses use, stood at around $2.5 trillion and projected to reach $6.5–$7 trillion in coming years. When real-time settlement arrived, the velocity of money increased, and with it, economic activity.

Stablecoins offered SMEs a direct advantage in cross-border trade. A small manufacturer paying an overseas supplier through the traditional banking system would typically wait two to four days for settlement, pay fees of 2–3 percent, and receive no real-time visibility into the payment's status. The same payment routed through USDC settled in minutes, at approximately 1 percent cost, with an immutable on-chain record of every step. Circle's annual report showed USDC had processed $18 trillion in transactions, growing 50 percent year on year, with wallet holders rising 45 percent to 3.9 million. In November 2024 alone, USDC processed $1 trillion in transactions. Standard Chartered's Zodia Markets minted $4 billion in USDC to streamline settlements between Asia-Pacific and the United States.

UK businesses were meanwhile losing £992 million annually in foregone interest by holding £103.5 billion in low-yield deposit accounts. Eighty percent of corporate operating cash globally sat in bank accounts earning little or nothing. Tokenized money market funds, $9 trillion in assets globally, traditionally required 2–3 business days to access. Tokenized versions of the same instruments were beginning to offer same-day redemption and hourly interest accrual. Ramp, a US fintech, offered businesses a treasury product enabling them to earn up to 35 times more on operating cash than the national average, extending working capital by an average of three days through optimized payment timing and AI-assisted cash forecasting.

From automation to intelligence: Payments 5.0

The evolution of payments technology moved through recognizable phases. Payments 1.0 meant physical currency and checks: trust derived from tangibility and counterparty confidence. Payments 2.0 introduced card networks from the 1950s onward: global scale, digital settlement, standardized infrastructure. Payments 3.0 brought digital wallets and e-commerce, PayPal, Apple Pay, Google Pay, moving transactions into the digital realm while the user remained the direct initiator of every action. Payments 4.0 delivered real-time rails: the UK's Faster Payments Service from 2008, FedNow, TIPS, UPI, PIX — instant settlement infrastructure across which money moved in seconds.

Each phase removed friction and shortened the settlement lag. But in every phase, the user was still the pilot. The machine executed instructions; it did not consider them.

Payments 5.0 is something different. An AI agent in this model does not wait for a user to instruct "transfer one hundred pounds to my supplier." Instead, a corporate treasurer expresses intent, "ensure my bills are paid on time while minimizing fees and maximizing loyalty points", and the agent designs and executes the entire multi-step financial plan: routing payments across the cheapest available rails, selecting settlement currencies dynamically, scheduling transfers to avoid congestion windows, and adjusting the plan in real time as conditions change. For an overseas payment, the agent might route through a CBDC rail for transparent T+0 settlement; for a domestic transfer, it might delay until a low-cost batch window, provided the payment deadline is not breached. The plan is fluid. The execution is autonomous.

The appetite for that shift was already measurable. A Gartner survey published in early 2025 found that 64 percent of enterprise technology respondents planned to deploy agentic AI within their operations, a trajectory encompassing treasury management, accounts payable automation and real-time cross-border settlement execution. The financial industry's proof-of-concept phase for autonomous payment systems was ending.

McKinsey had issued a warning about the economic stakes of this transition. Banks could lose up to $170 billion in global profits, approximately 9 percent of the total, as AI agents began automatically moving consumer deposits from low-yield checking accounts into higher-yield instruments. Approximately $23 trillion in deposits were currently held in near-zero-rate accounts, kept there by the inertia of the existing system and the friction of moving them. Agentic AI removed that inertia entirely.

The Bank of England's Jonathan Hall had asked publicly whether increasing use of AI models could harm financial stability — "monsters in the deep," in his phrase. The 2010 Flash Crash, in which algorithmic trading bots erased $1 trillion in equity value within minutes, had already shown what happened when autonomous financial systems operated without adequate oversight at scale. Visa's research found that 90 percent of stablecoin transactions were being executed by bots, with only $149 billion of $2.2 trillion in monthly stablecoin volume driven by genuine human-initiated payments. The infrastructure of tomorrow's payment system was already largely automated before most people had noticed it had changed.

The question of the rails

The cross-border payments system of 2030, if it follows the trajectories visible in 2025, will look nothing like the system of 2010. SWIFT will likely still exist, but it will carry a smaller share of global settlement. Correspondent banking relationships will persist, but their intermediation premium will have been eroded by stablecoins, real-time rails and programmable settlement. The nostro/vostro liquidity trap, trillions locked in pre-funded accounts earning nothing, will have partially dissolved as instant settlement eliminates the need for pre-funding. The remittance market, worth hundreds of billions annually and currently extracting 6 percent of the money sent by the world's most economically vulnerable workers, will have been permanently disrupted.

But none of that resolves who controls what replaces it. If Walmart and Amazon issue their own stablecoins, private dollars circulating through their global ecosystems, they become, as one analysis framed it, informal extensions of US monetary policy. The more dollar-backed stablecoins proliferate globally, the more demand is created for US Treasuries, the lower American borrowing costs fall, and the more deeply the dollar is embedded in the digital financial systems of nations that formally hold other currencies. The GENIUS Act's provision allowing Big Tech and commercial firms to own non-bank stablecoin issuers was being analyzed by legal academics as the potential creation of "shadow deposits": stablecoin instruments that functioned economically like bank accounts without carrying the same regulatory safeguards and which could, in a stress scenario, create contagion risks reminiscent of the subprime mortgage instruments that preceded the 2008 crisis.

On the other side of the ledger, nations that chose to develop their own payment infrastructure, PIX in Brazil, UPI in India, Cross-Border Interbank Payment System in China, were demonstrating that it was possible to build fast, inclusive and low-cost payment systems not dependent on Western infrastructure or private American capital.

The argument running through all of this, through programmable money, stablecoins, AI-driven treasury management and real-time national payment systems, was ultimately a single question framed in the language of technology: who decides what money can do, where it goes, and what it costs to move? The code was already being written. The chapter in which governments, institutions and regulators attempted to answer that question was just beginning.

The contest over payment rails is inseparable from a broader question about the two most significant forms of digital money currently under development. Stablecoins, issued by private actors and backed by commercial interests, are racing ahead of the regulatory frameworks designed to govern them. Central bank digital currencies, issued by governments and anchored to sovereign monetary authority, are moving more cautiously but, in many jurisdictions, they are moving. In the next chapter, we examine what happens when these two visions of digital money meet.

Chapter 7: Stablecoins vs CBDCs

At an international monetary conference in late 2025, an unnamed official from a Group of Seven central bank gave voice to something many of their peers had been thinking but few dared to say aloud. "There is a wall of shit money coming our way," they told a room of assembled policymakers, "and we're doing nothing about it." It was not the kind of language one expects from the guardians of monetary stability. But then again, these are not the kinds of times that monetary guardians have been trained for.

The official's frustration was directed at stablecoins: digital currencies issued by private actors and denominated in national currencies, predominantly the US dollar. By the time they spoke, USDC alone was processing eighteen trillion dollars in transactions per year, backed by some of the largest financial institutions in the world: Goldman Sachs, BlackRock, Fidelity. These were no longer fringe instruments of crypto speculation. They had become a parallel payment infrastructure operating at scale, outside the institutions that had spent centuries designing the architecture of money.

The contest between stablecoins and central bank digital currencies is not simply a technical competition between two forms of digital payment. It is a proxy war over who controls the future of money, what values that money embodies, and whether the sovereignty that governments have exercised over currency for three centuries is now negotiable.

The ghost of Libra returns

To understand how we arrived here, it helps to revisit a moment in 2019 that most people in finance have never fully left behind. Facebook, then not yet Meta, announced Libra, later renamed Diem, a digital currency that would allow its two billion monthly users to transfer value across borders at minimal cost. Visa, Mastercard and a string of global financial institutions initially lined up to participate. It was, by any measure, an audacious proposal: private money, issued by a private company, operating at the scale of a nation-state.

The central banking community's response was swift and coordinated. Within months, the key commercial partners had withdrawn under regulatory pressure, and the project was redesigned into a much tamer instrument before being wound down in 2022. The message was clear: the official sector would not allow the monetary system to be disrupted from Silicon Valley.

John Orchard, chairman of the OMFIF Digital Monetary Institute, has spent years straddling the line between central banking and private finance. His assessment of what has happened since is blunt. "The world is bifurcating," he told Digital Bytes in July 2025. The Libra episode had taught the official sector that private digital money could not be stopped, only deferred. And now it was back: rebranded, repackaged, and this time carrying the explicit backing of the United States government.

The vehicle was the GENIUS Act, passed in 2025 following an executive order from President Trump in January of that year. The order prohibited the United States from developing its own central bank digital currency while simultaneously designating dollar-denominated stablecoins as the mechanism through which American monetary influence would be extended into the digital era. Where Libra had been suppressed, the GENIUS Act elevated stablecoins into a structural pillar of the US financial system.

The effect was immediate and disorienting. One senior central banker returned from the IMF-World Bank Annual Meetings that autumn "profoundly unsettled." The United States was, in effect, outsourcing the internationalization of the dollar to private operators, and expecting the rest of the world to absorb the consequences.

Scale, speed, and the end of the neutral dollar

The numbers tell their own story, and they are not comfortable reading for anyone who assumed the dollar's digital future would be managed through official channels.

USDC's eighteen trillion dollars in annual transaction volume is not abstract. The Bank of

England's own analysis found that an amount equivalent to 23 percent of UK GDP, approximately £2.53 trillion, was already being transacted in USDC annually. At the 50 percent annual growth rate the instrument had maintained, the UK would see stablecoin volume pass 50 percent of GDP equivalence within two years. Andrew Bailey, the Bank of England Governor, acknowledged thc scale of the challenge in characteristically measured terms: "If we were to assume there are no benefits of digital technology in the world of payments, we would probably be failing the test of imagination." His analogy was the iPhone. When Apple launched its device, no one demanded that telephones remain attached to walls.

Beyond payment volumes lay a more consequential question about what stablecoins could enable that CBDCs were slower to support: the tokenization of real-world assets at scale. In conversations with industry participants on Digital Bytes in 2025, the most vivid use cases had begun to emerge. Stock market infrastructure was being rebuilt on blockchain rails. Digital exchanges like Archax in London and Swarm in Switzerland were enabling fractional ownership and instant settlement of securities that traditional market infrastructure required days to reconcile. Private company equity – estimated at more than $330 trillion in global market value, sitting entirely outside public markets, accessible only to institutional investors – was beginning to be tokenized. A financial startup could now issue equity tokens representing fractional ownership, settle them instantly, and execute complex operations like conditional secondary offerings or dividend distributions without intermediaries. For real estate, the implications extended to mortgage markets: a property-backed stablecoin could carry within it smart contracts automating rent collection, maintenance disbursement and tenant protections — programmable real estate where every contractual obligation was executable by code, not lawyers.

The advantage stablecoins offered over CBDCs, in these applications, was precisely their lack of central authority. A central bank could not move fast enough to support the iterative experimentation that asset tokenization required. Private stablecoin networks, operating on public blockchains, could. CBDCs could follow eventually. By then, stablecoins would have established the technical standards and market practices that CBDCs would inherit.

But Bailey's measured tone stood in contrast to the alarm being expressed elsewhere. SWIFT data was already showing the dollar rapidly displacing the euro in worldwide transactions, a trend analysts were calling "de-Euroization." Twenty major eurozone banks, Nordea's Ville Sointu revealed, were quietly assessing the mandatory financial impact of a digital euro. The ECB described its work on the digital euro as "crucial for bolstering European sovereignty." The language was telling. This was no longer a debate about payment efficiency. It was a debate about power.

Against this backdrop, the OMFIF Global Public Investor survey for 2025 carried the force of a collective institutional statement. Of the central banks surveyed, collectively representative of five trillion dollars in global reserves, not one held digital assets. Ninety-three percent had no intention of doing so. Eighty-two percent neither used distributed ledger technology nor intended to.

The reasons were not ideological, or not entirely. Larry Hathaway of Franklin Templeton laid them out directly: reserve managers would not hold no-yield stablecoins. To do so would be to hand the seigniorage, the economic benefit of issuing money, to a private operator. As Orchard explained: "Why would they? They say, why bother do that? I'll have the little bit of yield that the US government will give me, rather than donate the seigniorage, essentially, to the stablecoin issuer." The logic was impeccable. Reserve management is not a business that tolerates negative carry.

Daniela Klingebiel of the World Bank's reserve advisory and management program added the other dimensions: legal risk, counterparty risk, custodial complexity, de-pegging exposure. These were not theoretical concerns. When Silicon Valley Bank collapsed in 2023, Circle's USDC had briefly lost its peg. The memory had not faded among those whose job was preserving national wealth.

There were outliers. The Czech National Bank's Jan Kubíček offered a more exploratory posture: "We can pretend there is no such thing as Bitcoin, or gain some hands-on experience." It was a pragmatic observation, not an endorsement, but pragmatism is not nothing.

The picture among sovereign wealth funds and public pension schemes told a different story. Seven percent already held digital assets. Twenty percent intended to. The institutions with the longest time horizons and the smallest political exposure were leaning in while central banks stood back. President Trump had already announced a strategic Bitcoin reserve for the United States. Something was shifting at the edges of official tolerance, even if official posture remained frozen.

The singleness of money – and its paradox

At the heart of the official case against stablecoins sits a concept that the Bank for International Settlements invokes with quiet reverence: the "singleness of money." The principle holds that a functioning monetary system depends on all forms of money being interchangeable at par, that a pound in one account is worth the same as a pound in another. CBDCs, backed by the full authority of the central bank, preserve this singleness. Private stablecoins, the argument runs, cannot guarantee it.

The ECB's case was stark. Senior policymakers in Frankfurt predicted that stablecoins, left unregulated, could replicate the pro-cyclical crises of nineteenth-century American charter banking, an era when hundreds of competing private bank notes circulated at fluctuating discounts to face value. Before the Federal Reserve's creation in 1913, twelve thousand different banknotes had circulated across the United States. Some were worth face value; others were not. No one always knew which was which. A senior BRICS central banker was equally uncompromising: "We should not give stablecoins the sheen of respectability by regulating them." The implication was that acknowledgment itself was a form of legitimization.

But there was a problem with the singleness of money argument, and it became harder to ignore the more carefully it was examined. Approximately 97 percent of all money in circulation is not central bank money. It is commercial bank money: created by private institutions in the form of loans, existing as ledger entries, redeemable in central bank money only on demand. The fractional reserve banking system, which has operated since London goldsmiths first began lending out the gold of their depositors in the seventeenth century — already breaks the singleness principle in a significant and largely unacknowledged way. Every current account balance is an unsecured claim on a private institution.

Deposit protection schemes exist precisely to paper over this crack. The UK's Financial Services Compensation Scheme protects deposits up to £85,000. The EU's Deposit Guarantee Scheme covers €100,000. The US Federal Deposit Insurance Corporation insures up to $250,000. These are not proof that commercial bank money is safe; they are an admission that it might not be. A stablecoin backed one-for-one by US Treasury securities could, in a technical sense, be argued to offer stronger collateralization than the average bank deposit, and Orchard acknowledged as much. "Plenty of digital native people argue exactly that, that if you've got a stablecoin, which you could argue is a money market fund or even a narrow bank, you can't have runs on the bank happening the same way." They were not wrong.

The boardroom where the future was argued

The ambivalence that runs through the official debate is mirrored in the private institutions most affected by its outcome.

Orchard described a meeting he witnessed at one of the world's largest transaction-services banks. A major consultancy firm at the table disclosed, with some matter-of-factness, that it was already using stablecoins for internal cross-border remittances because they were so much cheaper than traditional channels. "There was a sharp intake of breath from the bank concerned." The bank, whose revenue model depended on exactly those flows, was not amused.

But on the other side of Orchard sat a senior representative of one of the world's largest multilateral development banks. That voice was more cautious: "I don't know if I'm going to do that. I'd much rather this bank, my bank that provides treasury services to me, found a way to use this technology, even if it's stablecoins in the background, to make remittances cheaper than they are now. But I would then rather have the bank as my counterparty risk to conduct that business than go in and out of a stablecoin."

The exchange captured something precise. The consultancy firm represented one axis of the argument: stablecoins are more efficient, the economics are undeniable, adoption will follow. The multilateral development bank represented another: efficiency is not the only value. Trust, familiarity, and accountability matter too. Both positions were rational. Neither was obviously wrong.

The human dimension

Beneath the institutional debate lies a question that economists tend to underemphasize and citizens tend to feel most directly.

Dr. Jameel El-Iman, a technologist and honorary senior fellow at Imperial College London, put it plainly in a conversation with Digital Bytes in 2025. A former software engineer with four decades in digitalization across pharmaceuticals, manufacturing and financial services, El-Iman had sat on a panel examining the future of money and come away troubled. "We are trading our privacy for these conveniences," he said. "I think it's important that we slow down a bit and look at the human aspect of technology, and validate whether these technologies that we're deploying are actually for the benefit of society, or are they another control block in managing people?"

His concern was not that digital money would fail. It was that it would succeed, and that in the process, the granular monitoring of economic behavior that programmable money enables would become permanent, normalized and invisible. A cashless establishment that refuses legal tender is already a minor coercion. A fully programmable monetary system, without choice or fallback, would represent something more fundamental. "Before it happens," El-Iman argued, "there has to be some societal debate. There have to be some considerations beyond what the techies are saying: how governments govern, and our freedom, our privacy, our anonymity. All of these things will completely change when digital currencies become mainstream."

"Technology is like a speeding train," he observed. "No one knows where it's going, but no one can afford not to be on it." The remark is uncomfortable precisely because it is accurate. The history of digital platform adoption, from social media to ride-hailing to contactless payments, suggests that network effects tend to foreclose choice long before most people have consciously decided anything at all.

The Bank of England's "monsters in the deep" speech made a related point about AI in financial markets: rather than dampening volatility, artificial intelligence might amplify it in ways that current models are not equipped to anticipate. The same logic applies to programmable money at scale. The failure modes of systems we do not fully understand cannot be derived from the behavior of systems we do.

The bifurcation and what comes after

The direction of this contest is becoming clearer, even if the destination is not.

Europe and the UK are moving toward wholesale central bank digital currency, digital money operating at the interbank level, as a mechanism for keeping public money at the center of the financial system without the political complications of retail CBDC. The ECB has developed what Deutsche Bundesbank officials describe as a "quick and dirty" interim platform to link TARGET2, the eurozone's real-time gross settlement system, to distributed ledger infrastructure. The BIS Project Agorá and the Hong Kong Monetary Authority's Project Ensemble are experimenting with unified ledgers that would allow tokenized central bank money and commercial bank deposits to coexist on shared programmable infrastructure.

The United States is doing the opposite. By allowing private stablecoins to become systemic, Washington is betting that dollar-denominated private money will extend American monetary reach more effectively than any official digital dollar ever could. The bet is not without risk, the echoes of the pre-Federal Reserve era are audible to anyone who has studied that history, but it is a considered wager, and it is already affecting behavior in every other major financial center.

Tony McLaughlin, a payments strategist and long-time Digital Bytes contributor who developed the Regulated Liability Network concept, perhaps the most intellectually serious attempt to design a hybrid public-private digital money architecture, has, according to those close to the debate, stepped back from that framework. The direction in private finance is away from grand unified theories and toward narrower, more practical instruments: a clearing entity to de-risk stablecoins, a settlement layer agnostic about what it is settling.

Orchard's read of where it ends is historically grounded. "I've seen many times in my career the banking sector, helped by regulators, co-opting new technologies. You might think of Visa as an example." Visa began life as a bank cooperative in payments. It is now a global infrastructure company processing fifty trillion dollars per year. The stablecoins that today alarm officials gathered at the Sintra Central Banker Forum may, in fifteen years, be the back-end rails of the same institutions currently expressing alarm.

The OMFIF analysis for 2025 offered a formulation that cut to the heart of the paradox. Given the pace of stablecoin adoption relative to the caution of official digital money projects, a troubling hypothesis had emerged: that private sector actors, for all their interest-driven motivations, might at this rate become the de facto protectors of the singleness of money — rather than the public sector institutions whose principal duty it is.

That is not alarmism. It is a hypothesis the evidence supports. And it is exactly the kind of question that regulators in Washington, Frankfurt, London and Beijing have, however belatedly, begun to take seriously.

The architecture of the middle ground

Lewis McLellan of the Digital Monetary Institute, discussing the new US regulatory posture on The Digital Bytes Podcast in December 2024, drew attention to a technical development that the political debate had largely overlooked. The previous assumption that regulated financial instruments could not operate on public, permissionless blockchains had been overtaken by a practical discovery: compliance controls did not need to be applied at the infrastructure layer. They could be embedded in the token itself.

A stablecoin issued by a licensed trust bank under the GENIUS Act framework, the structure the Office of the Comptroller of the Currency had now explicitly sanctioned, could sit on Ethereum's public network while carrying rules that restricted its transfer to wallets whose holders had completed identity verification, blocked transactions involving addresses on OFAC's Specially Designated Nationals list, and permitted immobilization of holdings in response to a court order or regulatory instruction. "You're not banning the infrastructure," McLellan observed. "What you're doing is putting control mechanisms on the actual products that are running through and using the blockchain." The permissionless network became, in effect, the settlement layer. The compliance obligations were encoded in the instrument that moved across it.

The distinction mattered to the stablecoins-versus-CBDCs contest in a specific way. A CBDC issued by the Bank of England or the ECB would, by construction, carry state oversight at every step: the issuing authority would know every transaction, every balance, every payment destination. A stablecoin issued by a private institution on a public blockchain, with KYC embedded at the token level and reserve disclosures published to a public ledger, could offer verifiable compliance to any regulator with access to the chain data, without requiring the centralization of payment information in a government database. Whether that model was adequate to the duties of central banks, financial stability, monetary transmission, lender-of-last-resort capacity, was the question this chapter has traced. That it was technically feasible was no longer in doubt.

The contest between stablecoins and CBDCs could not be resolved without a framework: laws, licenses, and limits that both sides could live with. In 2025, that framework began arriving at speed, across multiple continents and through multiple legislatures and regulatory agencies. The next chapter examines what happened when politics finally caught up with the market.

Chapter 8: The Regulatory Reckoning

For years, the standard complaint from every serious player in the digital assets industry was the same: we cannot build if we do not know the rules. Banks cited regulatory uncertainty as their reason for holding back. Institutional investors cited it as their reason for staying out. Prudent entrepreneurs watched less prudent ones accumulate market share in a vacuum of oversight, then watched regulators arrive years too late with enforcement actions that looked more like punishment than policy. The financial world had coined a phrase for it: regulation by enforcement. It was not a system. It was an absence of one.

In the summer of 2025, that era ended.

In a display of bipartisan consensus that Washington had not managed on a technology issue in a generation, the United States Congress passed, and President Trump signed, a package of legislation that fundamentally redrew the map of digital finance. The Guiding and Establishing National Innovation for US Stablecoins Act, known by its acronym, passed the Senate 68 to 30 and the House 308 to 122 during what Capitol Hill was calling "Crypto Week." Alongside it came the Digital Asset Market Clarity Act, which drew a clear line between digital commodities and digital securities; and the CBDC Anti-Surveillance State Act, which prohibited the Federal Reserve from developing a central bank digital currency without express congressional approval. Three bills. Three different signals about the direction America had chosen.

The direction was unmistakable: the United States was not going to build public digital money. It was going to domesticate private digital money and deploy it in the service of American strategic interests.

The debt problem behind the legislation

To understand what the GENIUS Act actually is, it helps to begin not with the digital assets industry but with the US Treasury's balance sheet. By 2025, the national debt of the United States had surpassed $36 trillion, with a debt-to-GDP ratio exceeding 120 percent, its highest level since the Second World War. More immediately, Wells Fargo estimated that over $14 trillion of that debt would mature within the next three years, requiring refinancing at rates significantly higher than the 3.27 percent average the government currently paid. The projected additional annual interest cost: $300 billion. Annual deficits were tracking between $1.7 and $1.9 trillion. Moody's had downgraded the US credit rating in May 2025. The arithmetic was punishing.

Scott Bessent, the Treasury Secretary, stated the solution with notable directness: "We are going big on digital assets." His specific claim was that stablecoins could trigger two trillion dollars in T-bill demand. Citibank's estimate was more expansive: $3.7 trillion in stablecoin assets by 2030. The BIS had already documented the transmission mechanism: each wave of inflows into stablecoins reduced three-month US Treasury yields by approximately two to two and a half basis points within ten days. The logic was simple. The GENIUS Act requires every dollar-denominated stablecoin to be backed one-for-one by US dollars or short-dated Treasury securities. Every stablecoin minted creates a mandated buyer of American sovereign debt. The entire multi-hundred-billion-dollar stablecoin market becomes, in effect, a captive buyer at the short end of the yield curve.

This was not merely regulatory housekeeping. It was fiscal engineering.

1863: The return of national banking

The historical parallel, once you see it, is difficult to dismiss.

Kelly Kennedy, a law student at UC Law San Francisco working on GENIUS Act implementation at the law firm Perkins Coie, put it plainly in conversation with Digital Bytes: the legislation was "going backward in time to increase the stability of the US dollar." David Parsons, co-founder of the London Digital Exchange, developed the point further. The National Banking Acts of 1863 and 1864, signed by Abraham Lincoln, had allowed thousands of individual banks to issue their own printed notes – provided those notes were backed by US Treasury securities held in custody. The result was a proliferation of private money that was nonetheless anchored to sovereign debt, eliminating the wild discounting that had made the pre-war monetary patchwork unworkable.

"There were over 8,000 issuers of US dollars back in the 1860s," Parsons noted. "And so when some people say, oh, well, we've got Tether and we've got Circle, that'll be it. Why do we need another stablecoin? And then we hear of Airbnb, Wells Fargo, Morgan Stanley, BlackRock, Meta..." The list of entities publicly signaling interest in issuing GENIUS-compliant stablecoins was growing by the week. Bank of America's CEO Brian Moynihan had confirmed his institution would "go into stablecoins if regulation were passed." JPMorgan, Citigroup and Bank of America were reportedly in early discussions about a joint stablecoin venture. The irony was pointed: the institutions most threatened by stablecoin disruption were now racing to become stablecoin issuers.

For Parsons, the deeper significance was structural: the GENIUS Act was "removing the central bank from the issuance of currency directly to institutions who can hold the treasuries themselves and then issue their own dollar." The Federal Reserve System, established in 1913 precisely to rationalize the chaotic National Banking era, was, in a limited but meaningful sense, being partially bypassed. The question of who controls the US dollar in the twenty-first century was no longer purely academic.

What the law actually does

The GENIUS Act's mechanics are worth understanding precisely because the legislative debate often glossed over them.

At its core, the law requires all payment stablecoins to carry 1:1 reserve backing in US dollars or three-month Treasury bills. Cryptocurrencies cannot back stablecoins. Leverage cannot back stablecoins. Monthly public disclosure of reserve composition is mandatory; issuers above $50 billion in circulation face annual audits. The framework is tiered: issuers with market capitalizations above $10 billion fall under federal oversight through the Office of the Comptroller of the Currency or the Federal Reserve directly. Smaller issuers may operate under state-level regulation if their state's framework is certified as "substantially similar" to federal standards, but if they grow past the $10 billion threshold, they have 360 days to transition to federal oversight, obtain a waiver, or stop issuing new tokens.

Two features define the law's character. First, stablecoins are formally classified as neither securities nor commodities – removing them from SEC and CFTC jurisdiction and resolving one of the most bitterly contested questions in digital asset law. Second, issuers are explicitly prohibited from paying interest or yield on stablecoins. This restriction, combined with the legal tender exclusion, the Act states clearly that stablecoins are not legal tender, preserves an important distinction between stablecoins and bank deposits, one that regulators and the banking establishment had lobbied hard to maintain.

The Act also carries a long arm. Only "permitted payment stablecoin issuers" may issue to US persons. Foreign issuers in "qualifying non-US jurisdictions," determined by the Treasury, may receive an exemption, but must register with the OCC, maintain US-held reserves for domestic liquidity needs, and accept US legal jurisdiction. The international implications of that last requirement are still being absorbed by central banks from Frankfurt to Tokyo.

The legal tender question

The prohibition is clearly stated. The direction of travel is less clear.

Kennedy had spent months working on the Act's implementation pathway. Her reading: "They currently are specifically... in the GENIUS Act that explicitly says that they are not legal tender. But I think they could be heading in that direction." The specific barrier she identified was tax treatment. Under the IRS's classification established in 2014, all virtual currencies, including stablecoins, are property. Using USDC to pay a $5,000 tax bill technically requires the payer to calculate the acquisition cost of their tokens, compare it to market value at the time of payment, and report any capital gain. Even when a stablecoin has maintained a perfect one-dollar peg for its entire existence, the compliance burden of property treatment makes it functionally impractical for routine civic payments.

The question of legal tender turns, in Kennedy's analysis, on whether Congress or the IRS reclassifies stablecoins from property to currency. "If they allow for legal tender not to be taxed as property... then yes, they could be used to pay your taxes." That step, modest in technical terms, significant in political symbolism, would represent the full integration of private digital money into the fabric of American civic finance.

El Salvador demonstrated the outer limit of that logic in 2021, when it became the first country to adopt Bitcoin as legal tender. The implementation was troubled, volatility undermined everyday utility, and the Chivo state wallet saw low adoption, but the legal template was established. The Argentine province of San Luis later issued a blockchain-based digital asset for utility payments; Palau partnered with Ripple on a dollar-backed stablecoin for public transactions. These were test cases, not models, but they demonstrated that the boundary between private digital money and public finance was moveable.

Reeve Collins, co-founder of Tether and chairman of STBL, offered a vision of what comes next: "Stablecoin 2.0 takes this further with a dual token structure. Instead of embedding yield into the stablecoin, the system separates it, tokenizing both the dollar and the yield. One token functions as the spendable digital dollar, while the other represents the income stream from the underlying collateral." Collins's framing pointed toward a stablecoin ecosystem sophisticated enough to carry dividends, coupons, rent and interest on tokenized assets — programmable money that would make the yield prohibition look as temporary as every other financial restriction that market demand has eventually eroded.

The compliance arms race

The GENIUS Act also created a set of obligations that the digital assets industry was not prepared to meet.

The scale of the compliance challenge is not small. By mid-2025, Chainalysis documented that illicit addresses had received $40.9 billion in cryptocurrency during 2024 alone, a figure projected to rise above $51 billion as additional criminal wallets were identified. Stablecoins comprised 63 percent of all illicit transactions, an unprecedented proportion that reflected precisely the qualities that made stablecoins attractive to legitimate users: price stability, low transaction costs, near-instant cross-border settlement. The North Korean hackers who looted $1.46 billion from the Bybit exchange demonstrated the scale of what sophisticated state-level actors could accomplish against even well-resourced platforms.

Legacy compliance infrastructure was not designed for this environment. Traditional anti-money laundering frameworks relied on static rulebooks and sanctions list-matching. Retail Banker International estimated that up to 95 percent of AML alerts were inaccurate — producing an avalanche of false positives that consumed analyst time while genuine threats went undetected. Systems that updated on 24-hour batch cycles operated in a world where a stablecoin could be minted, transferred through dozens of wallets, and converted into another asset in minutes.

The GENIUS Act's requirement that issuers maintain the technical capacity to seize, freeze or burn tokens treated AI-backed real-time monitoring not as best practice but as a baseline legal obligation. Hong Kong's new stablecoin law, enacted in August 2025, imposed similar requirements: mandatory licensing, robust KYC, prohibition of services to anonymous wallets. The US Office of Foreign Assets Control had already signaled enforcement expectations, in 2025 alone it levied penalties exceeding $200 million against firms for sanctions failures. The compliance gap between regulatory expectation and industry capability became, almost overnight, a legal liability.

The global divergence

Washington's choice to champion private digital money rather than public was received differently in different capitals.

The World Economic Forum offered cautious optimism, noting that the GENIUS Act and the EU's MiCA framework pointed toward eventual regulatory convergence. The mechanics mapped broadly onto each other: licensing requirements, reserve standards, transparency obligations. But the underlying philosophies diverged sharply. The United States had banned CBDCs and staked its monetary future on private issuers. The European Union was still developing a digital euro and had proposed caps on individual holdings to prevent destabilizing bank runs. The ECB's digital euro project was being described internally as essential to European sovereignty. Washington's approach treated that sovereignty as a problem to be solved by commercial competition.

For emerging markets, the GENIUS Act's passage presented an uncomfortable choice: accept the incoming tide of dollar-denominated stablecoin liquidity and manage the monetary implications, or attempt to resist it and risk being left outside the infrastructure on which global commerce was increasingly being settled. Brazil's PIX, India's UPI, Kenya's M-Pesa had each proved that domestic digital payment systems could compete on their merits. Whether they could compete against a US stablecoin ecosystem carrying the combined backing of the Treasury, the OCC, and projected institutional flows in the trillions was a different question entirely.

What was left unresolved

The legislation answered many questions. It left others visibly open.

Critics had identified several gaps. The Act contained no prohibition on the President or members of his family holding financial interests in stablecoin businesses, a conflict that created the appearance, if not the fact, of regulatory capture from the moment of signing. Big Tech companies, including those with platforms operating at social network scale, were not prohibited from issuing stablecoins — raising the prospect of Meta or Apple creating digital currencies with hundreds of millions of users before the regulatory architecture for such instruments had matured.

The "Tether loophole", a provision that critics argued could allow offshore stablecoins to remain accessible on US decentralized exchanges without compliance — left a meaningful gap in the enforcement perimeter. The Act's provisions did not take full effect for eighteen months after enactment, leaving a transition period during which market participants knew the rules were coming but were not yet bound by them.

Most significantly, the prohibition on interest-paying stablecoins created a structural wedge between stablecoins and traditional bank deposits, but the sustainability of that wedge was uncertain. Reeve Collins's Stablecoin 2.0 dual token architecture was one route around it. Market pressure would find others. The law had drawn a line. The question was whether the line was in the right place, or whether it was simply the best approximation available to legislators working in real time against a technology that had not waited for them.

The disclosure standard being written

The regulatory reckoning described in this chapter was being given practical form by people whose earlier careers had been spent building exactly the kind of machine-readable compliance infrastructure the crypto industry was now required to develop. Jason Myers, chief executive of Auto Chain Labs, had been part of the team that implemented inline XBRL, the machine-readable financial reporting standard, at the United States Securities and Exchange Commission in 2009. That work transformed how public companies disclosed their finances: replacing static PDF documents, readable by humans but not systematically processable by machines, with structured data that regulators and market participants could query, compare and analyze at scale.

Speaking on The Digital Bytes Podcast, Myers described a direct parallel between what he had done at the SEC and what MiCA was now requiring of token issuers in Europe. MiCA required that token white papers, the primary disclosure document for any digital asset sold to the public, be filed in inline XBRL format. The UAE's Virtual Assets Regulatory Authority was requiring the same. The five SEC crypto task force roundtables in the spring of 2025, on token classification, trading venue requirements and investor disclosure standards, were the legislative process's first serious attempt to build those tools in consultation with the industry rather than against it. Myers attended all five. The confirmation of Paul Atkins as SEC chair in April 2025 had produced a regulatory environment oriented toward constructing a workable disclosure architecture rather than extracting penalties for the absence of one.

Globally, the regulatory reckoning was not confined to Washington, Brussels or London. Takatoshi Shibayama, founder of Copper Ltd and a specialist in Asia-Pacific crypto infrastructure, explained on Digital Bytes that Singapore had emerged as the de facto regulatory leader in the region, not because Singapore was soft on enforcement, but because it had made early, clear decisions about what could operate and under what conditions. "The countries that decide the rules early win. The ones that wait, and wait, and wait, they end up being followers." Asia's cryptocurrency adoption rates, measured by institutional custody, trading volumes and merchant acceptance in developing economies, were higher than Western adoption, despite Western regulatory attention. The advantage was not technical. It was regulatory clarity. Banks in India, Indonesia and the Philippines that would have supported stablecoin infrastructure were not doing so because they had no policy framework telling them it was permitted. Institutions in Singapore and Hong Kong, operating under clear guidelines, were actively building.

The global stablecoin regulatory race was not a West-versus-East competition. It was a competition between jurisdictions that had decided quickly and those still deciding slowly. Everyone was going to have to engage with the infrastructure eventually. The regulatory winners were the ones who would shape it while it was still malleable.

The GENIUS Act created a framework. What it could not create was the infrastructure on which that framework would run. Banks looking at the new regulatory landscape did not simply need to decide whether to issue stablecoins; they needed to decide what kind of digital money they were in the business of providing. The next chapter examines the answer the banking sector began to develop: tokenized deposits, and whether bank-issued digital money could compete with the private money that had drawn Washington's grudging legitimacy.

Chapter 9: Tokenized Bank Deposits

There is a particular quality to the silence of a large institution deciding what to do about something that threatens it. It is not the silence of paralysis. It is the silence of calculation. And throughout 2023, 2024 and into 2025, that is the silence that descended on the boardrooms and digital strategy units of the world's major commercial banks as they assessed the stablecoin question.

They could see what was happening. USDC and USDT were processing trillions of dollars in transactions annually. DeFi protocols were offering financial services, imperfect ones, without intermediaries. The GENIUS Act was creating a regulatory framework that would, for the first time, give institutional legitimacy to private digital money. And behind the regulation, the capital was assembling: Citibank projecting $3.7 trillion in stablecoin assets by 2030, Treasury Secretary Bessent talking about $2 trillion in T-bill demand. The question for every global bank was no longer whether digital money was real. It was whether the bank was going to be part of it, or watch from the outside as someone else built the rails.

The answer, increasingly, was a third option, one that the banks themselves were developing quietly, in pilot programs and white paper annexes, in partnership with regulators who were as keen as they were to avoid stablecoins running away from public oversight entirely. The answer was tokenized deposits.

What banks looked like before

To understand why tokenized deposits matter, it is worth pausing to consider what the banking system they are being built inside looks like today.

In 2023 alone, financial institutions spent over $205 billion on financial crime compliance: $65 billion in North America, $15 billion in South America, $85 billion across Europe, the Middle East and Africa, $45 billion in the Asia-Pacific. These were not investments in better outcomes. They were the cost of running legacy systems designed in a different era, against threats that had evolved into a different one. Transaction settlement still ran on batch cycles. Cross-border payments still moved through correspondent banking chains that added days, counterparty risk, and costs that a blockchain-native system would render structurally unnecessary. The global interbank settlement system was, in fundamental technical respects, still the interbank settlement system of the 1970s: computerized, yes; modernized, yes; but not reimagined.

What became clear when we looked at monetary infrastructure convergence in mid-2022 was the institutional calculation behind the industry's shift: tokenized deposits were not a response to DeFi's success, but an adaptation to the velocity gap that digital settlement had revealed. When a cross-border payment could settle in seconds on a public blockchain and a correspondent banking transaction required days, the friction was no longer incidental. It was existential. The banks were not choosing to build tokenized deposits because they wanted to catch up to DeFi. They were choosing to build them because the alternative, watching capital flows migrate to faster, cheaper settlement layers, was unacceptable. This was institutional self-preservation expressed as innovation.

Tokenized deposits were the banking system's response to that challenge: a way to capture blockchain's efficiency gains without abandoning the regulatory architecture that gave commercial bank money its special status.

The architecture of tokenized deposits

The concept, in its essence, is not complicated. A tokenized deposit is a digital representation of a bank deposit, the same deposit that sits in any corporate or retail account today, recorded on a blockchain rather than in a bank's internal ledger. From the bank's perspective, it remains a deposit liability. From the client's perspective, it retains the legal protections that come with regulated bank money: deposit insurance, recourse rights and regulatory supervision that no stablecoin, however well-backed, currently matches.

Peter Left, who heads Prudential Liquidity Management at Lloyds Bank, drew the distinction directly: "If you make a payment with commercial bank money and it goes wrong, you get protection. If you make payment with a stablecoin and you send it to the wrong address, no one's going to give you the money back." That asymmetry in recourse, invisible during normal operation, decisive in a dispute, was the commercial bank's strongest argument.

Oliver Wyman, the management consultancy advising large institutions on the digital money transition, defined tokenized deposits as blockchain-based digital representations of existing bank deposits, issued by regulated institutions. Unlike stablecoins, they were not issued by non-bank entities operating at arm's length from the supervisory framework. They were a digitized mirror of conventional money, with the addition of programmability and real-time settlement.

The pioneers

JPMorgan did not wait for regulatory consensus. In 2019, years before the stablecoin debate reached its current intensity, the bank launched what would eventually become Kinexys Digital Payments, its blockchain-based deposit platform. By 2025, it had processed over $1.5 trillion in transaction volume, with daily values often exceeding $2 billion. The platform enabled 24/7, multi-currency cross-border payments with near-instant finality. It was a proof of concept that worked.

Citi followed with Citi Token Services, an institutional infrastructure layer that embedded tokenized deposits into cross-border payments and trade finance. The platform used smart contracts and a private blockchain for continuous liquidity movement, and connected directly to the bank's work on the Regulated Liability Network. HSBC's FX Everywhere platform, used in conjunction with Wells Fargo, demonstrated on a different axis that distributed ledger technology could dramatically increase the efficiency of internal foreign exchange flows. As Richard Bibbey, HSBC's global head of FX and commodities, put it: "The global, cross-border nature of HSBC and its clients sees us conducting thousands of foreign exchange transactions within the bank, across multiple balance sheets, in dozens of countries. HSBC FX Everywhere uses DLT to drastically increase the efficiency of these internal flows."

In Switzerland, UBS, PostFinance and the digital asset bank Sygnum signed a memorandum of understanding to pilot deposit tokenization — backed by the Swiss Bankers Association and aimed at delivery-versus-payment settlement for interbank and financial asset transactions. In Germany, Deutsche Bank, DZ Bank, Commerzbank, UniCredit and Helaba tested commercial bank money tokens in a proof-of-concept project backed by the European Banking Authority, working alongside Siemens, Mercedes-Benz and BASF to explore 24/7 corporate payments and atomic settlement. The EBA's conclusion was significant: tokenized deposits were, from a regulatory standpoint, equivalent to conventional deposits. Not a new category requiring new rules. An old instrument on new infrastructure.

In the United Kingdom, six of the country's largest banks, including Barclays as the initiative's core supporter, were developing the Great British Deposit Token: a sterling-denominated tokenized deposit system built in collaboration with Quant and EY. The project represented something the UK financial establishment rarely managed: the major institutions choosing to build together rather than separately, recognizing that the systemic benefits of shared infrastructure outweighed whatever competitive advantage any single bank might gain from proprietary tokenized rails.

The standard the banks were defending

The programmability that came with tokenized deposits was not a flourish. It was the point.

Edward Budd at Adhara, whose technology underpinned several of the major bank tokenization projects, framed the endgame directly: "We see the seamless interoperability of tokenized deposits and wholesale CBDCs with intraday liquidity markets as the end game. Tokenized deposit solutions give banks a logical stepping stone to service clients better and connect them to this new ecosystem."

What this meant in practice was money that carried its compliance credentials with it. AML and KYC verification embedded in the transaction layer. Smart contracts that released payment upon delivery confirmation, without manual authorization, without bilateral reconciliation. Settlement that was atomic: completing fully or not at all, eliminating the counterparty risk that fractional settlement introduces. For corporate treasurers managing supply chains across dozens of countries and currencies, these were solutions to real operational problems that cost real money to manage in legacy systems.

The Deutsche Bank and UBS cross-border corporate payment experiment, run in partnership with Adhara and the Deutsche Bundesbank's Trigger Solution, tested precisely this capability for real business transactions: time-sensitive euro and FX payments settled across commercial bank money and central bank infrastructure simultaneously. The result was not a demo. It was a rehearsal for how the institutional payment system might operate at scale.

The problem the banks couldn't solve alone

The challenge that emerged from every pilot, every proof of concept, every bilateral partnership, was the same: fragmentation.

JPM Coin processed billions. But it operated within JPMorgan's network. A client of HSBC could not send tokenized deposits to a Citi counterparty on the same blockchain without a bridge. Deutsche Bank's CBMT pilot was not interoperable with Citi Token Services. The Great British Deposit Token was a sterling instrument; the Kinexys platform was primarily dollar-denominated. Every bank was building its own walled garden, and the result was promising technology that could not deliver on its most fundamental premise: seamless, universal liquidity movement.

Tony McLaughlin, a payments strategist and long-time Digital Bytes contributor, approached this problem from first principles. He had developed the Regulated Liability Network concept, a unified ledger on which central bank money, commercial bank money and other regulated liabilities could coexist and interoperate. By 2025, he had moved on from that framework. What the market needed, he concluded, was not a grand unified architecture. It needed a clearing system.

"The way that stablecoins become dominant on the planet," McLaughlin said in conversation with Digital Bytes in April 2025, "is I can send you stablecoins from 100 different issuers on five different blockchains, and you've got the ability to give them to your own bank or fintech and they give you par value... because they can go back to the issuers, burn those stablecoins, and transfer the actual cash." The analogy he returned to was the check clearing system. There were 4,500 banks in the United States. Nobody set up bilateral relationships between every pair of them. A clearing house allowed any check to be redeemed at par regardless of its issuer. The stablecoin and tokenized deposit market needed the equivalent.

McLaughlin's platform, Ubyx, was designed as that clearing mechanism, and to establish stablecoins as cash equivalents under international accounting standard IAS 32. The question sounds technical but the implication is practical. Under current treatment, a stablecoin on a corporate treasury's balance sheet is classified as a financial instrument, not a cash equivalent. This means corporate treasurers who receive stablecoins treat them as what McLaughlin called "hot potatoes": counterparty risk against the issuer, counterparty risk against the off-ramp, and an accounting treatment that makes them unsuitable for treasury policy. Until stablecoins can be recognized as cash equivalents, they cannot be systemic. The clearing system is the mechanism that would achieve that recognition by guaranteeing par value regardless of issuer.

A quiet but significant revolution

The commercial bank money token, in the view of those closest to its development, was not destined to replace stablecoins or CBDCs. It was destined to coexist with them, occupying a specific niche that neither could fully address.

CBDCs, where they were being developed, were suited to retail payments and public-sector use cases, anchored by sovereign backing. Stablecoins were suited to crypto markets, DeFi and the kind of permissionless cross-border liquidity that operated at the edges of the regulated system. Tokenized deposits were optimized for wholesale settlement, corporate payments and regulated environments where counterparty trust was paramount and recourse mattered.

The BIS had argued for years that the "singleness of money", the principle that all forms of money should be interchangeable at par, required public oversight at the center of the monetary system. Tokenized deposits were the banking sector's argument that singleness could be maintained through private infrastructure, not despite it. When a client of Deutsche Bank exchanged tokenized deposits with a client of Commerzbank through a shared clearing mechanism, the result was par value, the same pound, the same euro, regardless of which bank had issued the token. Not because of a central bank mandate, but because a market structure made it economically irrational for it to be otherwise.

Andrew Bailey had been cautious about banks issuing stablecoin-like products without sufficient regulation. But he had modified his position as the technology matured: "It should also be possible to have innovation in the form of money. It would therefore be wrong to be against stablecoins as a matter of principle. Indeed, I do not hold that view, recognizing their potential in driving innovation in payments systems both at home and across borders." The regulatory establishment was not hostile to bank-issued digital money. It was insisting that innovation happen within the regulatory perimeter rather than outside it.

That insistence was itself a form of validation. The institutions with the most to lose from the disruption of the banking model were, under pressure, becoming the institutions most actively developing the tools that would ensure their continued relevance. Tokenized deposits were not white flags. They were adaptive responses from institutions that had survived every previous disruption of the financial system, and intended to survive this one too.

The protocol above the account

The practical implementation of what tokenized deposits promised at the institutional level was being built, in a different register, by much smaller organizations working at the retail and commercial end of the same problem.

As described in the previous chapter, Adam Feiler of Minima and Alastair Constance of Mercury Electronic Money Institution had outlined an architecture that ran on the same logic as the tokenized deposit transformation: a smart contract layer sitting above conventional account custody, automating the conditions under which money moved while leaving the regulated holding of that money exactly where it had always been. The programmable bank account, where IoT sensors, smart contracts and FCA-regulated custody combined to settle an insurance claim without human authorization — was that principle expressed at the customer level.

The architecture resolved, in practical terms, what the BIS's "singleness of money" argument had been asking theoretically. The fiat currency holding, with its regulatory protections, its FCA oversight and its par value guarantee, remained intact. The layer that automated settlement conditions, provided an immutable audit trail and removed human discretion from the execution sat above it, not beneath it. Tokenized deposits, as this chapter has described, were the banking sector's claim that singleness could be maintained through private infrastructure. The programmable bank account was the same claim expressed at the customer level: that automation and smart contract execution could deliver the efficiency of DeFi without requiring anyone to step outside the regulated financial system.

The question that remained, the question that no regulatory framework, no pilot program and no clearing system architecture had yet fully answered, was what money was ultimately for. Whether it was a technology, a public good, a geopolitical instrument, or all three simultaneously. The final chapter asks where this convergence of digital money, programmability, sovereign interests and private innovation is likely to lead.

Chapter 10: The Future of Money

There is a moment when a shift that has been building for years finally becomes legible, when the forces accumulating in laboratories, policy committees, pilot programs and trading floors crystallize into something undeniable. For money, that moment arrived in 2025. Not with a single announcement or a crisis, but with a convergence: regulatory frameworks hardening, corporations entering the fray, sovereign strategies diverging, and the infrastructure of global payments quietly beginning to reorganize itself around blockchain rails.

The previous nine chapters have traced the journey that brought the world to this point. The inadequacies of a system built on correspondent banking relationships and settlement windows that closed on weekends. The emergence of Bitcoin as a protest and a provocation. The algorithmic collapse of Terra and Luna as a corrective shock. The careful, contested efforts of central banks to assert a digital presence. The transformation of payments, the regulatory reckoning, and the arrival of tokenized deposits as a bridge between the world that was and the world that is becoming. This final chapter asks what comes next, and why the answer matters far beyond the confines of finance.

Three tracks, one question

By the middle of 2025, it had become clear that the major economies were not converging on a single model for digital money. They were diverging, rapidly and deliberately, into three distinct strategic tracks, each a different answer to the same underlying question: who should control digital money, and in whose interests should it be designed?

The United States had made its choice with unusual speed and clarity. The GENIUS Act, which passed the Senate with bipartisan support, created a legal framework for private stablecoin issuance. The White House had already moved by executive order to ban central bank digital currencies, signaling that the administration's preferred model was private-sector innovation rather than state-issued digital dollars. Federal Reserve Governor Christopher Waller noted that private stablecoins could strengthen the dollar's dominance without requiring government overreach. The logic was consistent: extend the reach of the dollar digitally, leverage the existing trust in the US financial system, and let the private sector build the rails. It was, as Digital Bytes had observed earlier in the year, the third chapter in a long expansion, from the petrodollar to the eurodollar and now to the stablecoin, each phase extending dollar influence into new territory, new transaction types, and new corners of the global economy.

Europe was moving along a different axis. The European Central Bank had conducted extensive distributed ledger technology trials between May and November 2024, testing three interoperability models across sixty-four market participants in nine countries, settling approximately €1.6 billion through DLT infrastructure. The ambition was to build a digital euro that preserved the ECB's role as the anchor of monetary stability while adapting to a world where instant, programmable payments were becoming the norm. Yet progress remained cautious, and critics were direct. OMFIF analysts John Orchard and Katie-Ann Wilson argued that the ECB appeared to be "projecting the traditional bank run experience onto the very different context of stablecoins," warning that fears of large-scale digital euro redemptions were "largely irrational" in a system where assets were matched one-for-one. Europe's caution, they suggested, risked turning it into a flyover zone on the DLT map while others pressed ahead.

China, meanwhile, was playing a longer and less visible game. The e-CNY had been deployed quietly but systematically along Belt and Road corridors, facilitating trade settlement in digital yuan and reducing the friction, and the dollar dependency, that had characterized those transactions. The mBridge project, developed with central banks from the UAE, Thailand and Hong Kong, was building the cross-border infrastructure to make this permanent. Where the US was extending dollar power through private stablecoins and the EU was protecting monetary sovereignty through institutional caution, China was constructing an alternative monetary order, one payment corridor at a time.

Beneath the three-track competition sat a fourth dimension that none of the major powers fully controlled: the question of cross-chain settlement and multi-currency interoperability. If the US dollar stablecoin ecosystem, the digital euro and the e-CNY each represented sealed monetary orders, the real bottleneck would be trade between them. BRICS nations had recognized that payment settlement infrastructure was itself a form of monetary sovereignty, and that building neutral settlement layers, atomic swaps between different currency zones using distributed ledgers controlled by no single jurisdiction, was the infrastructure prerequisite for genuine monetary autonomy. The infrastructure being built for this final dimension was not state-led in any direct way. It was being constructed through DeFi protocols, cross-chain bridges and decentralized settlement systems whose governance was distributed across multiple jurisdictions. The three-power competition for digital money would ultimately be constrained or enabled by whether these borderless settlement mechanisms achieved sufficient scale and reliability to connect the sealed orders into a functioning global system.

The battle over digital money was not just about technology. It was about who set the rules. And in 2025, three very different rule-sets were competing for global adoption.

The clearing gap

Within these geopolitical contests sat the infrastructure problem the previous chapter had left open. The three-track world of dollar stablecoins, the digital euro and the e-CNY each assumed a monetary coherence at the technical layer that the market had not yet delivered. Every prior payment instrument that achieved mass adoption, checks, credit cards, wire transfers, did so because a clearing system made it fungible at par, anywhere, regardless of issuer. McLaughlin's work at Ubyx, and the accounting reclassification question under IAS 32, represented precisely that unfinished business: until stablecoins could be treated as cash equivalents rather than financial instruments, corporate treasurers would keep treating them as hot potatoes, and the proliferating ecosystem of bilateral issuer arrangements would remain structurally unscalable.

The defining investment of the stablecoin era, in this reading, was not picking the winning coin. It was building the plumbing that made every coin trustworthy: a clearing standard that guaranteed par value regardless of issuer and gave institutional participants the accounting certainty to hold rather than immediately convert.

The corporate reckoning

The third dynamic ran through the private sector, where the mathematics of adoption were accelerating independently of regulatory timelines. The interchange fee system, $187.2 billion extracted from US merchants annually by card networks operating at 60 and 70 percent profit margins, had always presented a structural incentive for any retailer large enough to contemplate an alternative. By 2025 that contemplation had become strategy. Amazon and Walmart were both exploring stablecoin issuance. PayPal's PYUSD had already settled invoices between SAP, EY and Google. Shopify had enabled USDC acceptance. Apple, Meta, Airbnb and X were piloting capabilities.

In the twelve months to February 2025, $6.3 trillion in stablecoin payments had cleared: fifteen percent of all global retail cross-border payments for the year, growing at twenty-one percent annually. The question was no longer whether the corporate sector would adopt stablecoins, but what market structure emerged when the largest technology and retail companies held their own digital currencies. Whether it resembled a competitive payment ecosystem, or something closer to vertical monetary integration — private money at the scale of governments, without any of the public obligations that role has historically carried.

The geopolitical consequence

Behind the corporate competition and the infrastructure debates lay a set of consequences extending well beyond the financial system.

David Parsons had framed stablecoins as the third chapter in the long dollar story, petrodollar, eurodollar, now stablecoin, but the mechanism this time was fundamentally different from its predecessors. There was no diplomatic agreement to negotiate, no banking relationship to establish, no correspondent network to maintain. A Venezuelan family holding USDT, a Kenyan freelancer paid in USDC, a Chinese trader settling commodity invoices in dollar stablecoins: each was a node in a network that extended dollar power without a single decision from the Federal Reserve or the US Treasury.

The implications for monetary sovereignty were serious and uneven. For the governments of weaker economies, those where, as the Latin American central banker had made plain in earlier discussion, monthly inflation was not a theoretical risk but a lived experience — access to a stable digital dollar was not a threat to sovereignty. It was a practical necessity. The stablecoin was less an instrument of dollar imperialism than a pragmatic alternative to currencies that had already failed their citizens.

But the consequences were different for more stable economies, and different again for the global system as a whole. If central banks lost a significant share of monetary transactions to stablecoin flows, their ability to steer economies through interest rate adjustments would diminish. Tax collection in local currencies would become more complicated. Capital controls would erode. The policy toolkit, built over a century of central banking practice, would begin to rust. The "Big Bang" of US stablecoins might seem quiet in its early phases, but in hindsight it might prove to be the most transformative monetary shift since Bretton Woods.

What money is for

The questions that open any serious examination of digital money are the same questions that close it. What is money for? Is it a technology, a public good, a geopolitical instrument, a unit of account, a store of value, a means of exchange? The answer, of course, is that it has always been all of these simultaneously, and the tension between those functions has always been the defining challenge of monetary governance.

What the stablecoin revolution and its surrounding infrastructure have done is make that tension visible in a new way. When a private corporation issues its own digital money and embeds it in the daily transactions of hundreds of millions of people, the question of who controls the unit of account becomes political in the most direct sense. When a US dollar-backed token circulates in a country where the local currency has collapsed, the question of monetary sovereignty is answered, de facto, by market adoption rather than by law. When a clearing system built on blockchain rails settles trillions of dollars of value without a correspondent bank in sight, the question of financial infrastructure becomes a question about who owns the pipes through which value flows.

Tony McLaughlin had articulated the aspiration clearly: a pluralistic ecosystem of thousands of issuers, multiple currencies and many blockchains, unified by clearing standards that guaranteed singleness of money, the principle that one dollar held in any form should be redeemable at par everywhere. That was, at its core, a social compact: an agreement, enforced by infrastructure and regulation together, that money was trustworthy regardless of who issued it.

Whether that compact could be extended digitally – whether the clearing infrastructure could be built, the accounting standards updated, the regulatory frameworks aligned well enough to create genuine interoperability across US, European, Asian and emerging markets – remained the central open question of the decade ahead. The technology, as every chapter of this book has demonstrated, was not the primary obstacle. The technology worked. The obstacles were institutional, political and jurisdictional: the legacy of a monetary system designed in an era of wire transfers and business hours, now being asked to accommodate an era of programmable money that moved at the speed of code.

What was already clear was that the old binary, digital money as either a fringe innovation or a systemic threat, had been replaced by something more complex and more interesting. Digital money was now a strategic instrument deployed by the United States to extend dollar dominance, a sovereignty project pursued by Europe with painstaking deliberation, a parallel monetary order constructed by China through patient infrastructure investment, and a lifeline adopted by individuals and businesses in fragile economies for whom the alternative was worse. It was simultaneously a corporate efficiency play, a financial inclusion mechanism, a geopolitical weapon, and a genuine reimagining of what money could be.

The journey traced in these pages is, at its deepest level, a story about trust: about the slow, contested, still-unfinished project of building in digital money the kind of trust that most people extend, without a second thought, to the banknote in their wallet or the balance on their bank statement. The institutions that managed to build that trust, whether through a clearing standard, a regulatory license, a reserve audit, or the sheer weight of network effects, would shape the monetary landscape of the twenty-first century.

The question was no longer who controlled the interest rate. The question, as the Big Bang expanded and its shockwaves reached every corner of the financial system, was who controlled the code that moved value. And the answer to that question would define not just the future of money, but the future of economic power itself.

What the next era is being built for

In our discussions of the US Clarity Act on The Digital Bytes Podcast in 2025, we returned repeatedly to a formulation that cut beneath the legislative details. The act represented, in our reading, the third iteration of a consistent American strategy. The petrodollar arrangement of the 1970s had extended the dollar's reach into the global oil market through a bilateral deal with Saudi Arabia. The eurodollar system had extended it into offshore markets by allowing dollar-denominated lending and borrowing outside Federal Reserve jurisdiction. The stablecoin era, and the Clarity Act governing it, represented the third chapter: extending the dollar into digital markets, cross-border commerce, and the tokenization of assets that had previously been illiquid, inaccessible, or unglobalizable — "tokenizing data, your car, your health records," as we observed during those conversations, listing the categories the act proposed to open to digital ownership and exchange, and in doing so, to the dollar-denominated settlement infrastructure that increasingly ran beneath them.

The United States Strategic Bitcoin Reserve, declared by executive order in March 2025, occupied the same strategic logic from a different direction: a sovereign hedge whose deeper story unfolds in *The Bitcoin Era.*

What both decisions reflected was a single underlying recognition: that the infrastructure through which value moved in the twenty-first century would be built on code; that code was jurisdictional, it operated under a legal framework that gave it meaning and enforcement; and that the country whose legal framework governed the most widely used code would exercise a form of monetary sovereignty that no quantity of gold reserves or interest rate decisions could replicate. The question of who controlled the code was the question of who controlled the future of economic power.

Chapter 11: Cross-Border Payments

The plumbing that runs the world economy

Every time a manufacturer in Stuttgart pays a supplier in Shenzhen, every time a Filipina nurse in London sends her monthly remittance back to Manila, every time a trading firm in New York settles an import contract with a counterpart in Lagos, the same creaking, invisible infrastructure springs reluctantly into life. Correspondent banking, a network of bilateral relationships between financial institutions, threaded together through a series of intermediary accounts held at one bank inside another — has served as the plumbing of international commerce for the better part of two centuries. It has worked, after a fashion. But working after a fashion is no longer good enough when the global economy demands something far faster, far cheaper and far more transparent.

The scale of what passes through this infrastructure is staggering. Business-to-business cross-border payments are projected to reach $43 trillion by 2025 and $56 trillion by 2030. B2B e-commerce alone, the digital trade between businesses rather than between businesses and individual consumers, is expected to grow from $34 trillion in 2024 to $67 trillion by 2029. These are not the transaction volumes of a niche financial product. They are the lifeblood of globalized trade, and the system carrying that lifeblood is, by every meaningful measure, unfit for the purpose it has been appointed to serve.

The average international wire transfer takes three to five business days to settle. Fees range from two to five percent of the transaction value, sometimes considerably more for smaller remittances to developing nations. A small exporter in Vietnam or a garment factory in Bangladesh may lose a meaningful fraction of every payment it receives simply to the cost of receiving it. The system operates only on banking days, in banking hours, through banking intermediaries that each extract their own toll. The nostro and vostro accounts that correspondent banks maintain with one another, essentially pre-funded pools of currency sitting idle in foreign institutions, lock up an estimated $25 trillion in liquidity at any given moment. That is $25 trillion that could be deployed productively, earning returns, financing growth, but instead sits dormant as the price of making cross-border payments work at all.

The stablecoin insurgency

Against this backdrop, the numbers coming out of digital asset infrastructure are beginning to tell a remarkable story. In 2024 alone, stablecoin transaction volume reached $27.6 trillion. To contextualize that figure: it exceeds the combined volumes processed by Visa and Mastercard in the same period by approximately 7.7%. These are not projections from a white paper. They are measurable transaction flows running through a parallel infrastructure that settled, in many cases, in minutes rather than days, for fees measured in fractions of a cent rather than percentages of principal.

Between January 2023 and February 2025, according to data compiled by multiple blockchain analytics firms, stablecoins facilitated $94.2 billion specifically in B2B cross-border payment flows. That represents identified, trackable business payments, not speculative trading volume, not DeFi arbitrage, not retail gambling on price movements. Actual international commerce moving through a different set of rails because those rails are faster, cheaper and increasingly regarded as reliable.

What our examination of cross-border payment acceleration in early 2022 identified was a threshold moment: when treasury managers began choosing digital settlement over correspondent banking, it was not because of ideological commitment to decentralization. It was because the velocity advantage was material and unmissable. A supply chain manager able to confirm delivery and trigger payment in 90 seconds rather than managing a four-day settlement window eliminated working capital friction that correspondent banking had encoded as permanent. The economic consequence was multiplicative: for a company processing millions of transactions annually, the saving in working capital financing cost, in payment failures from late settlement, in currency volatility exposure from extended settlement periods, was substantial enough to justify integration of entirely new payment infrastructure. This was the transition from crypto-as-novelty to crypto-as-operational-necessity: the point where the speed advantage became too significant for risk-averse institutions to ignore.

The global stablecoin market had reached approximately $170 billion in circulating supply by mid-2025, with USDC and USDT dominating flows but new entrants arriving from every direction. The commercial logic is not difficult to grasp. A business treasury manager who can settle a cross-border invoice in ninety seconds, with on-chain confirmation and automated reconciliation, at a cost of fractions of a cent, has very little reason to prefer a process that takes four days, involves three correspondent banks and costs three percent.

The implications reach further than the treasury departments of medium-sized exporters. Mastercard has begun integrating stablecoins into its payment network across parts of Eastern Europe. In Puerto Rico, 90% of small and medium-sized enterprises credit digital payment infrastructure, including stablecoin settlement, with enabling growth that traditional banking channels did not permit. In global corridors where correspondent banking relationships have thinned over the past decade as compliance costs drove large banks out of higher-risk markets, stablecoin rails have moved into the gap.

The corporate giants enter the arena

When merchants at the scale of Walmart and Amazon begin exploring their own dollar-backed stablecoin operations, the nature of what is developing ceases to be a story about fintech disruption at the margins and becomes something more fundamental. Both companies were reported in 2025 to be examining the possibility of issuing proprietary stablecoins, not because they want to become banks, but because stablecoins enable something that conventional financial infrastructure cannot: programmable money embedded directly into commercial workflows.

Programmable money means, practically, that payment mechanisms can carry conditions. A smart contract governing supply chain finance might release payment to a manufacturer not on a fixed date but upon verified confirmation that goods have cleared a particular customs point. The payment itself is not just a notification that value has moved, it is the action of value moving, triggered automatically, without the involvement of a bank processor, a treasury officer or a clearing house. For a company with millions of supplier relationships and billions of supply chain transactions, the operational efficiency gains from this kind of automation are substantial.

The precedent, however, is not without its warnings. Meta's attempt to launch Libra, later renamed Diem, was wound down in 2022 under a coordinated wave of regulatory hostility from governments and central banks that recognized, with some alarm, what a global private stablecoin operated by a platform with three billion users would mean for monetary sovereignty. The difference in 2025 is that the United States government has not just tolerated the emergence of dollar-backed stablecoins but actively encouraged them. The GENIUS Act, which passed the United States Senate, provides a regulatory framework for stablecoin issuance with explicit federal oversight, reserve requirements and consumer protections. The signal that legislation sends is unambiguous: Washington has decided that dollar-denominated stablecoins are a tool of American financial influence, not a threat to it.

The economic logic is compelling. A world in which international trade is increasingly settled in dollar-backed digital assets rather than through SWIFT transfers necessarily increases global demand for US Treasury bills, since stablecoin issuers are required to hold high-quality liquid assets, predominantly short-dated US government debt, as reserves. Tether alone, the issuer of USDT, was among the largest holders of US Treasury securities in the world by 2025. The proliferation of dollar stablecoins, viewed through this lens, is not an alternative to US monetary hegemony. It is its digital continuation.

The geopolitics of payment rails

Not everyone shares the American perspective. The exclusion of Russian financial institutions from SWIFT in May 2022, executed within days of the full-scale invasion of Ukraine, demonstrated with surgical precision that access to the international payment system is a geopolitical instrument as much as a financial one. Russia had previously been warned that such exclusion was possible. What the speed and completeness of the action demonstrated was that the warning had been underestimated.

The consequences have been instructive. Russia moved rapidly to expand the use of digital assets in cross-border trade, deploying the digital rouble for selected bilateral transactions and facilitating USDT-denominated settlement for oil exports to countries unwilling to risk secondary sanctions by transacting in conventional dollar flows. Iran, long familiar with the experience of sanctions-induced isolation, had developed similar workarounds. China, with rather more leverage, began pressing harder on yuan internationalization through its own channels: expanding the Cross-Border Interbank Payment System, deepening UnionPay's reach across South-East Asia, and contributing to discussions about a BRICS payment infrastructure that might reduce collective dependence on dollar-denominated clearing systems.

The Bank for International Settlements, recognizing that the geopolitical fragmentation of payment infrastructure presents systemic risks, launched Project Agorá in partnership with major central banks. The project aims to create a shared wholesale financial market infrastructure using tokenized central bank money — essentially, a way to move central bank reserves across borders using blockchain settlement. JPMorgan and DBS established Partior, a wholesale digital money network built to eliminate the nostro and vostro inefficiencies that correspondent banking has never solved. Japan launched Project Pax, a collaboration involving MUFG, SMBC and Mizuho alongside SWIFT and domestic infrastructure provider Progmat, specifically targeting interoperability between Japanese yen stablecoin settlements and blockchain platforms including Corda, Ethereum and Polygon.

What emerges from these parallel initiatives is not a single winner but a more complicated picture: competing digital payment infrastructures, each backed by different geopolitical interests and regulatory philosophies, operating alongside a fragmenting global economy in which the unipolar payment system of the SWIFT era is giving way to something more plural, more contested and considerably more complex.

The wildcat banking problem

History, as ever, offers a mirror. In the nineteenth century, before the United States had established a national banking system, individual private banks across the country issued their own paper currency. Hundreds of different notes circulated simultaneously, each backed by the reserves of its issuing institution, each redeemable in theory but harder to redeem the further you traveled from the issuing bank. The system served a purpose, it provided money supply in an economy that needed it, but it was unstable, prone to fraud and occasionally collapsed in cascades of bank failures that wiped out the savings of those who had trusted the wrong institution.

The parallels to the current stablecoin landscape are not merely rhetorical. Critics of the GENIUS Act and of the broader permissive stance toward private stablecoins point to the systemic risk of allowing hundreds of separate stablecoin issuers to create shadow deposit-like instruments without the full regulatory protections that apply to insured bank deposits. If a large stablecoin issuer fails, whether through fraud, a run, or a collapse in the value of its reserves, the ripple effects through the financial system could be severe. The characterization of excessive stablecoin proliferation as "Subprime 2.0" is hyperbolic, perhaps, but it contains a serious analytical point. Financial crises tend to originate in the places where credit creation happens outside the established regulatory perimeter. Stablecoins backed by complex or opaque portfolio assets rather than plain US Treasury bills sit uncomfortably close to that perimeter.

The European response has been characteristically more cautious. The Markets in Crypto-Assets regulation, MiCA, subjects stablecoin issuers operating in the European Union to licensing requirements, reserve standards and caps on transaction volumes for non-euro stablecoins. The digital euro, when it eventually arrives, is explicitly designed by the European Central Bank not merely as a retail payment instrument but as a mechanism to ensure that

European monetary sovereignty is not gradually ceded to American private issuers. Jean-Claude Trichet, former President of the ECB, has argued that the dollar-stablecoin strategy, however beneficial to American interests, represents a form of monetary colonialism for economies that allow it to displace domestic payment infrastructure without regulatory response.

The infrastructure being built

Beneath the regulatory debates and geopolitical maneuvering, engineers and product builders are assembling the actual infrastructure through which the next generation of cross-border payments will flow. The components are mostly in place. Stablecoin settlement provides the medium of exchange. Smart contracts provide the programmability. Blockchain infrastructure provides the transparency and immutability of record. What remains is integration: connecting these digital rails to the existing commercial systems that businesses actually use in their day-to-day operations.

Partior, backed by JPMorgan and DBS, is specifically focused on the correspondent banking replacement problem: moving interbank settlement onto a blockchain to eliminate the nostro/vostro inefficiency at its source. Rather than pre-funding accounts at dozens of correspondent institutions worldwide, banks using Partior's infrastructure exchange tokenized representations of central bank money on a shared ledger, settling with finality in seconds. Project Agorá extends this vision to the multi-currency, multi-central-bank level: a shared settlement layer for cross-border wholesale transactions between participating central bank jurisdictions.

For businesses lower in the hierarchy, the exporter in Vietnam, the small manufacturer in Ghana, the software contractor in Colombia receiving payment from a client in Germany, the relevant infrastructure is different but the direction is the same. Stablecoin wallets connected to banking rails via regulated on-ramps and off-ramps. Payment protocols that can move value from a dollar-denominated digital account to a local currency bank account in a single automated step. Remittance corridors where a migrant worker can send money home in seconds for ten cents rather than in three days for ten dollars.

The trajectory is clear even if the destination is not yet settled. The plumbing of international commerce is being rebuilt, not all of it at once, not without friction, not without the kind of regulatory battles and geopolitical maneuvering that attend the replacement of major financial infrastructure. But rebuilt it will be, and the rebuilding is already well advanced.

What this means for the future

The cross-border payments revolution is not, at its core, a technological story. It is a story about power: who controls the infrastructure through which value moves across borders, on what terms, at what cost, and subject to whose rules. For most of the past century, those questions had settled answers. The SWIFT network, dominated by Western institutions, served Western interests. The correspondent banking system, built on dollar primacy, reflected dollar primacy. Those not well served by the existing architecture, the unbanked, the sanctioned, small businesses in frontier markets, absorbed the friction as the price of participation.

What is changing is that the friction is now optional. The alternative infrastructure exists and is growing. The choice between old and new rails will be made by treasury managers choosing the system that settles faster, costs less and uses fewer intermediaries.

The dollar-backed stablecoin model will likely continue to expand, driven by American commercial and geopolitical interests. But it will not be unopposed. The digital euro, the digital yuan, and the interoperability initiatives from the BIS and from BRICS-adjacent monetary coalitions all represent competing visions of how the next chapter of international monetary architecture should be written. The result may not be a single global system at all, but a more fragmented landscape of competing digital payment corridors: faster, cheaper and more transparent than the correspondent banking era, but perhaps no less contested in terms of whose interests it ultimately serves in the real world of trade, capital and enforcement. That tension between efficiency and sovereignty, openness and control, and market logic and geopolitics will define cross-border payments.

Chapter 12: Sanctions and Geopolitics

The price of two trillion dollars

The United Nations has estimated that approximately $2 trillion is laundered through the global financial system every year: roughly 5% of global gross domestic product. That number has circulated in policy circles and academic papers for so long that it has acquired the comfortable familiarity of a statistic that no longer disturbs. And yet two trillion dollars, processed annually through the infrastructure of international finance, represents a staggering volume of criminal proceeds, terrorist financing and sanctions evasion finding its way through correspondent banking, trade finance, real estate, shell companies and a thousand other channels.

Against that backdrop, the criminal use of crypto assets has been a subject of intense regulatory and media attention. Chainalysis, the blockchain analytics firm that tracks illicit activity across public ledgers, has consistently estimated that criminal use of crypto represents approximately 0.7% of total transaction volume, a figure strikingly smaller than the volumes moving through traditional banking channels without detection. The point is not that crypto is clean; it is that the comparison is frequently distorted by the visibility that blockchain's public ledger creates. When every transaction is permanently and publicly recorded, criminal activity becomes, paradoxically, more auditable than when it passes through opaque systems with no equivalent transparency obligation.

This visibility cuts both ways. It makes crypto genuinely useful as a tool for financial investigators. It also makes it genuinely attractive to state actors with sophisticated technical capabilities and a motivation to find workarounds to Western sanctions — because the transparent public ledger, once you understand it, can be gamed through a set of techniques that legacy compliance systems were never designed to detect.

State actors and the weaponization of crypto

Russia's experience since May 2022, when it was excluded from SWIFT, has been a compressed laboratory experiment in what sanctioned states can do when they decide to find out. The answer, it has emerged, is quite a lot.

Russia has deployed the digital rouble in selected bilateral transactions, developed an alternative to SWIFT for domestic interbank communication, and facilitated USDT-denominated settlement for oil and commodity exports to countries calculating that secondary sanctions risk is manageable. Russian entities have also made extensive use of cryptocurrency for ransomware operations: attacks on critical infrastructure, hospitals and businesses that extract payments in Bitcoin or Monero and convert them through mixers, privacy coins and eventually into fiat currencies through jurisdictions with permissive regulatory environments. The combination of state tolerance for ransomware operators and state willingness to use crypto infrastructure for sanctions evasion has made Russia the most significant case study in how a major economy adapts to being cut off from the dollar-dominated financial system.

Our conversations with compliance technology leaders in early 2022 surfaced a structural insight: the sanctions evasion challenge was not a law enforcement problem that could be solved through detection and blocking. It was an architecture problem that could only be solved through infrastructure design. A compliant stablecoin system with mandatory freeze capability embedded at the protocol level, as the GENIUS Act would later mandate, transformed sanctions from a reversible action requiring real-time compliance monitoring to a permanent lock on value transfer that no amount of mixing or obfuscation could circumvent. This shifted the geopolitical calculus. Sanctioned entities could adapt SWIFT evasion through alternative payment corridors, but they could not defeat a technical architecture in which the underlying asset could be frozen by its issuer in response to a sanctions designation. The result was a race between sanctions infrastructure that could reach into digital value systems and alternative digital infrastructures built specifically to operate outside the jurisdictional reach of sanctions enforcement. This was how monetary architecture became directly relevant to geopolitical competition.

Iran's experience predates Russia's by a decade and provides a longer-term perspective. Iranian entities have mined Bitcoin using heavily subsidized electricity, at one point accounting for an estimated 3% or more of global Bitcoin mining capacity, and used the resulting holdings for international trade, including oil exports sold to China, Russia and Venezuela in Bitcoin-denominated transactions that bypass the dollar system entirely. The Iranian government launched the digital rial in 2024, partly as a domestic payments modernization initiative and partly as an infrastructure piece for a broader strategy of circumventing the SWIFT-dependent architecture of international commerce.

North Korea presents the starkest example of state-level criminal exploitation. The Lazarus Group, a hacking collective operating under the direction of the Pyongyang government, executed what became the largest cryptocurrency theft on record: the $1.46 billion attack on the Bybit exchange in February 2025. Lazarus used sophisticated social engineering to compromise validator keys, drained multiple wallets and then began converting the proceeds through a chain of obfuscation techniques, mixing services, cross-chain bridges, privacy coins, over-the-counter brokers operating in unregulated jurisdictions, that represent the current state of the art in money laundering through digital assets. The United States Treasury Department, UK OFSI and international partners sanctioned Lazarus entities, but the fundamental problem of attribution and enforcement against actors inside a jurisdiction with no interest in cooperation with international law enforcement is not solved by a sanctions designation.

The compliance industry responds

The scale of the problem has given rise to a compliance industry of considerable sophistication. The United Kingdom's Office of Financial Sanctions Implementation published its Cryptoassets Threat Assessment in July 2025, and the document made sobering reading for anyone still under the impression that the crypto compliance problem is marginal. Of all suspected sanctions breaches reported to OFSI during the assessment period, 7% involved crypto firms, a significant share for an asset class that still represents a fraction of broader financial flows. More striking still, 90% of those reports were filed after April 2024, suggesting that reporting culture and detection capability had improved dramatically in a very short time, but also that the absolute volume of crypto-related sanctions concerns was growing rather than declining.

The assessment identified several red flag indicators that compliance teams should monitor: large transactions executed immediately after a new sanctions designation announcement; chains of small transactions structured to fall below reporting thresholds; sudden jumps in activity involving jurisdictions not aligned with UK sanctions policy; use of privacy-enhancing services such as coin mixers or zero-knowledge swaps; and access to trading platforms through KYC-free services or anonymous wallet providers. Each of these behaviors, individually, might have an innocent explanation. Their combination in a single transaction chain is a different matter.

The case of Garantex illustrates both the scale of the problem and the limitations of the response. Garantex, a Russia-based crypto exchange, was designated by the United States Treasury in May 2022 for facilitating transactions on behalf of sanctioned entities. It continued operating. By 2025, intelligence gathered by blockchain analytics firms suggested that Garantex had processed $9.3 billion in the four months following its rebranding as Grinex, a new entity established in Kyrgyzstan with different ownership structures but substantially similar operations. The rebranding was not especially subtle, but it was effective. Creating a new entity in a different jurisdiction is not technically difficult, and the compliance obligation falls on counterparties, exchanges, banks, on-ramps and off-ramps, to detect the relationship between the old sanctioned entity and its successor. This is precisely the kind of challenge that legacy compliance systems were not built to meet.

Legacy AML infrastructure has a well-documented weakness: it generates false positives at an extraordinary rate. Estimates typically suggest 95% of flagged transactions are ultimately found to involve no criminal conduct, while batch-processing checks on twenty-four-hour cycles leave substantial windows during which suspicious activity can proceed undetected. A sophisticated criminal operation running through a crypto platform can execute, blend and move funds faster than a compliance department running end-of-day screening will ever observe.

Artificial intelligence and the arms race

The response to this challenge has increasingly come from artificial intelligence. Elliptic, Chainalysis and a growing field of specialist compliance technology firms have developed AI systems capable of cross-chain analysis: tracking value as it moves between different blockchains through bridge protocols that conventional transaction monitoring was never designed to follow. Natural language processing enables fuzzy matching against sanctions lists, detecting name transliterations and alias chains that defeat exact string searches. Graph analysis reconstructs the networks of wallet addresses and exchange accounts through which laundered funds flow, identifying clusters of related activity that no human analyst could assemble manually from raw transaction data.

Banking Circle, a European digital payments institution, has deployed MiCA-compliant AI screening that monitors its EURI euro stablecoin flows in real time against the full range of OFAC, OFSI and EU sanctions lists. The AI identifies not merely direct matches but probabilistic associations: counterparties that have transacted within a relevant number of hops from sanctioned entities, custody providers with known exposures to high-risk jurisdictions, transaction patterns resembling documented evasion typologies. This is compliance as an AI arms race, and for now the defenders have the advantage of the public ledger.

The criminals are also adapting. AI-driven mixing services have moved on from the simple coin tumblers of the early Bitcoin era to sophisticated systems that blend funds from multiple sources, swap between chains and currencies automatically, and generate transaction patterns calibrated to fall beneath the probability thresholds of standard screening models. Deepfake technology, audio and video forgeries convincing enough to pass for genuine, has been used to impersonate executives in payments fraud cases, authorizing large transfers to fraudulent accounts. Hundreds of thousands of euros in individual cases; the aggregate global losses are likely in the billions.

The GENIUS Act, in its provisions for stablecoin oversight, mandated that regulated stablecoin issuers must maintain the technical capability to freeze or burn tokens associated with sanctioned addresses. This is a significant step. It means that dollar-backed stablecoins operating under US regulatory oversight can, in principle, be rendered valueless in the hands of sanctioned parties within hours of a designation, a capability that SWIFT exclusion provided imperfectly and with longer lead times. Hong Kong's stablecoin licensing law, which came into force in August 2025, added similar requirements: licensed issuers must maintain KYC records for all token holders, maintain freeze capability and prohibit anonymous wallet access to regulated platforms.

The architecture of global compliance

What the combination of OFAC enforcement actions, OFSI assessments, the GENIUS Act and MiCA adds up to is the beginning of a genuine global compliance architecture for digital assets. It is incomplete, contested and full of gaps. But the direction is clear.

The Financial Action Task Force, the international standards body for anti-money laundering, has pushed consistently for the adoption of its Travel Rule across crypto service providers: the requirement that exchanges and wallet providers transmit identifying information about transaction originators to recipient institutions, replicating the standard that already applies to wire transfers above certain thresholds. Adoption of the Travel Rule in crypto has been slow and uneven, with larger regulated exchanges in major jurisdictions implementing it while smaller platforms in jurisdictions with lighter-touch enforcement continue to operate without it.

The enforcement actions of 2025 demonstrated that regulators are willing to impose significant penalties on institutions that fall short. OFAC imposed sanctions-related penalties exceeding $200 million on GVA Capital and $11.8 million on Interactive Brokers for failures in crypto-related sanctions compliance. These are not token fines designed to send a message; they are numbers that concentrate the mind of a board of directors and a general counsel.

The cat-and-mouse dynamic that has always characterized financial regulation, new controls prompting new evasion techniques, which prompt updated controls, is fully operational in the crypto space. Regulators have the advantage of blockchain's permanent record. Criminal actors have the advantage of speed, technical ingenuity and the availability of jurisdictions willing to host services that more stringent regulators have banned. The balance between these advantages will shift over time, as it has in every previous episode of financial crime and regulatory response.

What is different about the crypto compliance story is the international dimension. The sanctioned state actors, Russia, Iran, North Korea, are not individual criminals whose operations can be disrupted by a single enforcement action. They are sovereign governments with the resources, motivation and technical capability to continue developing and deploying crypto evasion infrastructure for as long as the sanctions themselves remain in place. The geopolitical question of how financial sanctions interact with a decentralized payment infrastructure that no single government controls is not a compliance question. It is a question about the future architecture of international power.

Compliance as geopolitics

The United Kingdom's OFSI assessment, the American GENIUS Act requirements, Hong Kong's stablecoin licensing regime and the EU's MiCA framework are not simply regulatory documents. They represent national and regional decisions about who gets to participate in dollar-denominated, euro-denominated or sterling-denominated digital financial infrastructure, and therefore, indirectly, about who participates in the global economy at all.

When a sanctioned entity discovers that its stablecoin holdings have been frozen by the technical capability that the GENIUS Act mandated issuers to maintain, it discovers something more significant than a compliance failure. It discovers that the digital currency it was using as a sanctions workaround was, structurally, not outside the reach of American financial jurisdiction. The custodian of the asset is still subject to American law. The freeze capability is always there.

This is why the development of alternative digital payment infrastructure in Russia, Iran and China is not merely a technical project. It is a project to create financial infrastructure over which American jurisdiction cannot be asserted. The race between that aspiration and the technical, economic and political difficulties of making non-dollar payment infrastructure genuinely viable is one of the defining financial stories of the current decade.

The compliance industry operates in the gap between these competing forces, doing the painstaking work of identifying, reporting and blocking the flows that the rules prohibit. The AI tools are getting better. The regulatory frameworks are getting denser. But the fundamental tensions – between sovereignty and openness, between privacy and oversight, between the speed of digital finance and the pace of regulatory adaptation – will not be resolved by compliance technology alone. They will be worked out, slowly and imperfectly, in the same international political forums where every previous contest over the architecture of global finance has been conducted.

That process is now well underway, and its outcome will determine not merely who can use digital money, but who gets to write the rules governing the digital economy.

Chapter 13: Zero-Knowledge Proofs

The oldest problem in digital finance

Every financial system must answer the same fundamental question: how do you verify that someone is telling the truth without requiring them to reveal everything? The banker extending credit needs to know the borrower can repay, but the borrower's full balance sheet contains information they would prefer not to broadcast. The regulatory compliance system needs to know that a transaction is not connected to terrorism financing, but the compliance check necessarily involves collecting and storing personal information that might be misused, leaked or demanded by governments hostile to the account holder's interests.

The tension between verification and privacy is as old as finance itself. In the physical world, it was managed through trusted intermediaries, the bank, the lawyer, the notary, who sat in the middle, verified what needed verifying, and were presumed to protect what did not need broadcasting. The digital world has not improved on this arrangement so much as replicated it at scale, creating centralized databases of extraordinary sensitivity that have proven, repeatedly and expensively, to be attractive targets for theft, state surveillance and commercial exploitation.

Zero-knowledge proofs represent a genuinely different approach. They offer a mathematically rigorous method of proving that something is true without revealing the information that makes it true. The implications for digital finance, identity verification, regulatory compliance and the architecture of privacy in an increasingly digital world are significant, and the technology has matured rapidly from a theoretical curiosity to a production-grade component of blockchain infrastructure.

The mathematics of saying nothing

The intellectual origins of zero-knowledge proofs lie in the work of Shafi Goldwasser, Silvio Micali and Charles Rackoff, published in 1985 in a landmark paper exploring the question of whether it was possible, in interactive proofs, to transfer zero knowledge between a prover and a verifier. The answer they demonstrated was yes: under specific conditions, a prover can convince a verifier of the truth of a statement while revealing no information beyond the fact that the statement is true.

To understand the intuition, consider the analogy of a friend who claims to know where Waldo is hidden in a complex illustration. You are skeptical. They want to prove their knowledge without revealing the location. They could solve this problem by covering the entire picture with an opaque sheet, cutting a small hole precisely over Waldo, and showing you that hole. You can verify that Waldo is indeed visible through the hole without learning anything about where in the picture Waldo is located. The knowledge that Waldo exists in the picture has been demonstrated. The location, the useful information itself, has been revealed to no one.

Formally, a zero-knowledge proof system has three essential properties. Completeness means that an honest prover with genuine knowledge can always convince an honest verifier. Soundness means that a dishonest prover cannot convince an honest verifier of a false statement, or can only do so with negligible probability, approaching zero as the proof system parameters are tightened. Zero-knowledge means that a verifier learns nothing from the proof beyond the truth of the specific statement being proved. These three properties, working together, define what makes zero-knowledge proofs genuinely useful rather than merely theoretically interesting.

The practical challenge, for most of the technology's early history, was that zero-knowledge proofs required interaction. The prover and verifier had to exchange multiple messages in a challenge-response protocol before the verifier was satisfied. This was fine for academic demonstrations but impractical for financial infrastructure. The development of non-interactive zero-knowledge proofs, particularly zk-SNARKs, which stands for Zero-Knowledge Succinct Non-Interactive Arguments of Knowledge, changed the picture entirely. A zk-SNARK allows a prover to compute a single compact proof that can be verified by anyone, in seconds, without any back-and-forth communication.

Privacy in practice: Zcash and ZK rollups

Zcash was among the first blockchain projects to deploy zk-SNARKs at production scale. Launched in 2016, Zcash allows users to conduct transactions in which the sender, receiver and amount are all kept private, with a cryptographic proof demonstrating that the transaction is valid, no coins were created from nothing, no coins were spent twice, without revealing any of the information that would normally allow a blockchain observer to trace the flow of funds.

This is a significant technical achievement with significant practical implications. It demonstrates that it is possible to maintain a public ledger, with all the security properties that come from a large network of validators checking each other's work, while providing genuine privacy guarantees to users. The two requirements, public verifiability and transactional privacy, were widely assumed to be in tension. Zcash showed they need not be.

The application of zero-knowledge proofs to blockchain scalability, through what are known as ZK rollups, proved even more consequential than their application to privacy. A ZK rollup is a system in which a large number of transactions are processed off the main blockchain, bundled together and then submitted to the main chain as a single proof demonstrating that all the bundled transactions are valid. Instead of every transaction requiring every node in the network to process and verify it independently, the entire batch is confirmed by checking a single compact proof.

The consequences for throughput are dramatic. Ethereum, processing transactions individually on its main chain, handles in the region of fifteen to twenty transactions per second. ZK rollup systems built on top of Ethereum have demonstrated throughput several thousand times higher, with settlement security guaranteed by the underlying main chain. Starknet, zkSync, Polygon zkEVM and other rollup systems have moved from experimental status to active production use, processing significant volumes of financial transactions. This is not merely a technical optimization. It is the difference between a payment infrastructure that can handle the transaction volumes of a serious financial system and one that cannot.

The Bitcoin protocol itself, despite its comparatively modest transaction throughput on the main chain, has been enriched by cryptographic advances including zero-knowledge proof frameworks that extend the privacy properties originally embedded in its design. Bitcoin's immutability at the protocol layer, the certainty that a transaction recorded on the ledger cannot be reversed through any exercise of authority, has always depended on the cryptographic security of its proof-of-work architecture. As attackers grow more sophisticated and computing power accelerates, zero-knowledge proof systems have become essential to proving the validity of Bitcoin transactions and the integrity of the ledger without requiring every participant to process every transaction in full.

The regulatory frameworks governing digital asset settlement, across jurisdictions from Switzerland to Singapore, now explicitly recognize zero-knowledge cryptography as a core security standard, not an optional enhancement but a foundational component of financial infrastructure that meets institutional-grade security and audit requirements. Privacy at the protocol layer, achieved through zero-knowledge proofs, has shifted from a feature associated with anonymity to an operational requirement for institutions that must satisfy compliance obligations without surrendering the security guarantees that cryptographic verification provides.

Identity without exposure

The applications of zero-knowledge proofs extend well beyond transactional privacy and blockchain scalability. Consider the seemingly mundane problem of age verification. A website selling age-restricted products needs to know that a user is above eighteen years old. The user's actual birthdate, day, month and year, is not relevant to this determination. In the current digital world, however, systems routinely collect the full birthdate, along with identity document details, and store them in databases that become targets for data breaches. Zero-knowledge proofs offer a different path: a cryptographic system in which a user proves they are over eighteen, demonstrating the truth of the statement, without transmitting any of the underlying information from which an adversary could determine their actual age or identity.

Microsoft's ION project, built on the Bitcoin blockchain, explored this principle in the context of digital identity. Rather than creating a centralized identity registry, another database of sensitive personal information, ION allows users to anchor cryptographic identity credentials to the Bitcoin blockchain in a decentralized way. The user controls which attributes of their identity they choose to reveal and to whom, with zero-knowledge proofs providing the mechanism by which specific claims can be verified without full disclosure.

In healthcare, the implications are considerable. Medical researchers studying the incidence of a particular condition across a large population need statistical access to patient data without requiring, or being able to obtain, personal identifying information. Zero-knowledge proof systems can allow a researcher to prove the truth of a statistical claim about a dataset without the data itself ever leaving the secure environment of the healthcare provider. The research can proceed. The privacy obligation is discharged. No additional compliance risk is created, because no personal data has moved.

Financial services present the most commercially significant application set. The customer due diligence and AML obligations that financial institutions carry require them to verify customer identity, check names against sanctions lists, assess transaction histories for suspicious patterns and satisfy regulators that they have done so. All of this currently requires the collection, storage and transmission of personal data at a scale that creates substantial compliance costs, data protection liabilities and privacy risks for customers. A zero-knowledge proof-based KYC system could allow a regulated identity provider to certify, on behalf of a customer, that the customer has been properly identified, is not on a sanctions list, is resident in a permitted jurisdiction and meets the financial institution's customer acceptance criteria, without transmitting any of the underlying personal data to the financial institution at all. The institution receives the verification it needs. The customer's personal information never leaves the identity provider's secure environment. GDPR is satisfied by design rather than as an afterthought.

Fully homomorphic encryption: the adjacent frontier

Zero-knowledge proofs sit close to another area of cryptographic research with potentially significant implications: fully homomorphic encryption, or FHE. Where zero-knowledge proofs allow statements about data to be verified without revealing the data, fully homomorphic encryption allows computations to be performed on encrypted data, in the cloud, on someone else's hardware, with the result returned in encrypted form, without the computing party ever seeing the underlying data at all.

The analogy is of a bank vault with slots through which mathematical operations can be passed and completed, with the results returned through the same slots, while the vault itself remains closed throughout. A financial institution could, in principle, send encrypted transaction data to a cloud AI service for fraud analysis, receive the fraud score back in encrypted form, and decrypt the result for its own use — without the AI provider ever having access to the underlying transactions. The privacy properties are significant. The current computational cost remains substantial, though it has fallen dramatically from the near-impractical levels of FHE's early deployments. Commercial applications are emerging, and the combination of FHE with zero-knowledge proof systems represents a direction of cryptographic development with substantial implications for data privacy in financial services.

Challenges and the path forward

The deployment of zero-knowledge proof systems is not without difficulty. The computational requirements for generating a proof are significantly higher than for standard cryptographic operations. Generating a zk-SNARK proof requires considerably more processing time and energy than executing the underlying transaction without the proof. This constraint is becoming less binding as hardware improves and as proof generation is optimized, but it remains a factor in the cost structure of ZK-based systems.

There are no universally agreed standards for zero-knowledge proof systems, which means that proofs generated by one system are not automatically compatible with verifiers built for another. This fragmentation increases integration costs and complicates the multi-chain architectures that modern finance is beginning to require. The cryptographic parameters of many proof systems also require periodic trust ceremonies, structured multi-party computations, to establish the initial parameters: processes that must be conducted with care to ensure that no single participant can compromise the system.

And there is, always, the possibility of misuse. The same privacy properties that protect a patient's medical data, a whistleblower's identity or a legitimate business's commercially sensitive transactions also protect the activities of criminals who do not wish their financial flows traced. This is not a problem unique to zero-knowledge proofs, cash provides stronger privacy guarantees with far lower technical barriers, but it is a challenge that regulators will need to engage with thoughtfully rather than reflexively. Blanket prohibition of privacy-preserving cryptography would not merely inconvenience criminals; it would foreclose a set of capabilities that are genuinely valuable to legitimate financial infrastructure and to individual privacy rights.

The trajectory of development points toward integration rather than isolation. Zero-knowledge proofs are increasingly built into the infrastructure layer of blockchain networks, providing privacy and scalability simultaneously. AI systems are being combined with ZK proof frameworks to enable privacy-preserving machine learning: models trained on sensitive data without the data being exposed to the model trainer. The combination of quantum-resistant cryptography with zero-knowledge proof systems is an active research area, anticipating the day when the mathematical foundations of current cryptographic systems will need to be updated.

The privacy frontier in digital finance is not a static line. It is being actively contested and extended, by mathematicians, engineers, regulators and the users of financial systems who have an interest in participating in the digital economy without surrendering the last remnants of their financial privacy. Zero-knowledge proofs represent the most technically rigorous contribution to that contest yet seen, and their influence on the architecture of digital money will only grow.

Chapter 14: What Is Tokenization?

In the spring of 2025, with gold touching $3,000 an ounce for the first time in history, Philipp Pieper pulled up a browser screen. Pieper is co-founder of Swarm, a Berlin-based platform that has spent the better part of a decade working out how to bring traditional financial assets onto decentralized networks. What he showed was a non-fungible token, a unique digital record on a public blockchain, that pointed to a specific gold bar in a Brinks high-security vault. The bar had a serial number. It was weighed, verified, and legally tied to that token alone. Anyone holding the token held the gold: not as a bookkeeping entry in a bank's ledger, not as a futures contract traded on an exchange, but as a provably unique claim on a physical object sitting in a vault. The token could be transferred instantly, to anyone, anywhere, at any time. It could be posted as collateral in a decentralized lending protocol. It could be sold at midnight on a Sunday. The bar would never move.

That, in essence, is tokenization.

The word has accumulated an unfortunate amount of hype over the years, which tends to obscure how simple the underlying idea actually is. Tokenization is the process of representing rights to an asset, any asset, as a digital token on a blockchain. The token is programmable, transferable, and verifiable without the involvement of any intermediary institution. It carries the same legal claim on the underlying thing as a title deed or a share certificate, but it operates on rails that are always on, borderless, and interoperable with the broader digital economy. Gold bars are one application. Real estate, government bonds, money-market funds, carbon credits, music royalties, time itself, all of these have now been tokenized in production, by real institutions and real communities, operating in live markets.

From wild west to regulated infrastructure

Pieper described the arc of the past decade with precision on the 2Tokens Podcast in early 2025. In 2016 and 2017, the tokenization space was what he called a "wild west": ICO frenzies, speculative tokens with no underlying assets, founders raising fortunes through white papers. The period taught the market brutal lessons. What followed was a retreat, a consolidation, and eventually something more durable: platforms that had survived the crash, secured regulatory licenses, built institutional-grade custody infrastructure, and were operating within frameworks that central banks and financial regulators could recognize.

The arrival of MiCA, the European Union's Markets in Crypto-Assets regulation, changed the legal landscape significantly. For the first time, issuers of asset-backed digital tokens operating in Europe had a specific compliance framework rather than a patchwork of national rules and unanswered questions. Swarm operates under a German regulatory license. The gold tokens on its platform are MiCA-compliant. The $18 trillion global gold market had, in other words, acquired a credible on-chain infrastructure layer, one that was not a workaround or a gray-market instrument but a regulated financial product.

The broader opportunity sits at a scale that dwarfs gold entirely. Erich Schnoeckel, representing the 2Tokens Foundation, a Dutch organization that has spent years advising governments on digital asset policy, put the figure into perspective on the same recording: an estimated $2.2 quadrillion of traditional assets exists in the world, across equities, bonds, real estate, commodities, and derivatives. Virtually none of it is on-chain. McKinsey's estimates suggest that perhaps $2 trillion of assets could be tokenized by 2030 in a conservative scenario. Boston Consulting Group's comparable analysis reaches $16 trillion by the same year. Even in the most modest projections, the shift underway is structural rather than marginal.

Laws designed for paper

Not every jurisdiction is positioned equally for what comes next. The 2Tokens Foundation produced a detailed analysis for the Dutch Ministry of Economic Affairs that identified a specific warning: the Netherlands, despite its progressive self-image and strong financial services tradition, was falling behind the United Kingdom, France, and Germany in creating the legal and regulatory conditions for tokenization to flourish.

The diagnosis was precise. Dutch property law was designed around paper-based instruments and physical title. The concept of digital ownership, fractional, programmable, transferable without a notary or a registrar, sat awkwardly, or simply outside, its existing categories. There was no statutory recognition of tokens as legal property. Smart contracts had uncertain enforceability. And Web3 firms seeking to operate legitimately were finding it "extremely difficult" to obtain bank accounts in the Netherlands, creating a practical bottleneck that drove activity to more accommodating jurisdictions.

This is not a specifically Dutch problem, it is the clearest articulation of a challenge playing out across most legal systems simultaneously. The infrastructure for representing and transferring ownership was built for physical objects and paper documents, and retrofitting it for programmable digital tokens requires legislative effort that most governments have not yet made. The UK moved ahead with the Property (Digital Assets) Bill in 2024, formally recognizing digital assets as a category of personal property. Switzerland's Distributed Ledger Technology Act gives tokens legal equivalence to traditional securities instruments. Singapore's regulatory sandbox has enabled systematic institutional experimentation. The jurisdictions that move fastest on legal clarity are already seeing the tokenization industry respond accordingly, with firms, capital, and talent following the frameworks.

Time, energy, and the economics of inclusion

Tokenization is sometimes discussed as though its primary use case is to offer wealthy investors access to art or private equity. That framing misses a more significant story. Some of the most important applications are in communities where traditional financial infrastructure does not reach at all.

The Sarafu Network in Kenya, run by an organization called Grassroots Economics, operates a time-banking system on blockchain. Community members record the value they provide to their neighbors, childcare, labor on a smallholding, teaching, practical skills, as tokens on an immutable ledger. These tokens circulate within a local economy, functioning as a medium of exchange in communities where formal currency is scarce or unreliable. The Circles UBI project in Germany takes a related approach, issuing a basic income in the form of blockchain-based tokens that circulate within a trust network. Neither system requires a bank account, a national identity document, or access to any institution. They require an internet connection and a mobile phone.

The global population of unbanked adults stands at approximately 1.4 billion. Around 60 percent of them already have internet access. The constraint is not connectivity; it is that the financial infrastructure designed for formal banking was never built to serve communities at the economic margins. Blockchain networks engineered for low-bandwidth mobile environments, Celo, Stellar, and Mina Protocol among them, have been specifically designed for exactly this context. The Mina blockchain maintains a chain data size of approximately twenty-two kilobytes, small enough to run on a basic smartphone on a slow rural network.

Energy is another domain where tokenization is rewriting who gets to participate. The 2Tokens Foundation's "Power of the Many" white paper examined the emergence of the prosumer: a household or business that both generates and consumes electricity through rooftop solar, home batteries, and smart grid connections. The paper modeled what happens when an ordinary household, a school, or a community battery is tokenized, when the energy-generating capacity of a local network becomes a shared, tradeable resource rather than a private utility company's infrastructure. Peer-to-peer energy trading is already legally permitted in the European Union. The friction in expanding such systems is no longer primarily regulatory; it is the absence of market infrastructure that allows energy tokens to be issued, verified, and exchanged efficiently. That infrastructure is being built.

The waste dimension of the energy transition adds commercial urgency. As first-generation solar panels installed in the early 2000s reach end of life, the volume of materials entering the global supply chain has become significant: by 2023, 162,736 tonnes of aluminum had been generated by decommissioned photovoltaic panels alone; by 2050, some projections reach 2.9 million tonnes of steel per year from panels alone. Tokenized circular markets, where materials can be tracked, verified, and traded efficiently from decommission to reuse, represent one of the less-discussed but commercially serious applications of the technology.

Smart contracts and the problem of enforcement

Tokenization does not simply move ownership records from one ledger to another. It creates the possibility of programming the behavior of those records: building rules directly into the asset itself. This is most visible in debt. A conventional bond contract requires lawyers, trustees, and, in the event of default, lengthy legal proceedings to enforce a covenant or process a liquidation. A smart contract can execute the same logic automatically, triggering preset outcomes the moment specified conditions are met or missed.

El Salvador's Volcano Bonds and Kazakhstan's blockchain-backed debt pilots have explored this architecture in live sovereign contexts. MakerDAO and Aave, the decentralized lending platforms, operate large volumes of smart-contract-governed lending positions, with automated liquidation firing the moment collateral ratios breach specified thresholds. The potential to remove intermediary friction from debt markets, reducing settlement times from days to seconds and eliminating the need for manual reconciliation, is commercially significant.

But the model has a known vulnerability. Smart contracts depend on data feeds called oracles to know what is happening in the world outside the blockchain. And oracles can be manipulated. In 2022, oracle manipulation attacks cost decentralized finance protocols more than $400 million, according to Chainalysis. The market has responded with more sophisticated decentralized oracle networks, multi-source verification, and the emergence of platforms such as Kleros and LexDAO that function as decentralized dispute resolution courts: blockchain-native alternatives to conventional litigation for enforcing programmable contracts. These are live experiments. They remain incomplete. They represent, however, the first serious attempt to build a legal system capable of operating at the speed and scale that tokenized finance will require.

The machine economy

The most unexpected development in tokenization over the preceding two years had relatively little to do with human investors. A new class of participants had entered the market: AI agents — autonomous software systems that can hold assets, make trading decisions, and execute transactions without any human in the loop.

The Virtuals Protocol platform, which enables the creation and deployment of AI agent tokens with their own on-chain identities, provided data that told a sobering story about the maturity of this market. Eighty-eight percent of AI agent tokens launched on the platform had already ceased operating, with an average functional lifespan of just 17 days. The infrastructure was immature, the economic models were poorly constructed, and most of what emerged in the early wave resembled speculation rather than genuine utility. But the underlying problem those agents were trying to solve was genuine: autonomous systems operating across digital networks need a way to hold and transfer value. They need machine-readable assets available around the clock. They need rails that do not require a human to authenticate every transaction.

This is where the automation argument for tokenization becomes sharper than the liquidity argument. Twenty-five percent of all trading on the Robinhood platform in the United States already occurs outside regular market hours, executed by people and, increasingly, algorithmic systems at times when traditional exchanges are closed and post-trade settlement infrastructure is offline. Tokenized assets are programmable, composable, and always available. They can be incorporated into automated strategies without the friction imposed by a market structure designed for five-day trading weeks and human clearing cycles.

Larry Fink, Chief Executive of BlackRock, the world's largest asset manager, with more than $10 trillion under management, offered the most pointed version of this vision in his 2025 Chairman's Letter. Every stock, every bond, every fund, every real-world asset could, in time, be tokenized. He was not describing a distant technical horizon. He was describing an architecture that institutions he works alongside every day were already building, piece by piece.

There are now 55,000 publicly listed companies globally and an estimated 390 million businesses of all sizes. The fraction of them whose ownership, debt, or equity is represented on a blockchain is still vanishingly small. But the direction of travel, and the institutional weight beginning to press in that direction, is no longer ambiguous.

The enterprise case for tokenization extends beyond capital markets accessibility to a more fundamental restructuring of how organizations manage their internal financial operations. The real opportunity for enterprises lies in integrating three historically separate functions, the ledger that records transactions, the payment mechanism that moves value, and the compliance layer that verifies what can settle – into a unified system. Traditional finance required an organization to maintain separate infrastructure for each: a general ledger system, a SWIFT connection for international payments, a settlement institution, and a compliance framework that operated across all three. A tokenized architecture consolidates these, placing all three functions into a single layer where every transaction carries not just the movement of value but the conditions and verification necessary to permit that movement. For a multinational corporation managing operations across twelve countries, or a supply chain requiring conditional payment upon delivery verification, that integration represents a fundamental reimagining of how capital moves internally.

What the next decade decides

The competition to shape these standards is already under way. Swarm needed to work through more than thirty potential technology partnerships before finding the right infrastructure for its regulated securities platform. That figure is a proxy for the state of the ecosystem: the underlying blockchain technology is robust; the legal and custody infrastructure, in places like the UK, Germany, and Singapore, is now workable; the connections between traditional finance and on-chain markets are being assembled, slowly and expensively, by every institution that commits to doing the work.

Jurisdictions that have moved slowly, or that have treated digital asset regulation primarily as a risk-management exercise rather than an economic opportunity — are already watching capital, firms, and talent migrate to places with clearer rules. The Netherlands analysis is one data point. More will follow.

Tokenization did not begin in 2025. Its origins are older, its first serious test more visible, and its early mistakes more instructive than most histories tend to acknowledge. That story starts with the instrument that made the concept of programmable, verifiable digital ownership visible to a global audience: the non-fungible token.

The trillion-dollar laboratory

Lewis McLellan of the Digital Monetary Institute, speaking on The Digital Bytes Podcast in December 2024, offered a corrective to anyone still treating tokenized real-world assets as an experiment conducted at the margins of institutional finance. BlackRock, Franklin Templeton, Apollo, and Citi had all moved tokenized money-market funds onto public blockchains. Twelve to twenty different providers were offering competing products across Ethereum, Stellar, Polygon, Canton, and Base, five distinct chains hosting real financial instruments managed by real institutions with real clients. The Citi Global Perspectives and Solutions team had estimated that tokenized assets could generate up to $5 trillion in market activity by 2030. McLellan's assessment was unambiguous: "These are proper businesses with real revenue attached to these products. It's not like it's a weird experimental sideshow thing."

The structural improvement these products offered over their conventional counterparts was specific and identifiable. A conventional money-market fund is priced by the fund manager at the end of the trading day. The fund manager's interest in maintaining investor confidence creates an incentive to set valuations that are not perfectly aligned with the market's contemporaneous assessment of the underlying assets. A tokenized money-market fund trading on a secondary market against other tokenized instruments is priced by market makers against supply and demand in real time. The pricing is independent of the issuer's judgment, and regulators, institutional investors, and retail participants can all observe it simultaneously. McLellan noted that this independence was precisely what regulators and institutional risk officers found persuasive: the disclosure was not an after-the-fact document but a real-time observable.

The diversity of blockchains hosting these products was not, in McLellan's reading, a sign of fragmentation. It was the early phase of a competitive infrastructure market. Institutions were not yet committed to particular chains in the way they were committed to particular clearing systems. The multi-blockchain landscape created resilience: if one network was compromised or congested, activity could migrate to another. The laboratory was not yet standardized. The experiment was not yet over. But the assets being tested were not synthetic constructs: they were the same money-market funds that US investors had been accessing through conventional channels, now running on infrastructure that made them available around the clock, across borders, without minimum subscription thresholds, and with pricing that was independently verifiable by anyone with a wallet and an internet connection.

Tokenization's first chapter in public consciousness was written not by institutional fund managers or sovereign debt pilots, but by a market for digital art that briefly became one of the strangest financial spectacles in living memory. The next chapter examines what the NFT boom actually was, what it revealed about the underlying technology, and why its collapse may have been the most useful thing that could have happened to the broader tokenization story.

Chapter 15: NFTs: From Hype to Utility

On 11 March 2021, Christie's auction house concluded the sale of a digital file. The buyer paid $69.3 million, making Beeple's *Everydays: The First 5,000 Days*, a collage of five thousand individual digital images assembled over thirteen years, the third most expensive work by a living artist ever sold at Christie's, after two Jeff Koons sculptures. The transaction was completed on a blockchain. The buyer received a non-fungible token verifying ownership. No physical object changed hands.

The coverage was breathless. The figure was real. And for the next eighteen months, the technology that made the sale possible was treated as a synonym for the speculative excess that surrounded it: digital art flipping, celebrity drops, cartoon apes trading at prices that assumed perpetual appreciation. When the market collapsed in 2022, the coverage was equally breathless in the opposite direction. NFTs were declared finished.

Both readings missed what was actually happening beneath the noise. While speculators were trading images of bored primates, a Vatican librarian was examining how to make 180,000 fifteenth-century manuscripts accessible to anyone on earth with a browser. While commentators were writing obituaries for the technology, the Uffizi Gallery in Florence was exploring what it might mean to attach a verifiable digital provenance record to a Michelangelo. The $69.3 million sale was the most visible moment. It was not the most important.

The museums decide to participate

The Uffizi's decision to sell an NFT representing the *Tondo Doni*, Michelangelo's only completed circular panel painting, in 2021 was a small and largely unremarked event at the time. The museum received approximately $170,000 for a high-resolution digital representation of the work, paired with a token verifying authenticity and institutional origin. The money was modest. The concept was significant: a five-hundred-year-old state institution was testing whether blockchain could serve as verifiable provenance infrastructure for cultural heritage.

Then the Italian government intervened, ruling that publicly owned artworks could not be commercially exploited in this way by the institutions holding them. The experiment ended. But the impulse behind it had already spread. The British Museum, the Smithsonian Institution, the Los Angeles County Museum of Art, the Centre Pompidou in Paris, and the San Francisco Museum of Modern Art had all become either buyers or sellers of NFTs by 2022. The question these institutions were asking was not really about resale value. It was about whether verifiable digital ownership could solve problems that centuries of physical custody had not.

The problem that the Vatican's Apostolic Library was confronting is emblematic. The library holds approximately 180,000 manuscripts and 1.5 million printed volumes, many of them unique, most of them inaccessible to the vast majority of scholars who might benefit from studying them. Physical access requires institutional credentials, international travel, and appointments that take months to secure. The library had been working on digitization programs for years. What NFT technology offered was something different: a mechanism for attaching verifiable authenticity, controlled access permissions, and clear provenance to a digital copy, in a format that could circulate internationally without degrading or being forged. The preservation logic and the access logic converged.

Notre-Dame de Paris provided a different illustration of what blockchain-based cultural infrastructure could accomplish. After the fire of April 2019 destroyed the cathedral's spire and severely damaged the nave, a network of French and German museums assembled an augmented-reality touring experience, a way of taking visitors through the pre-fire building while reconstruction continued above it. The experience toured twenty institutions across both countries. What NFTs offered in that context was provenance and sequencing: visitors who engaged with the experience at multiple museums accumulated a digital record of that journey, verifiable and non-duplicable.

The inheritance problem nobody planned for

NFTs are most commonly discussed as a medium for art. The more economically consequential application may be estate planning.

The digital asset management market was worth $4.22 billion in 2023, growing at approximately 16 percent annually. That figure reflects a structural problem that has been accumulating for years without much public attention: ordinary people are dying with significant digital wealth that their heirs cannot access, do not know exists, or cannot legally claim.

Fidelity's research in 2024 found that fewer than 15 percent of digital asset holders had made any estate planning arrangements for their holdings. The consequences are already visible in the data. An estimated 3.7 million Bitcoin, roughly one in five of all Bitcoin that will ever exist, is believed to be permanently lost, locked in wallets whose private keys died with their owners. An estimated 5 percent of all Ethereum in existence is similarly inaccessible. The most frequently cited single case involves a hard drive accidentally discarded in Newport, Wales in 2013, whose lost private keys controlled eight thousand Bitcoin, a sum representing, at current prices, a loss in excess of half a billion pounds. What has since been attempted to recover it, and what that implies for the future of digital custody, is a story for later chapters.

The legal frameworks are evolving unevenly. Some American states have enacted versions of the Revised

Uniform Fiduciary Access to Digital Assets Act, granting executors statutory rights to access and manage digital accounts if explicitly authorized in a will. The UK's Property (Digital Assets) Bill, introduced in Parliament in 2024, formally recognizes digital assets as personal property under English law, giving executors clearer standing in courts. In Europe, the interaction between blockchain's permanent transaction records and the General Data Protection Regulation's right to erasure remains unresolved: the law that demands you can delete identifiable data sits in tension with the technology designed never to delete anything.

NFTs offer a structural solution to part of this problem. A token can carry embedded permissions — designating, at the point of issuance, that on presentation of a death certificate or a probate document, control should transfer to a nominated beneficiary. Multi-signature wallet architectures already allow this kind of conditional transfer. The legal wrapper to make such transfers enforceable in conventional courts is the piece most jurisdictions are still assembling.

Labor, science, and the next frontier

A cluster of platforms in 2022 and 2023 applied NFT logic to work itself. Braintrust and Gitcoin enabled freelancers, developers, and creative workers to build verifiable portfolios, not simply a resume of claimed skills, but an on-chain record of completed work, peer-rated contributions, and accumulated reputation. Mirror allowed writers to tokenize essays, articles, and newsletters as programmable objects that could carry royalty terms directly into any future transaction.

The underlying principle is the same as the museum provenance case: verifiable origin, programmable terms, and a record that cannot be retrospectively altered. For the tokenized labor market specifically, the stakes extend beyond wages. A developer in Lagos building for a South Korean firm, a designer in Guatemala contracting with a Swiss agency, the friction in these relationships is not primarily technical. It is the absence of trusted, portable reputation infrastructure that travels across jurisdictions, currencies, and institutional contexts. On-chain work records, attached to non-transferable tokens, represent one architecture for building that infrastructure.

A parallel economic model was being tested in gaming. Axie Infinity, a play-to-earn platform, had demonstrated by 2021 that token-based games could generate meaningful income for players in developing economies where traditional employment paths were limited. At its peak, the platform generated over $1.2 billion in annual transaction volume, with players across the Philippines, India, Brazil, and other emerging markets earning income streams that, in some cases, exceeded local minimum wages. The sustainability of play-to-earn models proved contested, many projects collapsed when speculative token prices fell, but Axie

Infinity's relative resilience over time suggested something more structural was at work. The game succeeded not because it was purely speculative but because it was genuinely playable: players engaged because they found the gameplay compelling, not because they expected perpetual token appreciation. The economic implication extended beyond gaming to any digital environment where users created value: creator platforms, open-source software communities, and collaborative content networks all represented potential applications for the same architecture. NFTs could enable economic models in which users were equity holders in the systems they populated, rather than employees or content providers subordinate to a centralized operator.

The scientific research community arrived at a similar conclusion from a different direction. The University of California Berkeley sold an NFT representing the original laboratory notebook and data behind a Nobel Prize-winning research project for $50,000 in 2021. The Molecule platform went further, developing what it calls IP-NFTs: non-fungible tokens representing intellectual property rights over a research project, enabling communities of investors to fund early-stage drug development without going through conventional pharmaceutical venture capital structures. The decentralized science movement, DeSci, working from this foundation, has begun funding research into neglected diseases, rare conditions, and therapeutic approaches that commercial incentives have systematically underfunded.

Copernic Space applied the same logic to Earth-orbit infrastructure, tokenizing data access rights to satellites and surface sensors and enabling fractional investment in space exploration by retail participants who could not previously access the sector at any price.

The tokenization market for this broader class of intangibles was valued at $5.02 billion in 2024. Projections from the sector's research community place it at $28.97 billion by 2033, growing at an annual rate of approximately 21.5 percent. The figures encompass a heterogeneous set of use cases, and aggregate projections for an immature market should be treated with appropriate skepticism. But the direction is clear: non-fungible tokens are becoming infrastructure for recording, verifying, and transacting rights across contexts that paper-based legal systems have historically handled clumsily, if at all.

Reforestation, verification, and the limits of trust

Some of the most commercially interesting NFT applications of 2023 and 2024 were environmental. Several platforms launched NFT-based systems for funding and tracking reforestation: each token represented a planted tree, linked to GPS coordinates and a verified planting event, with satellite imagery and IoT sensors providing ongoing proof of survival. The tokens could be held by donors, traded on secondary markets, and used by corporations as part of voluntary carbon offset programs.

The appeal is obvious. Climate finance has a chronic verification problem. Money raised for reforestation or renewable energy projects in developing countries frequently cannot be traced through to verified outcomes with sufficient granularity to satisfy institutional investors or regulators. The gap between what is claimed and what is measurable has made the voluntary carbon market a persistent target for both legitimate criticism and opportunistic greenwashing. Blockchain-based tokens, attached to real-world data feeds, were designed precisely to address this problem.

The difficulty is the assumption embedded in "verified." The NFT is only as reliable as the oracle that feeds it data, and the organization that controls the oracle. Verra and Gold Standard, the two dominant carbon credit certification bodies, have faced sustained criticism about methodology and double-counting. Digitizing their processes on a blockchain does not resolve the underlying certification problems, it makes fraudulent certification faster and more scalable. NFT-based environmental projects have attracted the same two-tier population that carbon markets always attract: genuinely motivated conservation initiatives alongside greenwashing exercises dressed in the technical vocabulary of proof-of-ownership.

The DAO model, where NFT holders collectively govern the conservation project they have funded, offers one structural response. If governance rights are distributed among token holders rather than concentrated in a promoter, the incentive for fraud is reduced and the scrutiny is increased. Community-governed reforestation DAOs operating in the Amazon basin, the Congo, and Southeast Asian peatlands have demonstrated that the architecture works at small scale. Whether it scales to the size where it could meaningfully affect global carbon markets remains an open question.

The record that could have saved a life

One illustration of the NFT's broader potential has nothing to do with art, finance, or speculation. A case discussed on The Digital Bytes Podcast in March 2024 involved a Do Not Resuscitate order, a documented medical instruction, signed, legally valid, and on file at the patient's primary healthcare provider. When he was admitted to a different hospital in a different state, the instruction did not follow him. It did not exist in that facility's records. His stated wishes were not honored.

The failure was not legal. The failure was infrastructural. Healthcare records, professional qualifications, legal instructions, and identity credentials all share a common characteristic: they are discrete, verifiable claims about individuals that currently exist in siloed systems maintained by intermediaries, invisible to institutions outside those systems and unreachable by the individuals whose lives they describe. The NFT's core capability — attaching verifiable digital ownership to a discrete record, creating an immutable ledger of provenance and authenticity readable by any permissioned party — is precisely suited to this class of problem.

The United Arab Emirates had moved further than most jurisdictions in making structured healthcare outcome data accessible: questions about comparative performance across providers could, in principle, be answered from available datasets. The United Kingdom, without a functional national digital identity system of its own, was using driving licenses and passports for online age and identity verification — building digital ID by necessity through the back door of existing documents rather than through deliberate infrastructure investment. Professional qualifications, academic credentials, and vocational licenses remained largely paper-based, stored in institutional archives rather than in formats their holders could present directly.

The NFT boom had been, in retrospect, an infrastructure test. It demonstrated that billions of people would engage with tokenized digital claims if the user experience was accessible and the perceived value was clear. That lesson was being absorbed in asset classes and institutional contexts that had nothing to do with the original test cases, and the most significant of them were not galleries or exchanges, but the places where people's legal, medical, and professional lives intersected.

What the hype cycle actually revealed

The 2021 boom and the 2022 collapse performed, in compressed form, a cycle that most new financial instruments go through over decades. It attracted speculative capital, produced absurd valuations for assets with no intrinsic use, and then washed most of that speculation away when sentiment shifted. What it left behind was a tested technology, a set of standards for interoperability, a market of platforms and tools, and a growing body of institutional knowledge about what NFTs can and cannot reliably accomplish.

The Christie's sale was not a prophecy about where the technology would settle. It was a proof of concept for a property that turned out to matter in a wide range of contexts that had nothing to do with digital art: the ability to attach verifiable, programmable ownership to any discrete object, claim, or record. That property is now being applied in fund structures, debt instruments, and corporate securities. The following chapter examines what happens when the same architecture reaches the institutional scale of bonds and funds, the trillions of dollars of capital that moves through them every year, and the structural changes that tokenization makes possible at that scale.

Chapter 16: Tokenizing Funds and Bonds

The annual Chairman's Letter from Larry Fink, Chief Executive of BlackRock, is read carefully by a specific audience. Fund managers, institutional allocators, pension trustees, regulators, the people who decide where very large amounts of money move. In 2025, Fink used that letter to make a declaration that the industry had been circling for several years without quite committing to. Tokenized funds, he wrote, would eventually look like exchange-traded funds. Every stock, every bond, every fund, every real-world asset could be tokenized. And when they were, it would remove the legal, operational, and bureaucratic frictions that had made investing inaccessible to most of the world's population.

It would also, Fink emphasized, require solving an identity problem. The same technology that removes friction from the movement of assets introduces a new requirement: if a tokenized fund can be transferred between counterparties in seconds, across jurisdictions, at any hour of the day, the infrastructure for verifying who is doing the transferring must be correspondingly robust. Tokenization democratizes returns. But if the identity layer is absent, it also democratizes the risk of fraud, money laundering, and sanctions evasion. The architecture of the financial system that follows will need both innovations simultaneously.

Fink was not announcing something theoretical. BlackRock had already demonstrated the direction of travel with BUIDL, its tokenized money-market fund launched on the Ethereum blockchain. The fund tokenized short-duration US government securities, offering institutional investors a vehicle that could be held, transferred, and used as collateral in decentralized finance protocols without ever leaving a regulated custodial framework. In 2024, the tokenized money-market fund market grew by 515 percent, reaching $4 billion under management. BlackRock's fund was its largest component and its most prominent proof of concept.

The bond market's structural problem

Bonds are the most traded securities on earth, and they are among the least efficient. In 2024, $7.1 trillion in bonds were issued globally — 18 percent higher than the previous year. The post-trade process for that volume of instrument involves correspondent custodians, clearing agents, paying agents, registrars, and reconciliation cycles that routinely extend over two or more days. Each intermediary takes a fee. Each delay creates counterparty exposure. Each manual reconciliation step introduces the possibility of error.

CashLink, a Frankfurt-based digital bond platform, quantified the savings potential with unusual precision. Its analysis suggested that tokenized bond issuance reduces costs by approximately 1.2 percent per transaction relative to the conventional process. Applied across 10 percent of global bond issuance, that figure represents approximately $85 billion in annual savings. The number is speculative as a projection but grounded in the documented costs of the actual workflows it would replace.

The European Central Bank provided the first institutional demonstration that this was operationally viable. In 2021, the ECB issued the first digital bond on the Ethereum blockchain, a small-volume pilot, but one conducted by the most significant monetary institution in the world. The Banque de France joined it in a combined central bank digital currency and bond settlement trial. In 2023, Siemens became the first major industrial corporation to issue a fully digital bond: €60 million, settled in one day rather than the customary five, without the intermediaries that would ordinarily be required. The Luxembourg Stock Exchange formalized its support for security tokens the same year. The infrastructure was demonstrably real.

Institutions begin building

The institutional engagement has not been evenly distributed. A cohort of major banks and asset managers has moved from observation to active deployment, while others maintain a watching brief.

Beneath these technical developments lay an institutional transformation that tokenized securities were enabling: the decoupling of capital raising from geographic jurisdiction and traditional intermediation. A corporation no longer needed to be listed on a specific exchange or route capital raises through investment banks in particular jurisdictions to access global capital. Tokenized securities, operating on public blockchains with permissioned infrastructure, allowed enterprises to issue debt and equity directly to investors globally, settling transactions instantly and programmably. The implications are structural: capital allocation is becoming borderless. A real estate investment trust can issue tokens representing commercial property interests, accessible to institutional investors in Tokyo, London, and Sydney simultaneously. A corporation can raise funds through tokenized bonds without requiring a credit rating agency assessment or an investment bank underwriting agreement — only a clear offering document and a compliant infrastructure layer. The institutions that have historically extracted rents from gatekeeping, stock exchanges, investment banks, custodians for specific geographies, face the choice of rebuilding their infrastructure around tokenized settlement or watching capital flows migrate to platforms that have done so.

Goldman Sachs and BNP Paribas collaborated in May 2023 to launch the Canton Network, a privacy-enabled blockchain infrastructure specifically designed for institutional financial markets. The network addressed one of the key objections to using public blockchains for regulated securities: the transparency of transaction data. Canton's architecture allows institutions to share the benefits of distributed ledger infrastructure, shared state, atomic settlement, programmable compliance, while keeping the details of each transaction private from parties who are not counterparties to it.

SWIFT, the messaging network that processes the vast majority of cross-border payment instructions between financial institutions, began live trials of digital currency settlement in 2025. The significance of SWIFT's participation is not technical but systemic: an organization that had credibly ignored the blockchain conversation for most of its existence was now running production experiments. HSBC launched its Orion platform, a digital bond issuance and settlement system covering both tokenized deposits and tokenized gold. Securitize, a digital securities firm regulated by both the SEC and FINRA, became the transfer agent of record for several tokenized fund issuers including BlackRock. The Depository Trust and Clearing Corporation, the organization that settles the overwhelming majority of US equity trades, ran a pilot with Chainlink called the Smart NAV program, exploring how fund net asset value data could be pushed onto blockchain infrastructure to enable real-time pricing of tokenized fund shares.

The Janus Henderson $11 million Anemoy Liquid Treasury Fund represented a smaller but symbolically important development: a mainstream global fund manager, not a crypto-native firm, choosing to build a fund product natively on blockchain infrastructure rather than retrofitting an existing one.

Private markets: where the transformation is largest

The funds story has a public component and a private one, and the private component is considerably larger in scale.

Publicly traded equities and government bonds are already relatively liquid. They can be bought and sold efficiently, owned in fractional amounts through ETFs, transferred in minutes through brokerage accounts. Tokenization improves the mechanics, but the underlying market functions. Private equity, private credit, and hedge fund investments, the asset classes that have historically delivered the best risk-adjusted returns in aggregate, do not function for most investors. Minimum investment sizes are measured in hundreds of thousands or millions of dollars. Lock-up periods span three to ten years. Valuation is infrequent and illiquid. Secondary markets are thin, expensive, and largely inaccessible to retail investors.

State Street's 2024 analysis of asset tokenization identified private equity as the most transformative opportunity across all asset classes. The private equity market was valued at approximately $540 billion in 2024. Projections place it above $1.35 trillion by 2034. The private credit market, direct lending to companies outside the public bond market, stood at $1.5 trillion in 2024 and is projected to exceed $3 trillion by 2028.

These are enormous pools of capital operating under structural constraints that tokenization was specifically designed to remove.

A tokenized private equity fund can set a minimum investment of $100 rather than $100,000. It can offer a secondary market where investors can exit positions before the end of a fund's life. Its net asset value can be updated continuously rather than quarterly. Its fund distributions can be paid automatically through smart contracts on the date they are declared rather than routed through a paying agent over several days. Each of these changes individually is useful. In combination, they represent a different kind of financial product, one accessible to a population of potential investors that the existing private market system has never reached.

Hamilton Lane, one of the largest private equity fund administrators in the world, was among the first to experiment with tokenized fund structures, partnering with Republic to offer retail investors access to private equity vehicles through fractionalized digital shares. Several funds have followed. The pattern is establishing itself: tokenize the fund, reduce the minimum, open a secondary market, and collect a new population of investors who could not previously access the asset class at all.

The quantified cost argument extends far beyond access alone. Calastone, one of the world's largest fund administration networks, calculated that tokenized fund operating costs could fall by 23 percent relative to conventional administration, a saving equivalent to

$135 billion per year for the global asset management industry at current scale. The UK manages approximately $11 trillion in assets, second only to the United States and representing roughly 8 percent of a $145 trillion global fund market, according to PwC. The case for upgrading the infrastructure through which that capital flows is not marginal.

The transformation also raises a structural question the fund management industry is only beginning to reckon with. If underlying assets, shares, bonds, commodities, can be tokenized directly and held by investors without an intermediary wrapper, the economic justification for the fund structure itself comes into question. A conventional fund charges 50 to 100 basis points per year to hold a diversified portfolio. A tokenized equivalent could, in principle, allow investors to hold individualized, directly owned positions in the same underlying assets, managed continuously by AI-driven allocation tools, without the cost of the intermediary layer. The fee pressure this creates on traditional asset management is structural rather than cyclical, and no amount of efficiency improvement within the existing fund model fully neutralizes it.

The 2025 scorecard

Each year, a set of predictions about the year ahead is made for the Digital Bytes newsletter and then, at year end, evaluated against what actually transpired. In 2025, three AI systems independently assessed the accuracy of the prior-year predictions: ChatGPT judged them 80 to 85 percent accurate; Grok reached 85 percent; Gemini gave 90 percent. The aggregate figure was approximately 85.9 percent.

The outcomes that came true: tokenized funds reached $33 billion under management. The London Stock Exchange Digital Market Infrastructure platform launched, creating regulated infrastructure for tokenized private credit and equity funds. Stablecoins grew from approximately $200 billion to $312 billion in total market capitalization. The United States Strategic Bitcoin Reserve was established by executive order in March 2025. Real-world asset tokenization, broadly defined, reached between $24 billion and $30 billion.

The prediction that proved too optimistic: broader RWA tokenization was forecast at $30 to $50 billion. The actual figure was at the lower end of that range, reflecting the persistence of regulatory fragmentation across jurisdictions and the continued difficulty of connecting on-chain token infrastructure with legacy custody and settlement systems. The UK permitted crypto exchange-traded notes for professional investors but stopped short of full retail crypto ETFs. Progress was uneven across markets.

The stablecoin figure, $312 billion in aggregate market capitalization, understates the significance of the asset class as financial infrastructure. Stablecoins are the settlement currency of tokenized markets. Every tokenized fund or bond that can be purchased requires a tokenized payment mechanism, and stablecoins currently perform that function. Their growth is a necessary precondition for the growth of everything else in the tokenized asset ecosystem.

The keys problem, revisited

Alongside the institutional progress, the human failure mode persisted. The private key problem documented in the previous chapter applies with particular force to institutional and sophisticated investors who hold more significant digital positions.

The James Howells story has become the most cited illustration of the irreversibility problem. Howells accidentally discarded a hard drive in 2013 containing the private keys to eight thousand Bitcoin. The drive is in a landfill site in Newport, Wales. He has repeatedly sought permission to excavate the site, deploying increasingly sophisticated proposals involving AI-enhanced sorting technology, environmental impact analysis, and revenue-sharing arrangements with the local council. The council has consistently refused. At prices prevalent during mid-2025, the lost keys represent in excess of five hundred million pounds — inaccessible and unrecoverable.

The UK government's Dormant Assets Scheme provides an instructive comparison. The scheme identifies financial accounts with no active owner, bank accounts, share certificates, insurance policies, and transfers the balances to a central fund for socially valuable purposes, subject to a right of reclaim if the original owner reappears. By 2024, the scheme had unlocked £745 million from an estimated £1.35 billion in dormant traditional accounts. The estimate of lost digital asset value, running into the hundreds of billions of dollars globally, dwarfs this figure by orders of magnitude, and comes with no recovery mechanism at all.

Multi-signature wallet architectures, institutional key management services, and smart contract-based inheritance protocols offer partial responses. A wallet requiring three of five named signatories to authorize any transaction is materially harder to lose completely than one controlled by a single private key on a single device. The professional custody market, State Street, BNY Mellon, Fidelity, Coinbase's institutional arm, has built precisely the kind of institutional-grade key management that individual holders routinely fail to implement. But custody creates its own risks, which are examined in detail later in this volume.

The money market migration

The scale of what was moving did not arrive without context. By mid-2024, the iShares Bitcoin Trust (IBIT), the BlackRock Bitcoin ETF launched in January of that year, had accounted for 23 percent of all BlackRock's net inflows in the first six months. For the world's largest asset manager to direct almost a quarter of its net investor intake to a single new digital product in that time was without precedent in the firm's history. The signal was not about Bitcoin specifically. It was about the speed at which institutional distribution infrastructure, once it committed to a new asset class, could redirect capital flows.

The conventional money market fund industry in the United States alone held approximately $6.5 trillion in assets. In the summer of 2024, American investors could see the competitive yields being offered on those assets advertised on roadside billboards: 5.1 percent, after years of near-zero returns. Lewis McLellan of the Digital Monetary Institute described the structural limitation that tokenized equivalents were designed to resolve. In a conventional money-market fund, shares could only be redeemed through a broker during market hours, subject to a standard two-to-three-day settlement window. Investors could not access their capital over a weekend, or outside business hours, or on a day when their particular brokerage was unavailable. In a tokenized money-market fund trading on a secondary market, the same assets were redeemable in minutes, at any hour, on any day of the week.

The independent pricing that resulted from secondary market trading was the improvement that McLellan and institutional risk officers found most structurally significant. A conventional money-market fund's net asset value was set by the fund manager. The tokenized equivalent's market price was set by the market. The difference was not merely operational, it changed the nature of the disclosure obligation and shifted accountability for valuation from the issuer to the trading infrastructure.

The fund and bond tokenization story, at its most optimistic, is about removing friction, expanding access, and enabling a global population of savers to participate in asset classes that have historically been closed to them. It runs alongside a more sobering story about what happens when sophisticated digital assets proliferate faster than the legal and technical infrastructure for preserving access to them. Tokenization creates ownership. It does not automatically preserve it.

The same dynamic, new ownership structures built on infrastructure whose risks are only partially understood, plays out with particular visibility in the most tangible asset class most people will ever encounter. The next chapter examines what tokenization looks like when the asset is a building.

Chapter 17: Real Estate on the Blockchain

Buying a house in the United Kingdom in 2024 took, on average, between twelve and sixteen weeks from offer acceptance to completion. The process required a solicitor acting for the buyer, a solicitor acting for the seller, a mortgage lender's legal team, a surveyor, a local authority search, a Land Registry application, and, in the event of any complications, an indeterminate extension to any of those timescales. Each party operated their own records. Each stage required the completion of the previous one. Settlement was sequential, expensive, and, until the final exchange of contracts, entirely reversible at the cost of losing legal fees.

This is not a failure of technology. The technology to record a property transaction and transfer title in hours rather than weeks has existed for years. It is a failure of coordination: the legal, administrative, and financial systems that govern real estate ownership were designed for paper-based transactions and have never been fully reconstructed around digital infrastructure.

Tokenized real estate does not simply apply blockchain to the existing process. It replaces several of its foundational assumptions. Ownership of a property, or a fractional share of one, is represented as a digital token on a blockchain. Transfer of that token constitutes transfer of the underlying ownership right. Smart contracts automate the conditions of transfer: completion only occurs when all specified conditions are verified on-chain. Settlement is atomic: ownership and payment exchange simultaneously, eliminating the period of counterparty exposure that characterizes conventional transactions. The entire system runs continuously, with no dependency on office hours, Land Registry queues, or the availability of nominated solicitors.

RealT and the geography of ownership

The platform most often cited in discussions of retail real estate tokenization is RealT, which has been operating since 2019. The model is direct: RealT acquires residential rental properties in the United States, primarily in Detroit, Cleveland, and other Midwest cities where yields are high and prices are accessible, and tokenizes the ownership. Each property is divided into a fixed number of tokens, typically several thousand, each representing a proportional share. Investors anywhere in the world can purchase tokens starting from approximately fifty dollars. Rent is collected and distributed automatically to the wallets of token holders in stablecoin, on a weekly basis, proportional to ownership.

The mechanics are operationally simple from an investor's perspective. The complexity is in the legal wrapper. RealT holds each property in a dedicated limited liability company under US law. Token holders own shares in the LLC; the LLC owns the property. The token is the mechanism for representing and trading those shares, not a direct deed of title to a physical object. This structure is legally necessary: property law in the United States, as in most jurisdictions, does not yet recognize a blockchain token as a valid title instrument. The LLC sits between the chain and the registry.

The consequence of this architecture is that the liquidity benefit, the ability to sell a fractional property holding instantly on a secondary market, depends on the secondary market actually functioning. RealT operates its own exchange; trading volume is modest. For illiquid tokens in less popular properties, finding a buyer at a fair price may take time. The promise of fractional real estate tokenization, true liquidity for an asset class that has always been illiquid, remains partly aspirational. The infrastructure is real. The depth of market is still developing.

Japan's largest bank enters the market

In parallel with the retail platforms, institutional real estate tokenization has moved from pilot to production in several markets. Mitsubishi UFJ Financial Group (MUFG), Japan's largest bank by assets, announced a program to tokenize commercial real estate and make fractional positions available to retail investors through its digital securities platform. The rationale was partly demographic and partly regulatory: Japan's aging population holds substantial savings in low-yield bank deposits and government bonds, and its securities regulator had created a framework explicitly designed to encourage digital securities products that could direct some of that capital toward higher-yielding real assets.

The South Korean securities tokenization market pursued a similar logic from a different angle. South Korean retail investors had already demonstrated a higher tolerance for digital asset investment than their counterparts elsewhere: approximately 15 percent of a population of 52 million had become registered cryptocurrency investors by early 2023, a figure that had grown by 21 percent in a single year. The Financial Services Commission released guidelines for Security Token Offerings (STOs) in February 2023. The first regulatory approval under those guidelines was an aircraft engine SPV tokenization: fractional investment in a pool of commercial aircraft engines leasing to airlines was opened, for the first time, to retail investors. Real estate followed as the most obvious next application.

The Bali resort tokenization, structured by the Tokeny platform in partnership with co-investment firm CofundX, represented a different geography but the same principle: dividing the ownership of a hospitality asset among a larger pool of investors, reducing the minimum ticket size, and using blockchain infrastructure to manage the ownership register and distribute returns automatically. The model was operationally straightforward. The challenge, as in every jurisdiction, was how token ownership interacted with local property and corporate law in the event of a dispute.

Agricultural and rural land

The case for tokenizing real estate is strongest where the assets are least accessible to conventional capital markets. A luxury Manhattan condominium is highly liquid by property standards: there is a large pool of buyers, transparent pricing, and professional transaction infrastructure. Farmland in sub-Saharan Africa or Central America is the opposite: high in potential productive value, in many cases legally controlled by communities without formal title, and effectively invisible to international investors who might otherwise provide development capital.

Projects in Honduras and Zambia have tokenized rights to agricultural land and crop outputs, not direct ownership, which in many cases would conflict with local land tenure systems, but verifiable claims on the economic value of the land's production. A token holder does not own a Zambian smallholding; they hold a fractional claim on the documented output of that holding, verified through GPS-tagged production records and distributed automatically through smart contracts when crops are sold. The model navigates the legal constraint without pretending it does not exist.

Honduras has gone further in creating legal infrastructure for these approaches. The Zone for

Employment and Economic Development (ZEDE) provides an alternative legal system within designated geographic zones, with contractual protections and dispute resolution mechanisms specifically designed for digital-native transactions. Tokenized land registries within these zones can function as legally valid title instruments, reducing the gap between the on-chain token and the off-chain property right.

The settlement problem in commercial real estate

The largest commercial real estate transaction to have been tokenized and settled on a public blockchain, a Manhattan condominium valued at approximately $30 million, demonstrated both the capability and the limits of the technology as it currently exists. The transaction was completed on the Ethereum public mainnet. Ownership transferred, payment settled, and the token was recorded in the buyer's wallet. The entire on-chain process took minutes.

The surrounding legal process, the months of due diligence, title search, mortgage documentation, and negotiation, took exactly as long as it would have for a conventional transaction. Blockchain compressed the execution phase. It did not compress the preparation phase, because the information required to execute safely was still produced by the same professionals, through the same processes, as in any other deal. The immutable record that tokenization creates is only as trustworthy as the information that was verified before the token was minted.

This constraint appears in every tokenized real estate application. The blockchain records what happened. It cannot, by itself, verify that what was recorded corresponds to physical reality, that the building exists, that there are no undisclosed encumbrances, that the seller has the right to transfer the title being claimed. Oracles, legal warranties, third-party inspections, and professional indemnity remain necessary components of any reliable tokenized real estate market. The technology reduces some friction. It does not eliminate the need for professional judgment about the underlying assets.

Inheriting a digital building

A distinct challenge emerges when tokenized real estate intersects with life events rather than market transactions. A person who holds fifty tokens in a tokenized apartment building in Detroit, a fractional share of a Bali resort, and a position in a Zambian agricultural scheme has accumulated exposure to real-world assets through three entirely different legal structures, on two or more blockchains, with access credentials stored on their personal devices.

When that person dies, their executor faces a question that property law has not yet resolved in any of these cases. In the LLC-based RealT structure, the executor's rights are determined by the LLC's operating agreement and the governing law of the state of formation. In the Bali resort structure, they may be determined by Indonesian corporate law and the terms of the digital securities contract. In the Zambian agricultural token, there may be no legal precedent at all.

The practical obstacle, access to the tokens themselves, is the same in every case: without the private keys or the platform credentials, the position cannot be claimed regardless of what any will or court order says. The digital inheritance frameworks discussed in the previous chapter apply here with particular force, because real estate is often the most significant component of an individual's estate. A token representing fractional ownership of a building is not self-evidently different, in economic terms, from a share certificate representing ownership in a company that owns a building. But the legal systems that enforce and transfer share certificates were built over decades to handle exactly the events that tokenized property systems are only beginning to anticipate.

The $380 trillion case study

Global real estate is estimated at approximately $380 trillion in total value, of which roughly 85 percent is residential. It is the largest store of private wealth on earth, larger than global equity markets and global bond markets combined, and the majority of it is owned in forms that make liquidity, divisibility, and cross-border participation structurally difficult. Land registries operate under national legal systems. Title transfer takes weeks or months. Mortgage instruments are not portable across jurisdictions. The unit of transaction is an entire building, not a fraction of one.

Philipp Pieper, co-founder of Swarm, described the specific opportunity this creates on The Digital Bytes Podcast. The home equity market in the United States alone was estimated at $30 trillion. American homeowners hold that equity locked in the structures they live in, accessible only through formal mortgage refinancing processes, home equity lines of credit, or sale. Pieper drew a contrast with decentralized finance, where users had grown accustomed to borrowing against their on-chain wallet balances continuously, at any hour, without paperwork or approval processes. "In DeFi, we've become very used to using whatever the wallet balance we have to be able to borrow against it," he said. Extending that capability to tokenized real estate equity would represent a fundamental change in how the world's largest asset class could be used, not merely held.

A pension fund managing assets across geographies could directly acquire fractional interests in commercial real estate portfolios without routing capital through geographic intermediaries. An insurance company could tokenize its real estate holdings internally, using them as collateral for financing operations without selling assets. A corporate development team could acquire property rights in multiple jurisdictions through a single unified ledger, settling all purchases simultaneously when all conditions were verified. The infrastructure being assembled, custody systems, tokenization platforms, identity verification, oracle networks, was functional piece by piece. The outcome it pointed to was visible: real estate, the least fluid of all major asset classes, was being reconstructed as a continuously tradeable, programmable, globally accessible capital markets asset.

Pieper's longer-term expectation was that the distinction between tokenized and conventional property ownership would eventually dissolve into infrastructure rather than remain visible at the surface. "I'm not quite sure that in due time we will actually need to know that something's tokenized or not," he said. The transaction would simply settle faster. The fractional ownership would simply be normal. The cross-border transfer would simply work. The mechanism would recede behind the outcome, as the TCP/IP protocols that carry data around the internet have receded behind the experience of using a web browser.

The direction of travel

Despite the constraints documented in this chapter, the trajectory of tokenized real estate is not ambiguous. The platform infrastructure, RealT and its counterparts in Europe, Asia, and the Gulf, continues to expand. The institutional programs led by banks like MUFG and platforms like Tokeny are moving from pilot into production. The regulatory frameworks in South Korea, Switzerland, Singapore, and the UK are creating explicit legal space for digital property rights. BCG's projection that $16 trillion in illiquid assets, a substantial portion of them real estate, will be tokenized by 2030 reflects institutional investment activity already under way.

What the real estate case illustrates, more clearly than almost any other application, is that tokenization is an infrastructure story as much as a technology story. The blockchain itself is only one layer. The legal instruments that give tokens meaning, the identity systems that verify who is transacting, the oracle infrastructure that keeps on-chain records connected to off-chain reality, and the custody systems that preserve access across ownership events: all of these must be assembled alongside the technology before tokenized real estate delivers on its potential.

The broader tokenized asset market, of which real estate is a large but not dominant component, was demonstrating that assembly in real time during 2024 and 2025. The following chapter takes the measure of the wider real-world asset moment.

Chapter 18: The RWA Boom

In August 2024, the Chief Executive of Coinbase reported that his platform had processed the first cryptocurrency transaction between two artificial intelligence systems, with no human initiating or authorizing the transfer. The AI agents involved were operating autonomously, holding digital assets in their own wallets, and settling a transaction between themselves in real time. The event went largely unremarked in the mainstream financial press. In retrospect, it marked something important: the moment the theoretical argument for machine-readable, always-on, borderless financial assets gained its first documented real-world example.

The argument had been made many times. Autonomous systems operating across digital networks need a way to hold and exchange value. They cannot wait for a bank to open. They cannot maintain accounts in the conventional sense. They need assets that are programmable, transferable without institutional intermediation, and available around the clock. Tokenized real-world assets, equities, bonds, commodities, money-market instruments, precisely fit that description. The AI-to-AI transaction was the proof of concept. The infrastructure being built around it, by financial institutions, technology firms, and regulators simultaneously, was the more significant story.

The financial infrastructure already in place

Before examining where tokenized real-world assets were going in 2025, it is worth establishing where the financial infrastructure already was. The United Kingdom, by most measures, held the most developed position. With 134 technology unicorns, 3,200 registered fintech companies, and an Investment Association representing 250 asset managers with £7.8 trillion under management, the country's financial ecosystem had the depth and institutional maturity to absorb new infrastructure models that smaller markets could not. The practical examples were already visible in mainstream financial services.

Lloyds Banking Group had deployed parametric insurance products: insurance contracts that pay automatically when a verified triggering event occurs, without requiring a claims investigation, reducing settlement times from forty-five days to forty-five minutes. That compression was not achieved through blockchain specifically, but through programmable contracts combined with verified data feeds, the essential architecture of tokenized finance applied to a product category that had existed for decades in a different form.

A parliamentary bill to clarify the legal status of digital assets as personal property was advancing through Westminster. A fintech adoption rate of 71 percent among UK consumers represented, in concrete terms, a population already comfortable with the digital financial products that tokenized assets would build upon. The infrastructure was present. The regulatory framework was developing. The capital base was there.

Visa, Mastercard, and the payments layer

The participation of payment network operators in the tokenized asset ecosystem provides a different kind of signal. Visa and Mastercard are the infrastructure through which retail commerce flows; their engagement with tokenization indicates that the technology is being integrated into the systems that process the most quotidian financial transactions, not just the bespoke institutional ones.

Visa launched its Token Asset Platform (VTAP) in October 2024. The platform allows banks and financial institutions to issue and manage tokenized fiat currency deposits using Visa's infrastructure. BBVA in Spain became the first institution to pilot the technology; the ambition was to enable institutional clients to move tokenized value across Visa's network in the same way that card payments move conventional currency. Visa processed 3.94 trillion transactions in the third quarter of 2024 alone. That volume represents the rails on which any mainstream tokenized payment infrastructure will need to operate.

Mastercard's Multi Token Network issued the first tokenized deposit in June 2024, demonstrating that both major card networks had reached the same conclusion: the future of payments infrastructure involves programmable, blockchain-native value, and the organizations that currently operate the dominant payment rails intend to be part of it. JPMorgan had reached that conclusion several years earlier, operating its JPMorgan Coin infrastructure for real-time interbank settlement and expanding the model through its Onyx platform. Goldman Sachs, HSBC with its Orion Digital Vault, and Société Générale with its blockchain bond program had each integrated tokenized asset capability into their core institutional offerings.

Gold, commodities, and the DeFi utility layer

The argument for tokenizing gold is straightforward: the $18 trillion global gold market is expensive to access, expensive to store, and illiquid outside standardized exchange-traded vehicles. Tokenizing specific gold bars held in custody, each token representing one troy ounce of a verified, serially numbered physical bar in a Brinks vault, eliminates storage costs for the investor, allows fractional positions, and enables settlement in minutes. PAX Gold and Tether Gold had established this model by 2023. What Swarm added was a DeFi utility layer.

Between January and March 2025, investors holding Swarm's xGold token and borrowing against it in a MetaStreet DeFi lending pool, using the tokenized gold as collateral to acquire additional exposure, generated returns of over 20 percent. In the same period, Bitcoin fell by approximately 15 percent. The comparison is imperfect: leveraged gold strategies carry their own risks. But it demonstrated something specific: tokenized gold, integrated with DeFi infrastructure, could behave as an active financial tool rather than a passive store of value.

The broader commodity tokenization landscape had expanded well beyond gold. Agridex was tokenizing wine, olive oil, cocoa, coffee, and livestock, providing farmers with faster access to capital and creating transparent, traceable supply chains. Sunified was issuing tokens backed by the production of solar energy. Paul Taylor was preparing to launch Token X, a MiCA-compliant stablecoin backed by a portfolio of European critical mineral assets — lithium, cobalt, and rare earth elements that sit at the intersection of the green energy transition and emerging geopolitical competition for resource control. The tokenized commodity market was beginning to encompass not just the most traded traditional assets but the most strategically significant materials of the coming decades.

Central bank gold accumulation added a macroeconomic dimension to this picture. Central banks globally had purchased more than a thousand metric tonnes of gold annually for three consecutive years by 2025. China's central bank increased its reserves for a fourth consecutive month in February of that year, reaching 73.61 million ounces valued at over $208 billion. BRICS nations collectively held more than 20 percent of the world's gold reserves at 6.2 tonnes.

Fort Knox, the United States depository holding a reported 147.3 million ounces valued at approximately $428 billion, had not been fully audited since 1953, a fact that acquired unusual political salience when the incoming US administration discussed the prospect of a live-streamed inspection.

The wallet as financial interface

The history of how people have kept records of what they own runs from Henry I's tally stick system, split sticks of wood, each half kept by one party to a transaction, functioning as legally enforceable proof of debt, through paper certificates, to the digital wallets that now manage everything from consumer purchases to institutional custody positions.

MetaMask, the browser-based crypto wallet, had more than thirty million monthly active users by 2025. Ledger's hardware wallets offered offline storage for digital assets. XDEFI served NFT collectors. TPX and Cheyenne Mint provided military-grade physical security for institutional-scale positions. The notable development was the evolution from passive storage to active interface: AI-powered wallets that could assess market conditions, recommend allocations, execute trades, and manage risk automatically — performing, for digital assets, what robo-advisers had begun performing for conventional portfolios. The wallet was becoming a decision-making hub rather than a container.

The conditions for mainstream adoption

The European Banking Authority surveyed 85 credit institutions in the European Economic Area in December 2024. Seventeen percent anticipated engaging with tokenized deposits within one to two years. The figure is notable less for its size than for what it implies: the majority of European credit institutions remained in a "wait and see" position, acknowledging tokenization's potential while declining to commit significant resources until specific conditions were met.

Those conditions, articulated consistently across institutions, followed a recognizable pattern. Regulatory clarity was essential: institutions required assurance that their tokenization programs would not encounter unexpected legal challenges. MiCA provided a European framework, but its interpretation across the twenty-seven member states remained uneven. Technical interoperability between different blockchain networks and between on-chain and legacy systems remained a significant barrier; without it, the efficiency benefits of tokenization could not be captured at scale. Institutional-grade custody solutions were a prerequisite for any major financial institution to hold or transfer tokenized assets on behalf of clients. And qualified specialists, the technology and compliance professionals capable of designing, operating, and auditing tokenized infrastructure, remained scarce.

The adoption trajectory, based on these conditions, was most plausibly described as a three-phase progression. The first phase, controlled pilots across limited asset classes, with regulatory-compliant designs and governance frameworks, was largely complete. The second phase, targeted deployments in high-value areas, increasing interoperability, expanding regulatory clarity, was under way. The third phase, where tokenized assets are integrated into mainstream financial infrastructure with standardized protocols and intuitive access for retail participants, was the destination institutions were building toward but had not yet reached.

Ripple's acquisition of Metaco, a crypto custody firm, for $250 million in 2023, followed by the purchase of HiddenRoad for $1.25 billion in 2025, was the clearest signal of what building toward that destination required. HiddenRoad worked with more than three hundred institutional clients and cleared in excess of $3 trillion in assets per year. The acquisition gave Ripple the full infrastructure stack, custody, payments, and market-making, that institutional tokenization required. It signaled that the conversation had moved from whether tokenization would transform finance to which firms would control the critical infrastructure when it did.

Prediction markets as signal

Two platforms provided an unconventional but revealing indicator of where institutional confidence in the tokenization sector was tracking. Polymarket and Kalshi, prediction markets where participants stake real money on the probability of future events, had become, by 2025, recognized tools for aggregating collective intelligence about uncertain outcomes. Kalshi processed $500 million in weekly volume and captured 62 percent of prediction market volume in September 2025. Intercontinental Exchange, the parent company of the New York Stock Exchange, committed up to $2 billion to Polymarket, pushing its valuation to $8 billion. Kalshi secured $300 million at a $5 billion valuation from a separate investor base.

These were not niche venues. The figures reflected institutional conviction, not just that prediction markets themselves have commercial value, but that the real-time probability assessments they provide about regulatory decisions, asset classes, and market events had become useful inputs for professional investors navigating a rapidly evolving tokenized asset landscape.

The scale that removed the doubt

Lewis McLellan of the Digital Monetary Institute, discussing the state of institutional tokenization on The Digital Bytes Podcast in December 2024, was precise about what made the real-world asset boom of 2024 and 2025 categorically different from the tokenized asset activity of previous years. The participants were different. The products were different. The revenue streams were real. "These are proper businesses with real revenue attached to these products," McLellan said. "It's not like it's a weird experimental sideshow thing."

BlackRock, Franklin Templeton, Apollo, and Citi were not conducting technology pilots. They were issuing instruments backed by actual portfolios of fund assets, distributing them to institutional and retail clients through regulated custody arrangements, and generating management fees on the volumes managed. Citi's estimate that the tokenized asset market could reach $5 trillion by 2030 was not a forecast made in a research vacuum: it was an estimate made by an institution that was itself building the infrastructure and distribution channels on which that growth depended. The estimate and the investment were part of the same strategic commitment.

Philipp Pieper, describing the integration challenge from the platform side, emphasized that the real-world asset boom would be measured not by the ambition of its proponents but by the quality of the connections it built between on-chain settlement and conventional financial market infrastructure. "It's more about making the on-chain markets work very efficiently with the traditional financial markets," Pieper said on The Digital Bytes Podcast. The blockchain was not replacing the conventional market. It was being assembled as an additional layer of settlement, distribution, and liquidity on top of it, extending reach, reducing friction, and creating new instruments, while the legal, custodial, and identity infrastructure that gave those instruments meaning operated in the same regulated environment it always had.

The scale of the shift

The real-world asset tokenization market reached $24 billion in June 2025, up 380 percent over three years. McKinsey projected the market would reach $2 trillion by 2030. Boston Consulting Group estimated that tokenized assets would represent approximately 10 percent of global GDP by the same year. Standard Chartered and Synpulse put the 2034 figure at approximately $30 trillion.

What underpinned the scaling was a specific category: interest-bearing tokenized assets. A tokenized bond paying regular interest can be programmed to distribute that yield automatically, in fractional amounts, to thousands of token holders simultaneously and continuously, with each distribution recorded as an immutable transaction and the interest calculation verified by an oracle network. A conventional bond distributing interest to paper certificate holders requires custodians, trustees, and clearing houses. A tokenized bond simply pays in a currency-denominated stablecoin to token holders at predictable intervals. The cost difference is not marginal, it represents the elimination of the intermediation layer that has historically extracted five to twenty basis points of every bond transaction. For institutional asset managers, this was not a technology feature. It was an economics transformation.

These are projections, not certainties, and they depend on conditions, regulatory convergence, technical standardization, institutional readiness, that are developing unevenly across markets and jurisdictions. But the direction of the shift, and the institutional weight now pressing into it, is no longer speculative. Nasdaq proposed formal rule changes to the US Securities and Exchange Commission in 2025 that would allow tokenized versions of equities and exchange-traded products to trade alongside their conventional counterparts, not as an experiment, but as permanent market infrastructure.

Nasdaq's Chief Executive, Adena Friedman, was direct: tokenized stocks and ETFs are the future as global markets move on-chain. The world's largest equity exchange was not waiting to see what would happen. It was attempting to define the standards by which it would happen, and in doing so, to ensure that the trusted, regulated intermediaries of the existing system remained the trusted, regulated intermediaries of the one that followed.

The carbon markets were discovering the same truth from a different angle, and with their own complications.

Chapter 19: Carbon Credits and Tokens

In 2005, a World Bank blog asked whether water would become the next oil, the defining scarce resource around which geopolitical competition and economic value would organize themselves in the century ahead. Two decades later, the question had acquired a practical dimension it lacked when it was posed. In 2025, a company called Portal.Lak3 was selling tokenized spring water: digital tokens representing verified ownership of a specific volume of water from a named source, tradeable on a blockchain, with the underlying physical resource stored and verified by an independent custodian. What had seemed a speculative metaphor in 2005 had become a live market.

Water is not yet the dominant story in the tokenization of natural resources. Carbon is. But the water example is worth holding in mind, because it captures something the carbon market debate tends to obscure: the question of whether tokenizing natural assets serves a useful purpose is distinct from the question of whether the specific mechanisms currently being used are working. The answer to the first question is almost certainly yes. The answer to the second is considerably more complicated.

Carbon markets and their structural failures

Carbon credits are instruments representing a verified reduction or removal of one metric tonne of carbon dioxide equivalent from the atmosphere. They are issued by environmental projects, reforestation programs, renewable energy installations, methane capture facilities, and purchased by corporations seeking to offset their own emissions as part of voluntary or regulatory net-zero commitments. In theory, they provide a market mechanism for directing capital toward projects that reduce emissions more efficiently than the purchasing corporations could achieve internally.

In practice, the global carbon market has been characterized by persistent structural failures. Verification processes are manual, time-consuming, and inconsistent across different standards bodies and geographical registries. The two dominant certification organizations, Verra and Gold Standard, have faced sustained criticism about methodology, with investigations in 2023 finding that a material proportion of forest conservation credits issued under one widely used standard had not produced the emissions reductions claimed. Double-counting, the same tonne of reduction claimed by both the project country under its nationally determined contribution and the corporations purchasing voluntary offsets — has proved difficult to eliminate. Prices vary enormously across linked and unlinked markets, which, combined with limited transparency, makes genuine price discovery almost impossible.

An estimated $41 billion in climate finance flows annually without clear accountability for where it goes or what it achieves. This is not primarily a fraud problem, though fraud exists. It is a coordination and verification problem: the information systems connecting climate finance to measurable environmental outcomes are inadequate for a market expected to expand dramatically as countries operationalize net-zero commitments.

The concentration of that value in large institutional players illustrates the gap. Tesla reported $10.7 billion in revenue from the sale of regulatory carbon credits in a recent financial year — credits generated by the avoided emissions attributed to its electric vehicles relative to conventional petrol cars. A single company, at sufficient scale, can extract billions from a carbon market that most households cannot access at all. A homeowner with rooftop solar or an electric vehicle generates carbon savings that are equivalent in principle to what Tesla monetizes through corporate regulatory channels. Without cheap, accessible infrastructure to verify, register, and trade those savings in small denominations, the individual's contribution flows to the grid at the utility's offered rate rather than reaching a carbon market at all. Tokenization changes that calculation: fractionalized carbon tokens, tradeable peer-to-peer through a smart contract, could open the revenue stream that currently flows only to actors large enough to navigate conventional carbon credit channels.

Tokenization as the transparency layer

The argument for applying blockchain to carbon markets is grounded precisely in the problems described above. A carbon credit represented as a blockchain token carries its provenance as part of its structure. The project of origin, the verification standard, the issue date, the retirement date, the custodial chain, the methodology used to calculate the emissions reduction, all of this metadata can be encoded in the token and is immutable once written. Fraudulent duplication becomes effectively impossible: the blockchain's consensus mechanism ensures that each token exists exactly once, and that its retirement, the act of consuming it to offset emissions, is permanently and publicly recorded.

Redbelly and CarbonHood are among the platforms that have moved carbon credit tokenization from concept into production. Toucan Protocol and KlimaDAO created the earliest large-scale experiments in on-chain carbon credit infrastructure, bridging credits from conventional registries onto blockchain networks to enable transparent tracking and DeFi-integrated trading. These experiments exposed both the capability and the risks: DeFi liquidity allowed rapid trading of carbon tokens at speed and global scale, but the connection to underlying verification quality was only as strong as the bridge between the blockchain and the originating registry. Credits that should not have been issued could still be tokenized, traded, and retired — doing so more efficiently than conventional systems, but not doing any less harm.

The infrastructure was, in a fundamental sense, solving the wrong scarcity. The bottleneck in carbon markets was not liquidity or tradability. It was verification quality and the assignment of liability for false or overestimated credits. A blockchain could make the trading mechanism infinitely liquid, but if the underlying carbon reduction claim was fraudulent, distributed ledger immutability meant that fraudulent claim would be permanently recorded. This was not a different problem from the carbon market's existing verification crisis. It was the same problem with higher stakes — because the transparency revealed the failure more conclusively.

The solution is not better blockchain infrastructure alone. It is a more robust oracle architecture, the real-world data feeds that report on forest coverage, project outcomes, and verified emissions reductions, combined with governance mechanisms that ensure the individuals and organizations certifying credits cannot simply declare a favorable outcome. IoT sensors, satellite imagery, and independent verification organizations are components of this architecture. So is the DAO model: distributing governance rights over the verification process among a broader set of stakeholders, including the local communities and landowners on whose land projects operate, reduces the single points of control that corruption most easily exploits.

The futures market for carbon tokens

A spot market for carbon credits, where tokens are bought and sold for immediate delivery, addresses one dimension of the carbon financing problem. A futures market, where participants can buy or sell contracts at predetermined prices for delivery at a future date, addresses another: the problem of investment planning for long-duration conservation or renewable energy projects.

A reforestation project in the Congo Basin that will sequester carbon over fifty years requires investment today. The investors who fund it need visibility over what the resulting credits will be worth across that timeline. A regulated blockchain-based carbon futures market provides exactly the forward price discovery that conventional carbon markets have struggled to produce. Smart contracts automate complex trading terms, margin calls, and settlement conditions; counterparty risk is reduced because the clearing and settlement mechanics are written into the contracts themselves. Settlement cycles compress from days to minutes.

The integration of wholesale central bank digital currencies, or, where those are not yet available, regulated stablecoins backed by high-quality liquid assets, into carbon futures settlement would add institutional credibility and cross-border accessibility. Carbon credits are global instruments, but current settlement systems are fragmented along national and currency boundaries. Atomic settlement in programmable digital currency removes those boundaries while maintaining the regulatory compliance that institutional participants require.

Water, minerals, and the politics of resource ownership

The question that Portal.Lak3 and its equivalents are beginning to raise reaches beyond carbon markets into the fundamentally political territory of how natural resources are owned, governed, and traded in a blockchain-enabled world.

Water rights are increasingly being considered for tokenization in regions where allocation disputes are intensifying. In Australia and California, pilot programs have explored blockchain-based water trading platforms: smart contracts that automate water allocations, enforce usage caps, and facilitate peer-to-peer trading between farmers. The practical logic is sound: water trading systems that rely on manual records and brokered transactions are slow, opaque, and susceptible to corruption. Blockchain-based systems offer speed, transparency, and auditability.

The ethical question is whether access to water, which the United Nations has recognized as a fundamental human right, should be structured as a tradeable commodity at all, and whether digital liquidity, by making water rights easier to trade, increases the risk that they accumulate in the hands of well-resourced actors at the expense of rural communities without digital access or financial sophistication. The blockchain records the transaction accurately. It does not resolve the question of whether the transaction should have been permitted.

Critical minerals — lithium, cobalt, nickel, the rare earth elements required for electric vehicle batteries, wind turbines, and semiconductor fabrication — present the same tension at a higher political temperature. These materials are concentrated in a small number of countries, many of them with fragile governance systems and limited capacity to capture the economic value that their extraction generates. Tokenization could, in principle, give local communities fractional ownership of the resources beneath their land, enabling them to participate in the value stream that currently flows primarily to mining corporations and their shareholders. Nigeria's pilot blockchain registry for oil royalties and Mongolia's experiments with mineral-rights transparency reflect this potential.

The risk, articulated by critics of resource tokenization, is a digital re-run of the colonial extraction dynamic: infrastructure designed by technology companies and traded on global blockchain networks capturing the value of sub-Saharan or Indonesian minerals, with local communities retaining residual rights that look like ownership but offer limited practical control.

Māori, First Nations, and co-designed governance

The most credible responses to this concern involve designing token systems with, rather than for, the communities whose resources are being represented. Projects in New Zealand led by Māori iwi, tribal groups with collectively held land and resource rights under the Treaty of Waitangi framework, have demonstrated that blockchain infrastructure can be built around governance models that originate with the community rather than being imposed on it. The token is the mechanism for representing and trading the value. The community's existing governance structures determine who has authority over the underlying resource, and those structures are encoded into the smart contracts rather than overridden by them.

First Nations organizations in Canada have pursued analogous approaches, using blockchain for land title registration and resource management in ways that strengthen rather than undermine the community's sovereignty over its territory. The technology does not resolve the underlying legal and political questions about indigenous land rights, those remain contested in most jurisdictions. But it provides a mechanism for recording and enforcing rights that communities have already established, rather than requiring them to translate those rights into the vocabulary of corporate property law before they can be recognized.

The token that proves the energy

Alex Bausch, chief executive of 2Tokens and co-founder of QTokens, described on The Digital Bytes Podcast an application of tokenization to the energy sector that resolved, in practical terms, several of the problems identified above in voluntary carbon markets.

The 2Tokens organization, which Bausch describes as a "do tank" rather than a think tank, an organization built to implement rather than advise, had started working in 2019 with a consortium that included the Port of Rotterdam, Dutch universities, and several of the country's major banks. Its initial use cases were in trade finance; the energy application came later, and proved more consequential.

The core concept was straightforward. A solar panel produces energy in measurable, time-stamped intervals. In the Netherlands, energy regulation requires that output be measured in fifteen-minute blocks. If each fifteen-minute interval of production from a specific panel is tokenized as a discrete digital asset, each token represents not merely a claim about the energy that was produced but a verifiable record of where and when it was generated, attached to the panel's identification number. "As soon as you tokenize the solar panel, you can also tokenize what comes out of it," Bausch said. Each production token was, simultaneously, a green energy token and a carbon certificate, the proof of origin that the voluntary carbon market had spent years attempting to create through paper-based certification chains.

European Union legislation had changed in 2019 to permit peer-to-peer energy trading: a household with excess solar production could now legally sell that surplus to a neighbor rather than being required to sell it back to the grid at wholesale rates. Tokenized energy production made this commercially viable at small scale. A municipality pilot in the Netherlands had taken the model a step further, creating token wallets for local residents that could be used to purchase goods and services from participating local businesses. The energy token had become a local exchange instrument, its value derived from verifiable green production.

The longer-term application concerned the estimated one billion solar panels that will require recycling within the coming decade. Bausch's Green Energy for All initiative proposed that refurbished panels, tested using AI to assess remaining output capacity, then deployed to sub-Saharan Africa and other high-sunlight regions, each carry a product passport token encoding its production history, maintenance record, and remaining capacity. "Every panel gets its own product passport token," Bausch said. The energy-as-a-service model this enabled would allow communities in the sunbelt to access power without capital expenditure on grid infrastructure, while the offset generated by the output of those panels could be tokenized against power purchase agreements, creating a revenue stream that was both verifiable and transferable.

What transparency alone cannot do

The broader temptation in sustainable finance, the temptation that tokenization of carbon, water, and natural resources all face in different forms, is to treat the transparency layer as a solution to a governance problem. Blockchain records what happened accurately and permanently. It does not ensure that what happened was the right thing.

A carbon credit whose underlying project did not actually sequester emissions is still a fraudulent instrument whether it sits in a conventional registry or a blockchain token. A water allocation system that fails to protect the rights of vulnerable communities fails regardless of whether the failure is recorded instantly on an immutable ledger. A mineral extraction contract that disadvantages the host community is not improved by being executed through a smart contract.

The technology is a necessary component of a more transparent and accountable sustainability finance system. It is not a sufficient one. The governance choices — who controls the oracle feeds, who designs the certification methodology, who holds governance tokens in the DAOs that manage these assets — determine whether the transparency that blockchain provides serves accountability or simply makes exploitation more legible.

That distinction between the record and the reality it describes runs through every asset class that tokenization touches. It is particularly acute in sustainability markets, where the gap between claims and outcomes is most costly, and where the stakes, the credibility of the mechanisms through which the world is attempting to organize a response to climate change, are highest.

The creative economy has confronted a related version of the same problem. Musicians, artists, and researchers have long operated in systems where the record of who created what was legible to intermediaries and opaque to creators. The following chapter examines what happens when programmable ownership is applied to culture itself.

Chapter 20: Art, Music and IP

In 2021, the musician and DJ Justin Blau, known professionally as 3LAU, released a tokenized version of his album *Ultraviolet* and raised $11.7 million in twenty-four hours. The figure attracted considerable attention from the music industry, but it was not the number that mattered most. What mattered was the accompanying structure. Holders of the tokens did not simply own a digital collectible. They owned a percentage of the streaming royalties from specified tracks: meaning that every time the music was played on Spotify, Apple Music, or any other platform, the revenue was split automatically between the artist and the token holders, without an intermediary processing the payment or taking a cut of the transaction.

It was a proof of concept for something the music industry had spent decades failing to deliver: a mechanism by which the value created when someone listens to a piece of music flows directly and transparently to the people who created it, and to those who invest in it at an early stage.

The royalty problem

The global recorded music market was worth approximately $28.6 billion in 2024, having recovered from the structural disruption caused by streaming's displacement of physical sales and digital downloads. But the economics of that market remain deeply skewed. Streaming platforms pay rights holders fractions of a cent per stream. The rights holders are typically music publishers and record labels, not the artists themselves, who receive royalties only after recouping advances and other charges against their accounts. An artist generating ten million streams per month might receive a monthly payment of several thousand pounds: before deducting the share owed to their label.

The further complication is opacity. The chain from stream to payment involves collecting societies, sub-publishers, digital service provider interfaces, legacy accounting systems, and contractual arrangements that in some cases predate the digital era entirely. Artists routinely report receiving royalty statements that they cannot verify and cannot query effectively. In jurisdictions where copyright is not registered in a central database, which includes most of the world, the legal chain of ownership is frequently unclear even to the parties involved.

Blockchain addresses each layer of this problem in a specific way. Smart contracts can encode royalty splits at the point of the original licensing agreement, automating payment distribution each time a commercial trigger is met without requiring intermediary processing. Every transaction is recorded immutably, meaning that the accounting for each stream, each use, each licensing event can be reconstructed in full at any point. Tokenized ownership of royalty streams is divisible and tradeable, enabling musicians to monetize future revenue today by selling fractions of their catalog to investors who receive ongoing income in return.

Royal, Audius, and the architecture of music tokenization

Royal, the platform 3LAU co-founded, operationalizes this model. Artists upload their work and determine what fraction of royalties they wish to tokenize. Buyers purchase those tokens, structured as limited digital assets, and receive their proportionate share of streaming revenue at regular intervals. The platform provides the interface; the underlying payment mechanics are handled through smart contracts and stablecoin distributions.

Audius, a decentralized music streaming platform with over seven million registered users, approaches the problem from the distribution end rather than the investment end. Artists on Audius upload content directly to a network of nodes run by the platform's community; plays are recorded on a blockchain; and AUDIO tokens, which govern the platform and incentivize participation, flow to creators based on engagement. The platform operates outside the conventional digital service provider model, meaning that its royalty structure does not pass through the intermediaries that consume the margins in mainstream streaming.

Together, these platforms illustrate the spectrum of what tokenized music infrastructure looks like in practice. Royal is an investment instrument: fans and investors stake capital in exchange for income. Audius is a distribution and governance infrastructure: musicians publish directly and participate in the platform's economics. Both are live, both are growing, and both exist in a legal gray zone: the regulatory status of tokenized music royalties under the securities and financial instruments regimes of most jurisdictions has not been definitively settled.

Visual art: from marketplaces to provenance systems

The role that the Beeple sale played in forcing the art world to take digital ownership seriously brought considerable speculative energy into the art NFT market, most of which had dissipated by 2023. What remained was a more durable set of questions about the infrastructure needs of the art market that blockchain is genuinely well-positioned to address.

Art provenance is notoriously unreliable. Physical records of ownership change hands imperfectly, documentation is lost, and the art market's traditional resistance to transparency has created conditions in which disputed attribution and outright forgery are both more common than the industry acknowledges. A blockchain-based provenance system does not replace the physical authentication process: establishing whether a painting is genuine still requires specialist expertise, material analysis, and art-historical scholarship. But it creates an immutable, auditable record of every subsequent ownership transfer, insurance event, and exhibition loan, accessible to any future purchaser and admissible in legal proceedings.

Major museums, from the British Museum to the Smithsonian to the Uffizi Gallery in Florence, had begun exploring NFTs not as a financial instrument for speculative trading but as a technical solution to a curatorial problem. The Vatican Apostolic Library holds 180,000 manuscripts and 1.5 million volumes, many of them unique. Access requires institutional credentials and months of advance notice. Tokenizing the digital representations of these works, paired with smart contracts managing access permissions, enables scholars anywhere on earth to study high-resolution images of documents that have been locked in physical archives for centuries. The British Museum extended this logic further: rather than merely making collections available digitally, it was exploring how NFTs could attach verifiable metadata to cultural objects, dating, provenance, conservation history, creating a distributed record that enhanced rather than replaced the physical curatorial infrastructure. The logic was less about monetization than about expanding access and deepening the documentary record around cultural treasures. These institutional applications bore almost no resemblance to the celebrity NFT drops and profile-picture collections that had dominated media coverage in the hype cycle. They represented instead an attempt to apply the provenance and metadata capabilities of blockchain technology to the genuine curatorial needs of cultural institutions managing irreplaceable collections. That use case, less visible than speculative art markets but considerably more substantial in impact, defined longer-term value more credibly than any of the profile-picture projects had managed to do.

Maecenas and Artory have developed platforms operating in this space. Maecenas enables fractional investment in high-value artworks that would otherwise be accessible only to wealthy private collectors or institutions. Artory has focused on registry infrastructure: a digital record-keeping system for the art market, designed to be interoperable with existing gallery and auction house processes. Both operate in partnership with conventional art world institutions rather than attempting to replace them, which is precisely the integration model that has proven most durable across every sector where tokenization has gained traction.

The fractional ownership argument for art is that it expands the pool of investment by disaggregating assets that are currently too large for most investors to access. A work valued at £50 million is, in practice, accessible only to the very wealthy. Tokenize it into a thousand shares worth £50,000 each, and the effective accessible price falls dramatically while the work's overall liquidity increases. The practical constraint is the same as it is for tokenized real estate: the secondary market for these tokens remains thin, and the legal framework linking token ownership to enforceable rights in the physical work requires jurisdiction-specific legal wrapping that adds friction and cost.

Patents and the tokenization of intellectual property

The patent system was designed for an industrial economy in which the creation of inventions was separable from the process of commercializing them. A company invests in research, files a patent, and licenses it to manufacturers. The economic return rewards the inventor and incentivizes further research. In principle. In practice, the system has accumulated structural inefficiencies that impose substantial costs on the economy without generating proportionate innovation benefits.

Patent litigation is expensive, slow, and disproportionately weaponized by non-practicing entities: organizations that own patent portfolios purely to extract licensing fees, not to produce anything. The process of discovering which patents are relevant to a given technology area, assessing their scope and validity, and negotiating licenses is opaque and time-consuming. Small innovators, particularly in the technology sector, often lack the resources to properly protect or exploit their intellectual property.

IPwe is among the companies applying tokenization to this problem. Its model involves creating digital representations of patents as tokens on a public blockchain, establishing a transparent marketplace for patent licensing and trading. The goals are efficiency (reducing transaction costs for patent licensing), discoverability (making the patent landscape more navigable for companies trying to build around or license existing inventions), and liquidity (enabling smaller companies and individual inventors to realize the value of their patents without having to build the commercial infrastructure to exploit them directly).

The legal architecture is complex. A patent is not a simple asset: it can be valid in some jurisdictions and not others, it has a defined duration, it can be challenged, invalidated, or narrowed. Representing it as a blockchain token requires legal documentary work in every relevant jurisdiction, and the value of the token is contingent on the survival of the underlying patent rights. But the inefficiencies in the current system are significant enough that the market for better patent infrastructure is substantial.

Scientific intellectual property and the DeSci movement

A different tradition of intellectual property tokenization has emerged from research science, motivated not by the commercial inefficiencies of the art or music markets but by the structural features of academic publishing and research funding that concentrate control of scientific knowledge in a small number of large publishers and grant-allocating institutions.

IP-NFTs, intellectual property non-fungible tokens, allow research institutions and biotech start-ups to represent ownership of early-stage research findings, drug candidates, or research licenses as tradeable digital assets. The implications for research funding are potentially significant. Under the conventional model, a biotech company with a promising drug candidate must either find pharmaceutical company partners willing to license it, raise equity from venture capital, or pursue a lengthy initial public offering process, all of which require the company to be at a stage of development that does not suit many early-stage research assets.

An IP-NFT allows the research asset itself to be traded and funded directly. Molecule is among the platforms enabling this: researchers can list their research as an IP-NFT, and investors, including scientific communities and patient advocacy groups, not just financial institutions, can fund it directly in exchange for fractional ownership of the resulting intellectual property.

The DeSci (decentralized science) movement, of which Molecule is a part, argues that this model can realign incentives in research funding in ways that the current system cannot. Research that is commercially marginal but scientifically or socially important, treatments for rare diseases, early-stage climate science, research on neglected tropical diseases, has historically been underfunded by a system that directs capital toward the largest commercial opportunities. Decentralized funding through tokenized research assets could, in principle, direct capital toward outcomes that communities care about rather than merely toward the outcomes that maximize the expected returns for venture capital portfolios.

Berkeley's BrainHub sold a Nobel Prize-winning neuroscience research NFT for $50,000 in 2021 as a largely symbolic demonstration of the concept. The more consequential developments are the live IP-NFT markets where drug development assets are actively changing hands, a market infrastructure that did not exist five years ago.

The commodification question

The chapter that dealt with NFTs in the aftermath of the hype cycle noted a persistent tension between the genuine utility cases, digital inheritance, scientific IP, institutional provenance systems, and the speculative froth that dominated public perception in 2021 and 2022. That tension runs through creative IP more broadly.

Music royalties, artworks, patents, research assets: these are not simply financial instruments to be optimized for liquidity. They carry cultural meaning, represent the creative labor of individuals, and exist in social and legal contexts shaped by values that are not easily encoded in smart contracts. A musician who tokenizes 30 percent of their future royalties has transferred an ongoing economic relationship with their audience from a personal one into a market transaction. Whether that is desirable depends on what kind of relationship between artists and their work the culture wants to sustain.

These are not objections to tokenization as a tool. They are constraints on the contexts in which it should be applied and the designs that should govern those applications. The music industry's exploitation of artists through opaque royalty systems and onerous contractual terms is not a problem that arises from transparency: tokenization's capacity to make those flows visible and auditable serves the interests of artists directly. The question is whether the investment instruments built on top of those flows serve them equally well, and whether the artists who use them understand what they are exchanging.

The record the creator controls

Tony McLaughlin, who had proposed the idea of a regulated liability network at Citi and had spent more than a decade working on the structural questions of digital money, identified a tension in how digital infrastructure had historically been organized that applies directly to the creative economy. He characterized systems as either Cathedrals — proprietary, controlled by centralized institutions, legible to intermediaries but opaque to the people whose activity they recorded, or Bazaars: open, interoperable, creator-controlled, and verifiable by any participant with access to the shared ledger. Traditional music royalty administration, publishing rights management, and research attribution systems were all Cathedrals. The platforms that intermediated between creators and audiences had historically captured the record of who created what and who received payment against it, and had used that record to extract fees and impose terms that individual creators had no practical means to contest.

Adam Feiler of Minima, a blockchain designed from the ground up to run on mobile devices without requiring institutional node operators, identified the capability most relevant to this structure. “Blockchain technology does one thing very, very well,” Feiler said, “which is to keep track of accounts.” Applied to creative work, this was not a metaphor but a direct description of the function: an immutable ledger that recorded authorship at the point of creation, timestamps that established prior art, and smart contracts that distributed royalty flows to recorded contributors automatically whenever a license was exercised. The intermediary that had previously held the rights administration database, and charged for its maintenance and operation, became optional.

The same logic extends to personal data. In a token-based system, sharing becomes a permissioned transaction that remains visible to the owner rather than a transfer of control to a platform that would use it for purposes the originator had not chosen. Applied to creative output, the principle is identical: the token encodes authorship, the smart contract specifies how and when royalties flow, and the immutable record of every license exercised persists in perpetuity — under the control of the person who made the work in the first place.

The question of who this infrastructure ultimately serves extends beyond individual creators to the households and communities for whom fractional tokenization may be the only practical route into investment at all. The next chapter follows that question into fractional ownership, and into the gap between the promise of inclusive finance and the difficulty of actually delivering it.

Chapter 21: Fractional Ownership

In the Netherlands, 42 percent of residential solar installations are on private homes or rental properties: panels owned by the household rather than by a utility. Dutch solar capacity grew by 22 percent in a single year. When a government working group and research consortium convened as 2Tokens published their whitepaper on energy communities, they were writing about an infrastructure shift that Dutch households could see from their own rooftops. The paper's core observation was simple and consequential: the prosumer, the household that produces as well as consumes energy, already existed at scale. What did not yet exist was the financial infrastructure to let those households participate in the energy economy as investors rather than merely producers.

The solution the whitepaper proposed was kWh Energy Tokens: blockchain-based instruments representing the right to a unit of renewable energy generated within a defined community network. A household with excess solar production would not simply sell it back to the grid at the utility's offered price. They would hold a token representing that excess production, tradeable within a marketplace of community members, or pooled into a virtual power plant whose aggregate output could be contracted and sold collectively. A household without rooftop access, a flat-dweller, a tenant, a small business, could purchase fractional shares in a solar park and receive a proportionate return in energy tokens or their economic equivalent.

This is fractional ownership applied to infrastructure. And it is one of the most significant ongoing experiments in what tokenization can actually mean for people without significant investment capital.

Who fractional ownership is for

The investment landscape before blockchain tokenization was structured by minimum transaction sizes that effectively excluded most people from most asset classes. Investing in commercial real estate required either the capital to buy property directly, or a position in a real estate investment trust, a pooled vehicle requiring brokerage access and a minimum investment that varies by territory but is rarely accessible to someone with a few hundred pounds to deploy. Private equity funds typically require seven-figure commitments. Fine art, private credit, infrastructure, and commodities are similarly accessible only to institutions and the wealthy. Even public equities present barriers of knowledge and access in markets where the most sophisticated intermediaries extract the most value.

The promise of tokenization is that fractional ownership can collapse those barriers. If a building, a solar park, a private equity fund, or a corporate bond can be divided into thousands of tokens at low or zero additional cost, the effective minimum investment falls dramatically. The Dutch household that cannot afford a rooftop panel can afford a token representing a hundredth of a community solar installation. The small investor who cannot access Hamilton Lane's private equity strategies directly can access Securitize's tokenized feeder fund at a fraction of the conventional minimum.

The argument is not simply about access for its own sake. Diversification, distributing risk across multiple uncorrelated assets, is one of the most robust principles in portfolio construction, and it has historically been available primarily to those with sufficient capital to build a genuinely diversified position. Fractional tokenization democratizes diversification. The same mechanism that lets a Dutch household buy a solar token also lets a Brazilian retail investor hold a small position in a US Treasury token, a fraction of a tokenized private credit instrument, and a stake in a Singapore real estate fund: a level of diversification previously available only to sovereign wealth funds and family offices.

Energy communities and the DAO governance model

The 2Tokens whitepaper went beyond ownership to governance. A community solar park owned by hundreds of small investors requires systems for making collective decisions: whether to expand, whether to upgrade, how to price access, how to distribute profits. The whitepaper proposed DAO governance as the natural complement to tokenized fractional ownership, not as an ideological commitment to decentralization, but as a practical solution to the coordination problem created by having many small stakeholders in shared infrastructure.

Renewable Energy Communities and Citizen Energy Communities, legal entities established under the EU Clean Energy for All Europeans package, provide the regulatory vessel into which this model fits. Member states are required to allow these community structures; the 2Tokens model proposed using smart contracts to automate the treasury management that conventional community governance handles through committee meetings and bank accounts. Contributions from member households flow into a smart-contract treasury; expenditure decisions are executed by the contract when they meet the threshold of approved votes held by token holders.

The governance architects consulted in the 2Tokens research identified a critical insight: the DAO governance model was not an ideological commitment to decentralization but a practical solution to a coordination problem that had proved intractable under conventional governance. A community solar installation owned by hundreds of small investors requires decisions about expansion, maintenance, cost allocation, and profit distribution that cannot sensibly be made by a central authority: because no single entity has the information or the legitimacy to choose.

Distributed governance, automated through smart contracts, made it possible to embed the decision-making authority into the infrastructure itself. The technological component was secondary to this organizational logic. What mattered was that tokenization made distributed ownership feasible, and smart contracts made distributed ownership governable.

The practical obstacles are real. Regulatory uncertainty across member states means that energy trading between community members remains legally complicated in many jurisdictions, even where it is technically straightforward. The technology stack, wallet management, transaction interfaces, and the user experience of participating in on-chain governance, is not designed for households whose primary interaction with finance involves a banking app on a mobile phone. And governance complexity in practice tends to concentrate effective decision-making in the hands of the most engaged and technically sophisticated participants, even in systems designed to be inclusive.

These are engineering and policy problems, not fundamental objections to the model. The EU's energy transition requires the rapid deployment of distributed renewable generation at a scale that exceeds the financing capacity of conventional utility models. Community energy, funded through fractional tokenized ownership, represents one of the few architectures available to bridge that gap: provided the regulatory and technological infrastructure catches up with the concept.

The institutional dimension: State Street and the custody question

While community energy experiments address fractional ownership at the retail end of the market, institutional investors are pursuing the same logic with much larger pools of capital and much more demanding requirements around custody, compliance, and risk management.

State Street's 2024 Digital Assets Study found that one-third of institutional respondents had increased their digital asset allocations in the preceding year, and 69 percent expected to expand their involvement over the following five years. These are not retail speculators. They are pension funds, insurance companies, asset managers, and sovereign wealth funds: institutions that will not deploy capital into any asset class without certainty about how it will be held, how it will be valued, and what happens when something goes wrong.

The digital asset custody question is substantially more complex than conventional securities custody. The global market for digital asset safeguarding was estimated at $57.77 billion in 2024, with 861 million users by 2025 representing approximately 11.89 percent of the world's population, a penetration rate comparable to the early internet. The IMF's warning, issued as crypto markets expanded tenfold, that the pace of growth demanded proportionate oversight was not alarmist: the systemic implications of institutional-scale capital concentrated in assets whose custody model is materially different from anything that existing regulatory frameworks were designed to govern are substantial.

At the market level, survey data sharpens the diagnosis. A study conducted by The Future of Finance into the barriers to broader tokenization in the UK found that 45 percent of respondents identified regulatory constraints as the primary obstacle, while 26 percent cited poorly designed tokenization products and services. Together, those two factors accounted for 61 percent of the identified barriers, a finding that locates the problem squarely in the interaction between product design and regulatory clarity rather than in any inherent technological limitation. The UK manages approximately $11 trillion in assets, and the institutional community operating within it is not indifferent to tokenization; it is waiting for the framework in which to act.

The architecture of digital asset custody differs from conventional securities safeguarding in ways that matter for institutional risk managers. Conventional securities are held by custodian banks under a legal framework that includes segregation requirements, insurance, and regulatory capital obligations. The custodian holds legal title on behalf of the beneficial owner; in the event of the custodian's insolvency, the client's assets are ring-fenced from the custodian's estate.

Digital asset custody operates on a three-tier model: addresses (the publicly visible location where assets are held, analogous to a post box), keys (the cryptographic credentials that control access to those assets, analogous to a door key), and entitlements (the legal arrangements, IOUs, custody agreements, contractual rights, that connect those technical structures to enforceable claims). The UK Share Association has described current segregation practice in digital asset custody as effectively an "honor system"; the legal treatment of digital assets in insolvency proceedings is unsettled in most jurisdictions. The UK Property (Digital Assets) Bill, introduced in September 2024, represents one of the first legislative attempts to clarify the property status of digital assets as a category distinct from conventional choses in possession or action.

What good custodianship looks like

Three pillars of robust digital asset safeguarding emerge consistently from analysis of the most durable custody arrangements currently in operation: technology, process, and law.

On technology: the key management architecture, hardware security modules, multi-party computation, hardware wallets, determines how resilient a custody arrangement is against both external attack and internal failure. No single person should control sufficient key material to execute a transaction alone. Access controls should be segregated according to function, and monitoring systems should generate alerts when access patterns deviate from the expected. The attack surface for digital asset theft is meaningfully different from the attack surface for conventional securities fraud, and custodians who apply conventional risk frameworks without modification are not adequately protected.

On process: the four-eyes principle, requiring two independent parties to approve any material action, must be implemented technically, not merely as a matter of internal policy. Whitelisting of permitted counterparty addresses reduces the risk that a compromised account can direct assets to an attacker-controlled destination. Incident response runbooks, tested regularly, ensure that when something goes wrong the organization can respond coherently rather than improvising under pressure.

On law: the trustee, bailee, and contractual custodian models represent different legal relationships between the custodian and the client's assets, with different insolvency protections and different obligations. Clients who do not understand which model governs their arrangement cannot reliably assess their exposure. The choice of governing law and jurisdiction matters; the UK, Switzerland, Singapore, and Abu Dhabi Global Market have each developed frameworks that address custody in materially different ways, and the choice between them has practical consequences that institutions should be making deliberately rather than by default.

Remaining risks at the frontier

Two risk categories remain inadequately resolved at the frontier of digital asset custody, even for the most sophisticated custodians currently operating.

Smart-contract-based assets present a governance risk that has no direct equivalent in conventional custody. When an asset exists on a blockchain governed by a smart contract, the rules that govern the asset can be changed by whoever controls the contract's upgrade mechanism. An institution holding tokenized assets whose underlying protocol is upgraded without its knowledge or consent may find that the rights it holds have been materially altered. This is not hypothetical: protocol governance disputes have resulted in contested upgrades across multiple blockchain networks. The due diligence required to understand the governance model of every protocol underlying a tokenized position is substantial.

Cross-chain bridge risk represents the second frontier challenge. As tokenized assets increasingly require interoperability between different blockchain networks — moving an asset from one network to another to access a different application or settle with a counterparty using different infrastructure — they must pass through bridge protocols that have proven to be among the most frequently exploited components in the digital asset stack. Over $2 billion in assets was stolen through bridge exploits in a single two-year period. Any risk management framework for diversified tokenized asset portfolios that does not explicitly address bridge exposure is incomplete.

The trajectory

The $57.77 billion custody market and the 861 million user base are not measures of a mature, stable industry. They are measures of an industry in rapid transition, in which the institutions that build durable structures are the ones that treat the technology as a genuine novelty requiring new frameworks, not as a variant of existing instruments that can be managed with existing tools.

Fractional ownership is one of the best arguments for tokenization as a genuinely democratizing technology. Community energy, tokenized art, fractional private equity, retail access to Treasury tokens: these are real improvements in economic participation available to real people. The challenge is ensuring that the infrastructure through which those improvements are delivered is as robust as the concept deserves. That requires regulatory clarity, custodial sophistication, and a public discourse about digital asset safeguarding that currently runs far behind the pace of adoption.

The fraction that places you in the market

Alex Bausch of 2Tokens, discussing the solar energy tokenization work his organization had developed, touched on a dimension of fractional ownership that financial commentary rarely addresses: its capacity to democratize participation in productive assets specifically for people whose housing circumstances excluded them from the most common form of household wealth accumulation. An apartment dweller in a Dutch city, without roof access and without the capital to install solar panels, could acquire fractional ownership of a virtual solar panel installed at a community facility or rural site. The production tokens generated by their fraction of that panel would accrue to their wallet in real time, in fifteen-minute intervals, representing both a financial return and a verified green energy certificate. The investment was not a fund unit delivered through a broker months after subscription. It was a live, continuously updating record of a physical asset generating output in the world.

Philipp Pieper of Swarm described a parallel dynamic in the property market. The $30 trillion home equity market in the United States represented wealth that most American homeowners held in entirely illiquid form, accessible only through formal bank lending processes, at the discretion of underwriters working on business-day timelines. In decentralized finance, the concept of borrowing against a wallet balance at any hour, continuously, without approval latency, had become an established expectation among regular users. "We've become very used to using whatever the wallet balance we have to be able to borrow against it," Pieper said. The extension of that capability to tokenized real estate equity, allowing a homeowner to post a fraction of their property's value as collateral against a short-term liquidity need, settled on-chain in minutes rather than through a mortgage refinancing process taking weeks — would change the financial lives of people who currently had no practical access to the equity they had spent years accumulating.

Adam Feiler of Minima added the infrastructure dimension: a blockchain running on IoT devices and mobile phones, with every device a node in the network, meant that fractional ownership was not merely theoretically accessible to anyone with a smartphone but practically anchored in the physical objects those people already carried. The custody question, the regulatory question, and the disclosure question all remained. The technology question, Feiler's work suggested, had already been answered.

The next chapter examines the legal and regulatory frameworks being assembled to close the gap between where the technology is and where the law has so far arrived, and the risks that accumulate in the distance between the two.

Chapter 22: Laws and Regulations

On the 21st of February 2025, hackers connected to North Korea's Lazarus Group stole $1.5 billion in Ethereum from the cryptocurrency exchange ByBit. It was the largest theft in the history of digital assets, eclipsing the $600 million Ronin Network attack of 2022 and dwarfing even the losses at Mt. Gox, the Tokyo-based exchange that collapsed in 2014 after losing 850,000 Bitcoin over several years of unauthorized extraction. The ByBit attack targeted a cold wallet, theoretically the most secure form of digital asset storage, through a sophisticated compromise of the signing infrastructure used to authorize large transfers. The funds were immediately dispersed across thousands of wallets and were being actively laundered at pace.

The attack was significant not only for its scale but for its timing. It occurred precisely as institutional capital was beginning to flow into digital asset markets at a volume that regulators and law enforcement had not anticipated. The ByBit theft was a reminder that the technological infrastructure underlying the tokenized economy, however sophisticated, was operating in a legal and regulatory environment that was still being assembled in real time.

That environment had matured enormously since the years of regulatory improvisation that followed the

Bitcoin white paper. But maturity and completeness are different things.

The deposit system and its digital evolution

The most conservative form of tokenized value is a tokenized deposit: a digital representation of a liability that a regulated bank already holds on its balance sheet. Unlike a stablecoin issued by a non-bank entity, a tokenized deposit remains within the regulated financial system, subject to the same capital adequacy requirements, deposit insurance frameworks, and supervisory oversight that govern conventional bank deposits. It is the digital money system's equivalent of a first step.

The UK's Regulated Liability Network, a proof-of-concept involving Citibank, JPMorgan, Visa, Swift, Mastercard, TD Bank, and a broader consortium overseen by the securities industry body SIFMA — tested interoperability among tokenized central bank money, commercial bank deposits, and regulated stablecoin instruments. The experiment's purpose was to determine whether a shared ledger infrastructure could support the settlement of financial transactions using tokenized forms of money, without requiring any participant to abandon their existing risk management frameworks or regulatory obligations.

Analysis of the Regulated Liability Network's design reveals a deep insight about regulatory evolution in crypto markets: the most significant regulatory frameworks were not being written by legislatures but by industry consortia working with central banks and supervisory authorities on proof-of-concept projects. The RLN was not a proposal for how tokenized deposits should work. It was a working prototype that regulators, central banks, and commercial institutions were building together. This collaborative infrastructure-building approach meant that regulatory clarity would emerge from practice rather than being imposed on practice. The risk was that the institutions building the proofs of concept would establish path dependencies that excluded smaller participants from the ecosystem. The benefit was that the regulatory frameworks that eventually crystallized would reflect the actual constraints operating financial institutions faced, rather than being based on theoretical assumptions that proved unworkable at scale.

Ryan Rugg, Citibank's head of Institutional Products, was candid in summarizing the timeline: progress was happening, but it was taking "longer than expected, to be honest." The friction is not primarily technical, the technology to settle tokenized deposits on a distributed ledger has been available for several years. The friction is legal and organizational: determining how tokenized deposits interact with central bank reserves, how cross-institution transfers are reported, and how existing consumer protection frameworks apply to instruments that are legally deposits but operationally different from anything those frameworks were designed to govern.

Fnality International, funded by Goldman Sachs, BNP Paribas, and others to the tune of $95 million in a November 2023 round, is developing payment infrastructure based on tokenized sterling held as central bank reserves, a form of wholesale tokenized money that sits above conventional commercial bank deposits in the hierarchy of financial claims. The Bank of Spain partnered with technology provider Adhara on a wholesale CBDC pilot for interbank settlement, one of several central bank experiments exploring whether the settlement layer of the financial system can be tokenized without disrupting the broader monetary architecture.

The Bank for International Settlements, in its 2024 work on the “Finternet”, a vision for the future financial system built on tokenization and unified ledgers, describes tokenized deposits and wholesale CBDCs as complementary components of a future settlement infrastructure in which the distinction between payment and delivery collapses: the transfer of ownership and the transfer of value occur in the same atomic transaction, eliminating the settlement risk that has characterized financial markets since modern securities trading began.

Corporate balance sheets and digital asset treasuries

The legal and regulatory evolution of digital assets on corporate balance sheets accelerated significantly in 2024 and 2025. The Financial Accounting Standards Board's ASU 2023-08, which took effect in early 2024, established fair-value accounting for cryptocurrency holdings: meaning that companies holding Bitcoin or other digital assets must mark them to market in their financial statements, recognizing changes in value in the period they occur rather than only on disposal. This resolved a longstanding accounting anomaly under which an institution holding Bitcoin was required to write down impairments immediately but could not recognize unrealized gains, a treatment that created perverse incentives and obscured the economic reality of digital asset positions.

The GENIUS Act, signed in the United States in July 2025, provided the first comprehensive federal framework for stablecoins, establishing reserve requirements, disclosure obligations, and redemption rights that brought regulated stablecoin issuance into a framework comparable to other forms of licensed money transmission. The US Treasury's accompanying guidance noted that CBDCs might eventually absorb the functions currently performed by private stablecoins, but acknowledged that private innovation would continue to lead the development of the payment technology stack.

Digital Asset Treasury (DAT) strategies emerged as a defined corporate finance model, with Bitcoin, Ethereum, and Solana the most commonly held reserve assets. BlackRock's BUIDL (the BlackRock USD Institutional Digital Liquidity Fund) and Franklin Templeton's OnChain US Government Money Fund reached a combined two billion dollars in tokenized US Treasury assets, demonstrating institutional-scale demand for yield-bearing on-chain instruments backed by the safest available collateral. JPMorgan's Onyx platform operationalized intraday repo using tokenized collateral, enabling institutional clients to deploy idle assets in overnight positions that settled and unwound within the same business day, a liquidity management capability without precedent in conventional money markets.

The risk that regulators and analysts identified in the DAT model is systemic: as more corporate treasuries hold digital assets, and as leveraged strategies built on digital asset holdings proliferate, the correlation between the prices of those assets and the financial health of the companies holding them creates a channel through which a digital asset market correction can propagate rapidly into corporate credit and equity markets. It is a new form of the interconnection risk that financial regulators have managed, with varying success, through every period of financial innovation.

Legal frameworks: where property meets code

The legal treatment of digital assets as property is still being developed across most jurisdictions. The UK's Law Commission concluded in 2023 that existing English law was capable of recognizing a third category of personal property — distinct from things in possession (tangible physical objects) and things in action (rights enforceable through legal action), that could capture the unique characteristics of digital assets. The Property (Digital Assets etc.) Bill, introduced in September 2024, proposed statutory confirmation of this conclusion: that a digital asset can be held as property, given as a gift, used as security, and included in an estate.

That last provision, inclusion in an estate, confronts a practical problem that no property law reform can fully resolve on its own. A digital asset's value is accessible only to whoever holds the private key that controls it. A private key is not a password stored in a bank's records or a share certificate held in a custody account. It is a string of cryptographic data that, if lost, renders the associated assets permanently and irrecoverably inaccessible. When James Howells lost access to a hard drive containing the private keys to 8,000 Bitcoin, now worth several hundred million dollars, he did not lose a legal claim to property that courts could subsequently restore. He lost the only mechanism by which the property could ever be accessed. Granting his estate a legal right to those Bitcoin would be formally correct and practically meaningless. The assets exist on the blockchain in perpetuity. They are simply permanently locked, absent the key.

This is the real frontier of digital asset estate planning, and it is more a technical and organizational challenge than a legal one. The solutions that have emerged are custody-based: institutional custodians who hold private keys on behalf of clients and maintain succession procedures that allow designated beneficiaries to claim assets following a client's death; multisignature arrangements in which no single private key can unlock an asset alone, and in which a predefined set of key holders, family members, solicitors, trusted institutions, must cooperate to authorize a transfer; and encrypted key storage services that hold key fragments in probate-accessible escrow. None of these solutions is convenient, and uptake among ordinary retail holders of digital assets remains low. The gap between the legal recognition that the Property (Digital Assets) Bill provides and the practical infrastructure that would make digital inheritance routine is real, and narrowing it will require both better tooling and a cultural shift in how digital asset holders think about the responsibilities they are taking on when they move value outside the conventional financial system.

The UK Economic Crime and Corporate Transparency Act 2023 went further in a different direction, giving law enforcement agencies powers to seize and destroy digital assets linked to criminal activity, a practical response to the operational challenge that the ByBit theft and similar incidents had made visible. The Act's digital asset provisions recognized that the asymmetry between the speed at which digital assets can be moved and the speed at which conventional asset-recovery processes operate made existing powers inadequate for the reality of digital asset crime.

The Ripple acquisitions of Metaco (for $250 million in May 2023) and HiddenRoad (for $1.25 billion) illustrate the private sector's response to regulatory evolution. Metaco provides institutional-grade digital asset custody; HiddenRoad, the prime brokerage and financing infrastructure, serves more than three hundred institutions and clears trillions of dollars of transactions annually. Ripple's thesis is that the critical components of the digital asset financial infrastructure, custody, payments, market-making, will converge into integrated platforms, and that institutions that fail to position themselves in that infrastructure during the current period will find themselves dependent on others who did. The crypto custody market is estimated to reach ten trillion dollars by 2030, according to Ripple's head of custody Sagar Shah.

Risk management: from exchange failures to systemic oversight

The history of digital asset risk management is substantially a history of failures from which better practice has slowly emerged. Mt. Gox's collapse in 2014 was attributable to a combination of internal fraud, inadequate security practices, and complete absence of regulatory oversight. QuadrigaCX's collapse in 2019, when the exchange's founder died as the only person holding keys to approximately $190 million of customer assets, demonstrated that the risks of single-point-of-failure custodial models were not limited to external attacks. Celsius, Voyager, and FTX illustrated the systemic risks arising from opacity in leverage, counterparty exposure, and asset segregation within interconnected digital asset platforms.

The response from both regulators and the industry has involved the application of conventional financial risk management tools adapted for digital asset specifics. Blockchain analytics providers, Chainalysis and TRM among them, enable both regulators and institutions to trace the movement of assets across public ledgers, providing forensic capability that is in some respects superior to what is available in conventional financial crime investigation. Smart contract audits, conducted before deployment and at intervals when code is updated, provide independent assessment of whether the logic governing an automated process behaves as claimed.

AI-powered risk models – detecting anomalous patterns in on-chain activity, flagging transactions that match the signatures of known attack vectors, monitoring liquidity conditions that precede market dislocations – are being embedded in digital asset risk management infrastructure at increasing sophistication. The interoperability risk between different blockchain protocols, already identified as a frontier challenge in the custody framework, is also a risk management challenge: when assets move across chain boundaries, they pass through components of the infrastructure whose risk characteristics are poorly understood by the institutions instructing the movements.

The International Monetary Fund's repeated warnings about the pace of growth in crypto markets and the insufficiency of oversight relative to systemic exposure are not, at this stage, warnings about an imminent crisis. They are structural observations: that a market with 861 million participants, trillions of dollars in daily value transfer, and deep linkages to the conventional financial system through tokenized deposits, DAT strategies, and institutional custody is now material enough that its failure modes matter to everyone, not only to those who participate in it directly.

The convergence the industry needs

Elliott Hentoff of State Street summarized the institutional view succinctly: tokenization is not a revolution in finance, it is "market evolution." The operational processes of financial markets are being digitized, the settlement infrastructure is being upgraded, and the range of instruments that can be created, transferred, and held is being expanded. The economic logic is not obscure. The obstacles are real but manageable.

The regulatory convergence the industry requires is toward equivalent standards for digital asset custody, market conduct, and systemic risk oversight as those that govern conventional securities markets, not identical rules, because the technology is different, but comparable protections. Switzerland's Financial Market Infrastructure Act, Singapore's Payment Services Act, and the UK's Financial Services and Markets Act 2023 represent different approaches to achieving that equivalence. None is complete. All are further along than the regulatory vacuum that existed five years ago.

The central insight of the legal and regulatory evolution described in this chapter is that the question of whether to regulate digital assets has been definitively answered. The live questions are how to regulate them, in what sequence, and who takes the lead in establishing the international standards that will determine whether the tokenized economy functions as a genuinely global infrastructure or fragments into incompatible jurisdictional silos.

The standard being written in practice

Jason Myers, chief executive of Auto Chain Labs, brought to the chapter's themes the perspective of someone who had built compliance infrastructure at the frontier of previous regulatory transitions. As part of the team that implemented inline XBRL, the machine-readable financial reporting format, at the United States Securities and Exchange Commission in 2009, Myers had been through the process of transforming opaque, document-based disclosure into structured, queryable data at institutional scale once before. He was building the same infrastructure for digital assets in 2025.

The Markets in Crypto-Assets regulation required that token white papers in the European Union be filed in inline XBRL format rather than as conventional PDFs. The UAE's Virtual Assets Regulatory Authority was requiring the same standard. The practical consequence was precisely the one Myers had observed during the equity disclosure transition: compliance review that had previously required manual examination of individual documents became a systematic, programmable process. Regulators did not need to read filings. They queried them. Anomalies, omissions, and inconsistencies that would have taken human reviewers weeks to identify could be detected algorithmically in minutes. At the scale the tokenized asset market was approaching, Citi's estimate of five trillion dollars by 2030 implied disclosure volumes that no manual review process could sustain, machine-readable standards were not an optional improvement. They were a structural prerequisite.

Lewis McLellan of the Digital Monetary Institute, examining the relationship between technology choice and regulatory design, offered a principle that the broader regulatory frameworks discussed in this chapter had approached from a different angle. "The market should be able to decide which blockchain to use," McLellan said, "and the regulators shouldn't really have their thumb on the scale either way." The implication was a regulatory architecture built around outcome standards rather than technology mandates: requiring that permissioned tokens carry verifiable KYC data, that custody meet specific protection standards, that systemic risk thresholds trigger specific reporting obligations — without specifying whether those requirements were met using Ethereum, Canton, Stellar, or any other infrastructure. The machine-readable disclosure standard Myers was building applied equally regardless of which chain the token lived on. That neutrality was not incidental. It was the design.

The next chapter steps back from the immediate regulatory timeline to ask what the tokenized world looks like at a distance, and what is visible on the horizon that most of the policy conversation has not yet turned to face.

Chapter 23: The Tokenized World

In late 2024, BlackRock published a short video on Facebook explaining the basics of Bitcoin investment. Three billion people have active accounts on that platform. The choice of channel was not accidental. Larry Fink, who had described Bitcoin as an "index of money laundering" in 2017 and had become one of the most prominent advocates for digital asset adoption by 2025, understood that the audience for the tokenized economy was not the early adopters who had been building it for fifteen years. It was everybody else.

Fink's YouTube short, released around the same time, made the case for tokenization in a register designed for general audiences: the frictions in financial markets, slow settlement, manual processes, restricted access, existed because the infrastructure was old, not because they were inevitable. Tokenization, he argued, could compress those frictions out of the system, making markets faster, cheaper, and accessible to a wider range of participants. Equities, real estate, commodities, bonds, funds, money, payments: the scope of what he described was not limited to digital assets as a peripheral asset class. He was describing the financial system itself being rebuilt on a new infrastructure layer.

The person who had steered the world's largest asset manager into that conviction had also been watching something else very carefully. In December

2024, Google announced that its quantum computing chip, Willow, had completed a standard computational benchmark problem in less than five minutes. The fastest classical supercomputer would take ten septillion years, a number larger than the age of the universe by many orders of magnitude, to complete the same problem. The announcement was technically qualified: the benchmark does not represent commercially useful computation, and a great deal of engineering work remains before quantum computers can perform the tasks that would make them economically relevant. But the direction of travel was unmistakable, and the implications for the infrastructure that Fink was advocating were profound.

The quantum threat to cryptographic security

The security of every blockchain-based digital asset, every tokenized bond, property, carbon credit, music royalty, and fractional solar investment discussed in this book, depends on the computational infeasibility of reversing the cryptographic functions that protect transaction signatures and wallet keys. The elliptic-curve cryptography that underpins Bitcoin, Ethereum, and most other blockchain networks is secure against classical computers because factoring large numbers is, on current hardware, computationally intractable. A quantum computer of sufficient scale and fidelity, a cryptographically relevant quantum computer, in the technical terminology, can execute Shor's algorithm to factor those numbers efficiently.

Google's Willow chip demonstrated quantum error correction at a scale and consistency that had not previously been achieved. It does not yet run Shor's algorithm against cryptographically significant key sizes. But it has advanced the credibility of claims that such a machine will exist within a defined future timeframe from plausible speculation to a well-supported engineering projection. The National Institute of Standards and Technology in the United States published its first set of post-quantum cryptography standards in 2024, creating standardized algorithms designed to resist quantum attack. The migration of existing digital infrastructure to these new standards is a multi-year undertaking.

For digital assets in particular, the concern extends beyond the usual migration challenges. Quantum computers that can break elliptic-curve cryptography would not only threaten new transactions; they would threaten the accumulated history of transactions on public blockchains, where the public keys associated with old wallets remain visible. The "store now, decrypt later" attack model, in which an adversary captures encrypted data or transaction records now, with the intention of decrypting them when a sufficiently powerful quantum machine becomes available — is a known threat that financial institutions holding long-duration digital assets must account for in their risk models today.

Preparing the infrastructure

HSBC's response to this challenge provides the most concrete example currently available of a major financial institution translating quantum risk into operational action. In partnership with Quantinuum, the UK-based quantum computing company spun out of Honeywell, HSBC trialed quantum-safe technologies for tokenized gold trading. The experiment involved converting tokenized gold holdings into ERC-20 tokens on the Ethereum blockchain, a technically standard operation, with the addition of cryptographic protections designed to resist both current attack methods and the quantum attacks that do not yet exist but which the threat models of long-duration financial instruments cannot prudently ignore.

The trial compressed multiple timeframes. It tested the current state of the technology. It identified the points of friction where quantum-safe cryptographic algorithms interact imperfectly with existing blockchain infrastructure. And it built institutional knowledge about the process and cost of migration, so that when quantum-safe standards become mandatorily required by regulators, or when the threat level rises to the point that discretionary migration becomes non-optional, HSBC will have implementation experience rather than laboratory theory.

Blockchain protocols themselves are not passive in this transition. Several layer-1 networks have quantum-resistant roadmaps incorporated into their long-term development plans. The upgrade of the Ethereum network to incorporate post-quantum cryptographic primitives is a process of coordination and engineering that will take years, but the protocol's governance model, through which upgrades are proposed, debated, and implemented by the validator community, provides the mechanism for that transition to occur without the central authority that would be required to mandate such a change in a conventional financial system.

The energy dimension of this transition is also worth noting. The shift from proof-of-work to proof-of-stake consensus mechanisms, completed by Ethereum in September 2022 and adopted as the default for most new blockchain protocols, reduced the energy footprint of those networks by more than 99 percent. The narrative that blockchain technology is inherently environmentally destructive, accurate for Bitcoin mining operations powered by fossil fuel grid electricity, does not apply to the next generation of blockchain infrastructure. Post-quantum cryptographic algorithms are more computationally demanding than their classical equivalents; the energy efficiency of proof-of-stake networks creates headroom to accommodate that additional computational load without the energy profiles reverting to the earlier pattern.

Three horizons

The preceding nine chapters have traced tokenization across a wide sweep of the economy: from the basic mechanics of representing assets digitally, through early NFT experiments, the institutional adoption of tokenized bonds and funds, fractional real estate ownership, real-world asset markets, sustainability applications, the creative economy, and the legal structures required to make all of it reliable. Set against that developing infrastructure is the longer-term challenge posed by quantum computing.

The clearest way to organize that picture is through three horizons.

The first horizon is the next two to three years. The infrastructure is largely built. The regulatory frameworks are in place in the leading jurisdictions. The institutional adoption curve is steep: the one-third of institutional investors who increased digital asset allocations in 2024 will be joined by most of the 69 percent who said they intended to expand in the following five years. Tokenized Treasury funds have demonstrated that the yield-bearing on-chain assets that institutional investors require can be built and held safely. The GENIUS Act has given stablecoins a regulatory home. The UK, Switzerland, Singapore, and Abu Dhabi have established competitive frameworks for digital asset business. In this horizon, the question is no longer whether, it is which jurisdictions, which protocols, and which institutional strategies will capture the greatest share of the transition.

The second horizon is five to ten years out. This is where McKinsey's projection of two trillion dollars in tokenized assets by 2030, Standard Chartered and Synpulse's thirty trillion dollars by 2034, and BCG's ten percent of global GDP converge on a common picture: tokenization as load-bearing infrastructure for a substantial portion of global asset management, lending, trading, and settlement. In this horizon, the questions become systemic. The Digital Asset Treasury strategies that are currently voluntary corporate finance experiments become standard practice for corporations above a certain scale. The integration of AI agents as autonomous participants in tokenized financial markets, placing orders, managing positions, executing cross-asset hedging strategies without human intervention, creates market dynamics that require new regulatory thinking. The cross-border interoperability of tokenized money systems creates a settlement infrastructure that is genuinely global in a way that the correspondent banking system, with its fragmented and expensive intermediation, has never been.

The third horizon is twenty or more years away. This is where the quantum timeline intersects with the tokenization timeline, and where the outcomes become genuinely difficult to predict. If cryptographically relevant quantum computers arrive before the migration to post-quantum cryptographic standards is complete, the security of the tokenized economy will face a challenge unlike anything it has previously encountered, not a hack of a specific exchange or protocol, but a potential compromise of the foundational cryptographic assumptions on which the entire infrastructure rests. If the migration is completed before that point, which is what NIST's publication of post-quantum standards and the HSBC quantum-safe trials are designed to enable, then the tokenized economy inherits the resilience that classical computing provides and extends it into the quantum era.

What the transition means for people

The framing of tokenization in terms of market capitalization, settlement efficiency, and regulatory frameworks is accurate but incomplete. The more important question is what the transition means for the households, communities, and individuals who are the ultimate beneficiaries or victims of changes in how the economy works.

The institutional adoption of tokenized assets also creates a structural incentive to widen access in ways the previous financial paradigm did not. When a bank can tokenize Treasury bonds, it can offer fractional holdings at almost any denomination rather than forcing investors into the hundred-thousand-dollar minimums that define much of conventional bond trading. When an asset manager can run a tokenized fund with real-time settlement and programmable rebalancing, it gains an efficiency advantage over competitors still relying on legacy architecture. This is not altruism. It is competitive pressure. The institutions moving fastest to adopt tokenization infrastructure will also have the strongest reason to broaden participation, if only to capture the network effects of larger markets.

Adoption research already suggests that each successive cohort expands the user base: first crypto-native firms, then TradFi entrants, and now insurers, pension funds, and sovereign wealth funds. Whether that access becomes genuinely democratic or simply extends privilege to a somewhat larger circle will depend less on the technology than on the governance choices around pricing, rules, and barriers to entry.

The Dutch household that can buy a fractional stake in a community solar installation. The musician in Lagos who receives streaming royalties in real time through a smart contract rather than waiting eighteen months for an accounting statement from a distributor that works in a currency she cannot easily access. The smallholder farmer in Zambia whose land title exists on a blockchain rather than in a physical register that can be lost, altered, or ignored by a more powerful actor. The investor in a developing economy who can hold a fraction of a US Treasury token as a savings instrument rather than having no safe store of value outside of cash. These are not abstractions. They are the actual people for whom the tokenized economy could function materially better than the one it is replacing.

The risk is equally real and equally personal. The loss of access to a private key deletes the financial history it unlocks, permanently and without recourse. The investor persuaded to put savings into a fraudulent token project by a convincing AI-generated pitch is no less harmed because the technology that defrauded them was sophisticated. The First Nations community whose traditional land rights are represented by tokens but whose governance over those tokens was designed without meaningful consultation is no better served by the precision of the blockchain record.

Larry Fink's conviction that every asset can be tokenized is correct in its technical dimension and correct in its economic logic. The difficult question is whether the systems being built to realize that vision are being designed with the people who use them as the primary consideration, or as an afterthought to the infrastructure. The history of financial innovation — from the mortgage securitization that financed generations of homeownership and then crashed the global economy in 2008, to the payment systems that serve the wealthy with instant settlement and the poor with checks and delays — is not a history of technology failing. It is a history of the choices made about who the technology would serve.

The decade ahead

The tokenized world is not a future state being approached from a distance. It is the present, being constructed in real time by the people and institutions documented in this book. The infrastructure exists. The capital is moving. The regulatory frameworks are being built. The experiments have produced enough evidence to identify what works, what fails, and what the genuine uncertainties are.

What the decade ahead requires is not more technology. It is the governance, the legal clarity, the multilateral coordination, and the deliberate inclusive design that will determine whether the tokenized economy serves the breadth of human interest or merely the subset of it that was already well-served by the financial system it is replacing.

That is not a technological question. It is a human one. And it is, ultimately, the same question that every significant economic transition in history has posed: not whether the new infrastructure is powerful, but whether the people who build it choose to make it just.

The world that doesn't know it's tokenized

Philipp Pieper of Swarm, asked what the mature tokenized economy would look like from the perspective of a participant in it, gave an answer notable for what it did not say. He did not describe blockchain interfaces, wallet addresses, or smart contract interactions. He described the outcomes: faster settlement, continuous access to capital, liquid markets in assets that were previously illiquid, and fractional participation in investment products that had previously required significant minimum commitments. "I'm not quite sure that in due time we will actually need to know that something's tokenized or not," Pieper said. The mechanism would become infrastructure. The experience would become normal.

The US Clarity Act's scope extends well beyond financial instruments: its proposed legal frameworks cover the tokenization of data, vehicles, health records, real estate, and intellectual property. This represents the continuation of a strategy the United States has pursued across two previous monetary eras. The petrodollar arrangement had extended dollar reach into commodity markets through a bilateral deal with Saudi Arabia. The eurodollar system had extended it into offshore capital markets through dollar-denominated lending outside Federal Reserve jurisdiction. Stablecoin legislation combined with broad tokenization law represents the third iteration: extending the dollar into the on-chain economy, the tokenized asset market, and the data-driven commercial infrastructure that will increasingly mediate global economic activity.

Alex Bausch of 2Tokens, reflecting on his seven years of practical tokenization work, a body of experience that included the Port of Rotterdam, major European banks, and dozens of implementation partners, offered what may be the most precise synthesis available. His background was energy and sustainability; his conclusion was not sector-specific. "Tokenization is digitalization of value," Bausch said. "We could take on any industry." Lewis McLellan of the Digital Monetary Institute, surveying the institutional landscape in December 2024, agreed from the institutional end of the same telescope. The infrastructure was no longer experimental. The participants were no longer early adopters. The question the decade ahead had to answer was whether the system being assembled would distribute the benefits of that infrastructure as broadly as its technical architecture permitted, or whether it would concentrate them in the institutions and jurisdictions that had moved fastest to control the rails.

The next chapter examines one of the oldest stores of value human economies have ever used, gold, and what happens when the asset that has served as a refuge from institutional failure for five thousand years is itself tokenized onto the infrastructure that has only just been built.

Chapter 24: Tokenized Commodities

Imagine owning a fraction of a gold bar resting in a high-security vault in Switzerland. Not a contract that gives you the right to buy gold at some future price, not a share in a company that mines gold, not an ETF that attempts to track gold's performance through a basket of derivatives. An actual, specific, identified quantity of physical gold to which you hold verifiable legal title, that you can sell on a digital marketplace at any moment of the day or night, transfer to another owner anywhere in the world in under a minute, or use as collateral in a decentralized lending protocol while it remains sitting undisturbed in its vault. This is not a theoretical possibility. It is what PAX Gold (PAXG) provides today.

PAXG is a gold-backed token where each token represents one troy ounce of physical gold stored in Brink's vaults and audited by independent custodians. When you hold PAXG you hold legal title to that specific physical gold. You can trade it twenty-four hours a day, seven days a week, on a range of digital asset exchanges. You can send it to anyone with a compatible digital wallet anywhere in the world, at essentially zero cost, in real time. You can use it as collateral in DeFi protocols to borrow stable-value digital assets. And you can, if you choose, redeem it for the physical gold itself. Every property that gold has always been valued for, stability, intrinsic value, protection against the debasement of paper currencies, combined with every advantage that digital infrastructure provides in terms of accessibility, divisibility, and mobility.

Philipp Pieper, co-founder of Swarm, which offers similar tokenized gold exposure through its xGold product, made the investment case precisely in those terms. He noted that between January and March 2025, investors who used xGold as collateral in a DeFi lending pool, borrowing against their gold position to reinvest in additional xGold exposure, saw returns exceeding 20 percent. In the same period, Bitcoin holders were down nearly 15 percent. The comparison is not merely about short-term performance; it is about the ability to activate a traditionally passive asset, turning a store of value into a position that can work within the programmable finance ecosystem without being liquidated or relinquished.

Gold's enduring significance

To understand why tokenized gold matters, it helps to understand why gold has mattered for twenty-six centuries. The first gold coins were struck in Lydia, modern-day Turkey, around 550 BC, and gold's role as a monetary anchor, store of value, and standard against which other currencies have been measured has persisted through the collapse of empires, the rise and fall of the Gold Standard, two world wars, and the creation of the modern fiat currency system that followed the Bretton Woods breakdown in 1971.

The World Gold Council has catalogued over 150 historical documents spanning 1660 to 1999 that trace gold's evolution from monetary anchor to investment asset to strategic national reserve. The pattern is consistent: whenever confidence in paper money falters, whenever political institutions are challenged, whenever inflation erodes the purchasing power of conventional holdings, gold attracts renewed attention as something that cannot be printed into worthlessness by a government decision.

That dynamic was on full display in the early months of 2025. Gold hit an all-time high above three thousand dollars per troy ounce against a backdrop of persistent inflation concerns, US-China geopolitical tensions, and central banks in multiple countries accelerating their accumulation of physical reserves. China's central bank increased its gold reserves for four consecutive months, reaching 73.61 million ounces valued at more than two hundred and eight billion dollars. BRICS nations collectively held over 20 percent of the world's gold reserves, approximately 6,200 tonnes, as part of a broader strategic shift away from dollar-denominated reserve assets. Globally, central banks had purchased over one thousand metric tonnes of gold annually for the third consecutive year.

Even Fort Knox, the physical symbol of American monetary credibility, reportedly holding 147.3 million ounces of gold, re-entered public discourse in 2025 when Donald Trump and Elon Musk raised the possibility of live-streaming an inspection of its contents. The fact that such an audit had not been conducted since 1953 had generated decades of speculation. The suggestion that the contents should be verified, publicly and in real time, is itself a reflection of gold's unique psychological position in monetary life: no other asset is quite so intertwined with questions of institutional trust and national credibility.

Beyond gold: the commodity tokenization landscape

Gold is the most advanced and most liquid example of commodity tokenization, but the technology and the commercial logic extend across the full range of tangible goods that form the backbone of the global economy. The broader significance of commodity tokenization is the democratization of infrastructure investment: taking markets that were previously available only to large institutions and making fractional participation accessible to participants anywhere in the world. This applies equally to energy, agriculture, minerals, and traditional commodities.

The Port of Rotterdam's blockchain-based peer-to-peer energy model demonstrated that when energy production is converted into tokenized units and settled through smart contracts, the settlement velocity changes the entire commercial model. What previously took days of billing and reconciliation through utility intermediaries now occurs in seconds through blockchain settlement. For industrial energy purchasers, this changes the effective cost of renewables by the magnitude of the financing cost embedded in conventional pricing. The structural implication is that democratized settlement infrastructure does not merely make commodity markets cheaper; it redistributes the economic surplus from payment intermediaries to the producers and consumers conducting the actual transaction.

Sunified has been developing tokens backed by the production of solar energy installations and associated carbon credits, enabling fractional ownership of renewable energy infrastructure and real-time settlement between producers and buyers through smart contracts. The appeal to institutional investors is the combination of inflation-linked returns, energy prices track input costs, with the liquidity and programmability that tokenization provides. The appeal to the energy sector is access to a broader pool of capital, including retail and institutional investors who could not previously access energy infrastructure investment except through large private funds with long lock-up periods.

Agricultural commodities represent another frontier. Agridex has developed blockchain-based infrastructure for tokenizing wine, olive oil, cocoa, coffee, and livestock, creating supply chains where every transaction is recorded on an immutable ledger from producer to consumer. For farmers, the benefit is faster access to capital: rather than waiting for a commodity to be physically delivered to a warehouse before receiving payment, a tokenized representation of the asset can be used as collateral for financing from the moment of production verification. For investors, the benefit is access to agricultural commodity exposure without the complexity of futures markets or the illiquidity of physical commodity storage.

Oil-backed stablecoins remain at the conceptual stage in most jurisdictions, but several sovereign-adjacent projects have explored the design in earnest. Venezuela's Petro, a state-issued token supposedly backed by oil reserves, was an early and unsuccessful experiment, undermined by the government's lack of credibility and the difficulty of independently auditing the claimed oil backing. More credibly structured oil-backed digital instruments, issued by regulated entities with genuinely auditable reserve mechanisms, remain a live area of experimentation as digital asset infrastructure matures.

Paul Taylor, who was developing Token X, a MiCA-compliant security token backed by a portfolio of European critical mineral assets, articulated both the commercial opportunity and the structural significance of the moment. Traditional funding mechanisms for critical mineral extraction, he observed, were broken: listed junior mining markets in London and other exchanges were starved of liquidity, leaving projects vital to the energy transition, lithium, cobalt, rare earth elements, unable to access the capital needed to develop them. MiCA's regulatory clarity, he argued, opened a path to funding these projects through digital token issuance in a way that was compliant, auditable, and accessible to a global investor base.

Taylor went further, connecting critical mineral tokenization to geopolitics: access to the physical materials needed for batteries, semiconductors, and defense systems is no longer merely an economic question but a matter of national security. A tokenized critical mineral fund, operating within a clear regulatory framework, could redirect capital toward supply chain resilience in ways that conventional equity and debt markets have failed to do.

The mechanics of making things digital

The process by which a physical commodity becomes a digital token is more rigorous than the breathless marketing materials of the early tokenization era sometimes suggested. For the tokenization to mean anything, the physical asset must be verified, authenticated, and held in custody by a party with the legal and operational capacity to guarantee the connection between the token and the underlying thing.

For gold, this means storing bullion in recognized commercial vaults, Brink's, Malca-Amit, and other specialist custody providers operate the secure storage infrastructure, and engaging independent auditors to verify that the claimed tonnage is present and correctly allocated. The token issuer, typically a regulated entity operating under a securities license, mints tokens on a blockchain in quantities that correspond precisely to the audited physical holdings. When tokens are retired, when a holder redeems them for physical delivery or when the issuer repurchases them, the corresponding physical holdings are adjusted. Regular audits confirm the ongoing one-to-one correspondence between tokens in circulation and assets in custody.

For less standardized commodities, the mechanics are more complex. Oil in a tank is not identical to oil in another tank; wheat grown in one region has different characteristics than wheat from another. The tokenization of these assets requires not merely custody but a standardized specification framework and an agreed method for auditing the physical inventory against the digital record. This is solvable — commodity markets have been doing something analogous with warehouse receipts and futures contracts for a century and a half, but it requires thoughtful design and robust governance.

Smart contracts automate the enforcement of contractual terms once assets are tokenized. A trade finance arrangement can be structured so that payment to a supplier is released automatically when a verified shipment notification is received from a logistics provider, without human intervention. An agricultural forward contract can be settled atomically when a verified quality inspection report is recorded on-chain. The programmability of tokenized commodity infrastructure adds a dimension of automation and reliability that conventional commodity finance cannot match.

Institutional adoption and the remaining barriers

JPMorgan and Goldman Sachs have both explored blockchain for commodity settlement. JPMorgan's Onyx platform has processed tokenized asset transactions for institutional clients. The interest from large financial institutions reflects a commercial calculation: if commodity settlement can be made materially faster and cheaper through tokenization, the competitive advantage of moving early is significant.

HSBC's foray into tokenized gold for retail clients in Hong Kong, and the subsequent quantum-safe cryptography trial it conducted in partnership with Quantinuum, demonstrates that the institutional interest is not merely hype. HSBC converted its gold tokens into Ethereum-compatible ERC-20 tokens as part of the Quantinuum trial, testing the resistance of its custody infrastructure against the kind of cryptographic attacks that quantum computers may eventually be capable of mounting. This combination, institutional-grade gold custody, blockchain distribution, and quantum-safe cryptographic protection, represents the direction in which serious commodity tokenization is heading.

The barriers that remain are real. Regulatory classification of tokenized commodities is unresolved in many jurisdictions, with different tokens attracting different treatment as securities, commodities, payment instruments, or some novel combination. Custody arrangements must satisfy both the technical requirements of blockchain infrastructure and the legal requirements of asset ownership, which differ by jurisdiction. Liquidity, for many tokenized commodity instruments, remains thin; secondary markets exist but lack the depth that institutional participants require. And the technical security of smart contracts, the risk that a coding error or a flash loan exploit could drain a commodity-backed pool, remains a concern that requires rigorous audit and ongoing monitoring.

None of these barriers is insuperable. Every mature financial market has solved analogous problems. What the tokenization of commodities requires is the same combination that every financial infrastructure innovation has required: technical reliability, regulatory clarity, institutional endorsement, and the gradual accumulation of trading history that transforms an experiment into a market. That accumulation is now well underway.

The reinvention of an ancient asset class

What is happening to commodities is, in some ways, the most intellectually interesting transformation in finance. Commodities are the oldest form of economically meaningful value, grain, metal, fuel, raw material, and they have been traded through increasingly sophisticated intermediary structures for millennia. Spot markets, forward contracts, futures exchanges, ETFs, commodity-linked bonds: each layer of financial innovation has added liquidity and accessibility while distancing investors from the physical reality of the underlying asset.

Tokenization does something different. It reconnects the financial instrument to the physical asset in a way that is direct, auditable, and legally binding, while simultaneously adding all the benefits of digital infrastructure: divisibility, programmability, global accessibility, real-time settlement. The result is a form of ownership that is simultaneously the oldest and the newest: the direct economic interest in a physical thing, expressed through the most advanced financial technology available.

Gold illustrates the paradox perfectly. It is twenty-six centuries old as a monetary asset. It is also, in its tokenized form with quantum-safe custody architecture and DeFi integration, one of the most technically sophisticated financial instruments in existence. That combination, ancient value proposition, modern infrastructure, is exactly what makes tokenized commodities significant for the long-term future of digital finance.

The next chapter examines a different kind of asset, scientific knowledge, and the decentralized movement attempting to reshape how research is funded, owned, and shared.

Chapter 25: Decentralized Science

Science, in the formal sense, is the most consequential collective undertaking in human history. The last two centuries of organized scientific research have produced the germ theory of disease, the green revolution, nuclear power, the internet, and genetic medicine. These achievements have been the product of institutions: universities, government research bodies, pharmaceutical companies, charitable foundations. Those institutions have provided the funding, the peer review mechanisms, the physical infrastructure, and the credentialing systems without which individual researchers could not have accomplished what they collectively achieved.

But institutions also impose constraints. The process by which scientific research receives funding is a bureaucratic exercise of considerable proportions: grant applications running to hundreds of pages, review committees subject to their own biases and institutional loyalties, funding criteria shaped by political priorities rather than scientific merit. The result is a system where established researchers in established institutions with established research programs receive the majority of available capital, while unconventional ideas, novel methodologies, and researchers working outside the recognized elite networks find funding exceptionally difficult to obtain.

Peer review, the mechanism by which the scientific community evaluates the validity of research before publication, is similarly constrained. Reviewers are anonymous, unpaid, and subject to their own intellectual commitments, which may or may not align with the actual quality of the work they are assessing. Research that challenges established paradigms, or that emerges from contexts without institutional prestige, faces additional skepticism that may have more to do with sociology than with scientific rigor. The average time from submission to publication in major scientific journals runs to many months. For fast-moving fields, this delay is not merely inconvenient, it can be the difference between timely knowledge that shapes decisions and retrospective documentation that describes what happened after the fact.

None of this is to say that the existing system has failed. It has produced extraordinary science. The question being posed by the emergence of decentralized science, DeSci, is whether it could produce more, better, and more equitably distributed science if the institutional architecture were redesigned from first principles using the tools that blockchain technology provides.

The DeSci proposition

The core proposition of decentralized science is straightforward, even if its implementation is technically demanding. Blockchain technology enables the creation of transparent, auditable governance structures, decentralized autonomous organizations, or DAOs, in which funding decisions are made collectively by token holders rather than by grant committees. Smart contracts can automate the disbursement of research funding in tranches tied to verifiable milestones: publication of results, completion of a trial phase, achievement of a specified outcome — removing the human discretion that currently sits between a funding decision and the actual delivery of money to a researcher. Tokenization allows intellectual property generated by research, discoveries, datasets, patents, publication rights, to be represented as digital assets that can be owned, traded, and monetized in ways that current academic IP frameworks do not permit.

But a deeper insight emerges from the infrastructure enabling this: the programmability of incentives through token economics. When research data becomes a tokenized asset, it becomes subject to the same economic incentive mechanisms that blockchain has developed for value distribution. A researcher who contributes a dataset to a DeSci platform can be compensated not merely for generating the data but for curating it, validating it, and making it available to others. Every subsequent use of that dataset generates a smart contract payment flowing back to the original contributor. This creates a continuous economic signal, across decades, that rewards the production of high-quality foundational data. The conventional academic system provides a one-time publication reward and then the data becomes part of the commons with no mechanism to compensate the original creator for subsequent uses. Token-based incentive structures flip this incentive: they make the production of quality data perpetually valuable. This is not incidental to DeSci; it is the mechanism by which decentralized science could fundamentally alter the risk-reward calculation of research careers, making it economically viable to pursue research that is scientifically important but commercially neglected.

VitaDAO, focused on longevity research, is perhaps the most prominent operational example. VitaDAO's token holders vote on which early-stage research projects to fund. The DAO has committed capital to researchers working on the biology of aging, accessing a funding stream for work that conventional pharmaceutical industry research programs, focused on conditions with large existing patient populations and established commercial paths to revenue, consistently underinvest in. The governance is on-chain: every funding decision, every vote, every transaction is visible and auditable. A researcher in Singapore, a token holder in Nigeria, an endowment in California, and a biotech investor in the Netherlands can participate in the same governance process on equal terms, subject only to the number of tokens they hold and the quality of the arguments they advance.

Molecule provides infrastructure for a different aspect of the DeSci model: IP tokenization. When a researcher using Molecule's platform generates intellectual property, a dataset, a discovery, a methodology, they can represent that IP as an NFT. The NFT functions as a financing instrument, allowing investors or research DAOs to purchase fractional rights to the IP in exchange for providing research funding. If the research leads to a commercial application, a drug that gets licensed, a technique that gets adopted, the IP NFT holders participate in the resulting revenue stream in proportion to their holdings. The researcher retains a portion of the economics of their discovery rather than assigning full IP rights to a university or a corporate employer in exchange for a salary. The incentive structure is fundamentally different, and the range of people who can participate in financing research is dramatically expanded.

AxonDAO operates at the intersection of biometric data, artificial intelligence, and decentralized governance, funding DeSci projects that use AI to analyze biological data. AxonDAO's approach reflects a broader point about the synergy between DeSci and the current AI moment: the most valuable thing that many biological and medical research programs produce is not a publication or a patent but a structured dataset that can be used to train AI models. The conventional academic system has no good mechanism for valuing, incentivizing, or monetizing dataset production. DeSci infrastructure, token incentives for data contribution, on-chain records of data provenance, fractional ownership of curated datasets, offers a new approach.

Transparency and trust in research

The scientific credibility of a system depends critically on its resistance to manipulation. This is where blockchain's core properties become particularly relevant to the DeSci proposition. If funding decisions, research milestones, and data records are recorded on an immutable public ledger, then the manipulation of those records becomes technically difficult in ways that manipulation of conventional institutional records is not. A university can quietly bury a research result that reflects poorly on a major donor. A pharmaceutical company can decline to publish negative trial results. A grant committee can favor a particular research program for reasons that never appear in the official record.

On a transparent blockchain, the published record cannot be retroactively altered. The history of a research project — what was proposed, what was funded, what milestones were claimed and when, what data was generated and when it was recorded — is available to anyone. This does not eliminate fraud; a researcher can lie about results in the initial record just as they can lie in a paper submitted to a journal. But it eliminates a particular category of institutional manipulation: the quietly buried inconvenient result, the funding decision that was made for reasons that could not survive scrutiny.

The implications for reproducibility, science's self-correcting mechanism, are significant. One of the most troubling problems in contemporary research is the reproducibility crisis: a substantial fraction of published scientific findings, when subjected to independent replication attempts, do not replicate. The causes are multiple: publication bias favoring positive results, inadequate documentation of methodology, statistical analysis choices made after the fact. Blockchain-based research records, in which protocols are pre-registered before data is collected and results are recorded against the pre-registered protocol in a timestamped and immutable form, could provide a structural remedy for some of these problems.

Open access to research data is another dimension of the DeSci vision that blockchain infrastructure facilitates. Much of the data that academic research generates is not publicly available. It sits in proprietary institutional repositories, behind journal paywalls, or in filing systems accessible only to the laboratory that generated it. Tokenization of research data creates a mechanism by which data can be monetized, researchers and their institutions can receive compensation for data use, while simultaneously making it accessible to a broader community. The economic incentive and the public interest case are aligned rather than in conflict.

The challenges of building on decentralized rails

The DeSci ecosystem is young, and its proponents are the first to acknowledge the gaps between the vision and the current reality. The most significant challenge is regulatory: the legal status of tokenized intellectual property, research DAOs, and IP NFTs varies dramatically across jurisdictions and is unsettled in most. A DAO operating a research funding program may or may not constitute an investment fund, a charity, or a business. The IP generated by research funded through a DAO may or may not be assignable, licensable, or enforceable in the relevant jurisdictions. Legal uncertainty of this kind deters institutional participation and creates risks for researchers who engage with DeSci platforms without understanding how their contributions will be treated under applicable law.

The quality assurance problem is also not trivially solved by decentralization. Peer review is imperfect, but it exists and it has a track record. Token holder governance in a research DAO provides a form of collective judgment, but those token holders may have interests that are misaligned with scientific merit: they may prefer research that is commercially attractive over research that is cosmetically less interesting but scientifically more important. The design of governance mechanisms that avoid the familiar pathologies of concentrated token holdings — early investors dominating decision-making, celebrity researchers attracting disproportionate capital regardless of merit — requires careful attention.

Data privacy is a recurring complication wherever health data is involved. The same immutability that makes blockchain records resistant to manipulation makes them difficult to reconcile with GDPR's right to erasure. Patient data contributed to a DeSci research program in good faith could, in principle, be irretrievably exposed if the governance of the relevant platform later breaks down or if sufficiently powerful analytics allow re-identification of supposedly anonymized records. Zero-knowledge proof techniques offer possible solutions, enabling queries against datasets without revealing individual records, but implementing this in practice requires substantial technical sophistication.

These are genuine difficulties, not merely theoretical objections. They will be resolved over time, through iteration of both technology and governance design, through regulatory clarification in the jurisdictions that choose to engage with DeSci constructively, and through the demonstrated track record that currently successful DeSci projects are beginning to build.

What decentralized science could become

The ambition underlying DeSci is not modest. It is nothing less than a restructuring of the social contract of scientific knowledge: one in which funding decisions reflect a broader community of interest than the existing institutional structure allows, in which the economics of discovery flow more directly to the people who make discoveries, in which data is accessible rather than hoarded, and in which the transparency of the research process is structurally guaranteed rather than institutionally promised.

The problems it addresses — research funding concentrated among elite institutions, publication bias, IP structures that do not reward early-stage discovery, barriers to data access, reproducibility failures — are recognized as serious problems within the scientific community itself. Incremental improvements to the existing system have been proposed and partly implemented for decades. DeSci offers a more fundamental structural alternative.

Whether that alternative matures into something that complements or competes with the existing scientific funding infrastructure will depend on factors that are currently unpredictable: regulatory openness in key jurisdictions, the quality of governance mechanisms developed by leading DeSci platforms, the willingness of established researchers to engage, and the commercial and scientific success of the research programs that DeSci infrastructure funds.

What is not in doubt is that the tools are real, the problems they address are real, and the global community of researchers, investors, and curious people willing to participate in reimagining how science is funded is larger and more sophisticated than most conventional scientific institutions have begun to appreciate. The digitalization of finance that blockchain technology enables is not confined to money. It extends to knowledge, and in the long run, the tokenization of knowledge may prove the more consequential transformation.

The twenty-five chapters of this book have traced a single arc: the emergence of a new financial and organizational infrastructure built on programmable ownership. From stablecoins and CBDCs to NFTs, tokenized funds, fractional real estate, carbon credits, creative IP, community energy, gold, and the funding of research itself, the same underlying capability, the ability to represent any asset or right as a digital token on a shared ledger, is being brought to bear on the most entrenched structures in the global economy. The conversation continues in The DeFi Revolution.

Appendix A: Key Concepts

This appendix collects the conceptual foundations on which this volume depends. It opens with a short set of foundational ideas that recur throughout the full series. The sections that follow cover the ideas specific to those chapters. This is not a glossary (those entries are in Appendix B) but an explanation of the logic behind the ideas, written for a reader who wants to revisit a specific chapter with a clearer frame.

Foundational Concepts

Four ideas recur across both volumes. They are introduced here once.

Smart contracts

A smart contract is code deployed to a blockchain that executes automatically when predefined conditions are met. The canonical example is a vending machine: deposit the correct amount, select your item, and the machine delivers, no human intermediary required, no possibility of the vendor renegotiating after receipt. The terms are in the code; the code is on the blockchain; the blockchain executes it automatically. Smart contracts make possible parametric insurance (Volume 2, Chapter 13), automated DeFi lending liquidations (Volume 2, Chapter 8), tokenized asset settlement (Chapter 7), and cross-border payment programmability (Chapter 4). They also introduce the oracle problem described below.

The oracle problem

A blockchain records what it has been told. It cannot independently observe the physical world. Whether a shipment has arrived, a temperature threshold has been breached, a property is free of encumbrances, or a corporate action has completed, all of this must be reported to the blockchain by an external data source, known as an oracle. Oracle networks such as Chainlink reduce manipulation risk by aggregating data from multiple independent sources before publishing on-chain.

The oracle problem manifests differently across contexts. In tokenized asset markets (Chapter 7), oracles connect digital tokens to physical reality, confirming that the gold in the vault is actually there. In DeFi protocols (Volume 2, Chapter 8), oracles report real-time asset prices; if prices can be manipulated by temporarily cornering a thin market, the smart contracts consuming them can be drained instantly. In enterprise deployments (Volume 2, Chapter 13), IoT sensors and satellite verification systems serve as oracle infrastructure for supply chains and trade documents. In every context, the quality of oracle infrastructure is, in the most literal sense, the foundation on which data-dependent smart contracts stand.

Tokenization

Tokenization is the representation of an asset, a bond, a bill of lading, a kilogram of gold, a property share, a carbon credit, as a digital token on a blockchain. The token carries a reference to the underlying asset and is governed by smart contract rules determining who can hold it, how it can be transferred, and what rights it confers. The blockchain provides an immutable chain of custody from issuance to current holder.

Tokenization does not automatically make assets more liquid or accessible; it creates the infrastructure on which liquid, accessible markets can be built. The commercial case is straightforward: if every transfer of ownership currently requires reconciliation between two separate ledgers, a shared ledger eliminates the reconciliation requirement, and at the scale of the global bond market, that saving aggregates to an enormous amount. The term *real-world assets* (RWAs) refers to the broad category of assets existing outside the crypto ecosystem that are being brought on-chain: equities, bonds, real estate, commodities, private credit. The RWA market, estimated at approximately $24 billion in mid-2025, is growing at hundreds of percent annually.

Zero-knowledge proofs

A zero-knowledge proof is a cryptographic technique allowing one party to prove a statement is true without revealing any of the underlying information. In a financial context: you can prove your account balance exceeds a threshold without disclosing the balance; you can prove you are a resident of a qualifying country without revealing your address; you can prove your funds did not originate from a sanctioned source without disclosing where they came from.

This is the technical resolution to a structural tension that runs through Volume 2, Chapters 8 and 13. DeFi's transparency, all transactions public on-chain, conflicts with user privacy, while KYC regulations demand identity disclosure. Zero-knowledge proofs allow compliance verification without data exposure: the protocol receives the confirmation it requires; the user retains their privacy. In digital identity systems (Volume 2, Chapter 13), ZKPs allow a credential holder to prove they satisfy a criterion without revealing the underlying data. Practical deployment is expanding rapidly, and its trajectory is toward becoming the compliance infrastructure of any system where privacy and regulatory accountability must coexist.

Chapters 1-13: The Future of Money

1. Electrified versus digitized

The payments system most people use today is digital in appearance but not in substance. When you make a bank transfer, an electronic instruction moves across a network, but the underlying money still sits in a commercial bank ledger, settling through batch processes designed for the era of paper. Charles McManus of ClearBank calls this "electrified." Truly digitized money is native to a ledger: it is the asset itself, not an instruction about it. Stablecoins, tokenized deposits, and CBDCs are digital money in this sense. The distinction matters because it is the difference between a faster fax machine and the internet: you can make the old system faster, but you cannot make it do things it was not designed to do.

2. You are a creditor to your bank

When you deposit money in a commercial bank, you do not hold that money in any direct sense. You hold a claim against the institution, an unsecured IOU that the bank can lend out, leverage, and use for its own purposes up to the limit that regulation permits. In the United Kingdom, deposits are protected up to £85,000 by the Financial Services Compensation Scheme. Above that threshold, you are an unsecured creditor, as the corporate depositors of Silicon Valley Bank discovered in March 2023, until emergency government intervention prevented the full consequences. Digital money held in bankruptcy-remote reserves, whether a well-structured stablecoin or a CBDC, is a qualitatively different instrument, and that difference in risk architecture runs through these chapters.

3. The four kinds of stablecoin

Not all stablecoins are the same instrument. *Fiat-backed* stablecoins, of which USDC and USDT are the largest, are digital tokens pegged one-to-one to a national currency, backed by reserves of that currency or short-dated government securities. *Crypto-backed* stablecoins use other cryptocurrencies as collateral, typically over-collateralized to absorb price volatility. *Commodity-backed* stablecoins are pegged to physical assets, most commonly gold. *Yield-bearing* stablecoins are tokenized money-market funds that pass interest to holders rather than retaining it. Terra/Luna's UST was none of these, it was algorithmic, and that distinction is precisely why it failed in the way it did.

4. The death spiral

TerraUSD maintained its dollar peg not through held reserves but through a software mechanism: users could always burn UST to mint LUNA, and vice versa, in a way that should, in theory, create arbitrage pressure restoring the peg. When a large redemption event broke the peg in May 2022, the system was forced to mint extraordinary quantities of LUNA to absorb the selling. That minting destroyed LUNA's value, which destroyed confidence in the mechanism, which created more selling. The feedback loop ran to completion in roughly seventy-two hours. Forty billion dollars was wiped out. The death spiral was not a bug, it was the mechanism operating as designed, in conditions the design had not anticipated and could not survive.

5. Singleness of money

A monetary system functions when all forms of money are interchangeable at par, when a pound in a current account, a pound in cash, and a pound in a digital wallet are each worth exactly one pound, without friction or discount. Economists call this "singleness of money." During the free-banking era of the United States in the nineteenth century, bank notes traded at discounts that varied by issuer and distance, and the monetary system was permanently chaotic as a result. The stablecoin era has reopened the question: whether a proliferating ecosystem of private digital currencies, each with its own reserve model and redemption guarantees, can maintain singleness of money, or whether it requires clearing infrastructure to enforce it.

6. The clearing gap

Every payment instrument that achieved genuine universality, checks, credit cards, wire transfers, did so because a clearing system made it fungible at par regardless of issuer. When you deposited a check drawn on an unfamiliar bank, you trusted it because both banks participated in the same clearing system. Stablecoins have no equivalent: each issuer operates bilaterally, with no common standards guaranteeing any holder can redeem any stablecoin at par at any time. This is the clearing gap, and it is why stablecoins, despite settling trillions of dollars annually, cannot yet be classified as cash equivalents under international accounting standards, and why corporate treasurers treat them as financial instruments rather than working capital.

7. Programmability

Digital money can be conditional. A smart contract can instruct money to move only when a shipment is confirmed delivered, only when a project milestone is verified, only when a bond coupon falls due. This is programmability: money that behaves according to preset rules without human intermediation. For a corporate treasurer, it eliminates reconciliation cycles and counterparty risk. For a government distributing welfare payments, it enables precise targeting. For a gig economy worker, it means settlement at the completion of each task. Programmability does not exist in the current banking system. It exists only in digital money natively built on programmable infrastructure.

8. Narrow banking versus fractional reserve

A commercial bank holds only a fraction of its deposits in reserve and lends the remainder out, the mechanism through which credit is created and most new money in a modern economy comes into existence. The risk is a bank run: if enough depositors demand their money simultaneously, the bank cannot pay. Narrow banking is the alternative: one hundred percent of deposits held in liquid, safe assets, and no lending. ClearBank operates this way; the most credible stablecoin issuers adopt a similar model, with reserves held in US Treasuries and overnight repo, not lent out, not leveraged. At scale, a fully reserve-backed system cannot create credit, and that is a genuine trade-off, not a resolved question.

9. The GENIUS Act and the T-bill machine

The Guiding and Establishing National Innovation for US Stablecoins Act, passed in 2025, required all US dollar-denominated stablecoins to be backed 100% by US Treasury bills or cash equivalents. This looked like consumer protection but functioned simultaneously as fiscal engineering: it created a structural buyer for US government debt at precisely the moment the deficit was expanding and demand from traditional foreign holders was uncertain. Citibank estimated the stablecoin market could reach $3.7 trillion by 2030, representing $3.7 trillion in captive demand for T-bills that required no foreign central bank to cooperate. The

Act was simultaneously innovation policy and sovereign debt management.

10. Three tracks, one geopolitical question

The contest over digital money ran along three distinct trajectories by 2025. The United States promoted dollar dominance through privately-issued dollar stablecoins, ensuring the underlying asset was always a US Treasury bill. The European Union built the digital euro through the ECB, emphasizing sovereignty, privacy, and regulatory control under MiCA. China constructed the e-CNY through patient state-managed infrastructure, deployed domestically first and then through bilateral trade corridors across Africa, Southeast Asia, and Latin America. Each track reflected different values and different strategic ambitions. The underlying question was the same for all three: in a world where money is programmable, whoever controls the code controls the flow of value.

Chapters 14-22: Tokenizing Everything

11. The token and the asset are not the same thing

A token is a digital record on a blockchain that represents a claim. It is not the asset itself. A token representing a share in a property does not move the bricks. A token representing a carbon credit does not remove carbon from the atmosphere. The value and enforceability of a token are only ever as strong as the legal, physical, and institutional infrastructure that connects the digital record to the real-world thing it claims to represent. Every chapter in this section is, in some sense, an examination of how well or badly that connection has been made in a particular context.

12. Atomic settlement

Conventional financial transactions settle in two steps: execution and payment, separated by time and handled by different systems. The gap between trade and settlement, two days in most equity markets, five days in some bond markets, is the window during which counterparty risk exists: one party might fail to deliver before settlement completes. Atomic settlement eliminates that gap. On a shared ledger with smart contract execution, the asset and the payment transfer simultaneously, and either both sides complete, or neither does. For the cost of collateral, the velocity of capital, and the ability of markets to operate continuously across time zones, this apparently technical detail has profound practical consequences.

13. Fungible versus non-fungible

A fungible token is interchangeable with any other of the same type. One tokenized ounce of gold is identical in every respect to any other tokenized ounce of gold; any buyer should be indifferent between them. A non-fungible token is unique, no other NFT is identical to a specific one, because uniqueness is the property encoded in the token itself. Most financial instruments, bonds, shares, currencies, fund units, are fungible. Most claims over cultural objects, specific properties, or individual intellectual works are non-fungible. The architecture of the token changes depending on which property is required, and the legal treatment, secondary market behavior, and appropriate regulatory framework all differ accordingly.

14. The keys problem

On a blockchain, whoever controls the private key controls the assets associated with it. The key is not a password that can be reset by a helpdesk. It is a cryptographic secret, and if it is lost, the assets it controlled are gone permanently and irreversibly, with no recourse available. An estimated 3.7 million Bitcoin, more than a fifth of the total supply that will ever exist, is believed to be permanently inaccessible because private keys have been lost. Managing this risk is the founding purpose of the digital asset custody industry, and it is why institutional adoption of tokenized assets has proceeded via custodied infrastructure rather than self-held wallets.

15. The legal wrapper

Most jurisdictions do not yet recognize a blockchain token as a valid legal title instrument for physical assets. A token representing a property does not, in most legal systems, constitute a deed. A token representing a fund share may or may not be a recognized security depending on how it was issued and where the holder resides. The legal wrapper is the structure, an LLC, a trust, a regulated vehicle, placed between the token and the underlying asset to make the ownership claim enforceable in conventional courts. The token provides programmability, transferability, and a transparent record. The wrapper provides legal enforceability. Neither is sufficient without the other.

16. Fractional ownership

Dividing an asset into many small tokens does more than lower the minimum ticket size for investors. It restructures how ownership works. When a building, a bond, or a community solar installation is owned by thousands of token holders rather than one, the governance model, liquidity profile, inheritance characteristics, and regulatory treatment all change. Fractional ownership at small denominations is what transforms tokenization from a back-office efficiency story into a financial inclusion story: the ability to hold a genuine, yield-bearing, diversified portfolio from a starting position of a few hundred pounds is only possible when assets can be divided to that scale. The technical capability exists; the legal and market infrastructure to make it fully liquid at small denominations is still being assembled.

17. The three-horizon structure of the transition

The tokenized economy is not arriving all at once. The first horizon, 2-3 years, is infrastructure consolidation: regulatory frameworks now in place, institutional adoption under way, stablecoin settlement rails being built. The second horizon, 5-10 years, is systemic integration: tokenized assets and AI-driven portfolio management as standard features of both institutional and retail investing, and policy focused on oversight of a transformed system rather than encouragement of an emerging one. The third horizon, 20 years and beyond, is where quantum computing intersects with cryptographic security: a technological environment that current digital asset infrastructure was not designed for, and toward which the post-quantum cryptography migration is already under way. Conflating these three horizons produces confusion about both the urgency and the scale of what is happening.

Appendix B sets out a glossary of key terms used throughout this volume. The companion Key Concepts appendix in Volume 2 covers Parts Three, Four and Five.

Appendix B: Glossary

Algorithmic stablecoin

A digital currency that maintains its peg not through held reserves but through software mechanisms, typically by allowing holders to mint or burn a companion token in a way that should, in theory, create arbitrage pressure that restores the target price. The problem is that the same mechanism that is meant to stabilize the price can also accelerate a collapse when confidence fails. TerraUSD is the defining case study: the algorithm worked as designed until the moment it destroyed itself.

Atomic settlement

The simultaneous exchange of an asset and its payment in a single, inseparable transaction; either both sides complete, or neither does. Atomic settlement eliminates the counterparty risk inherent in conventional systems where execution and payment are separated by time. On a shared blockchain ledger with smart contract execution, atomic settlement is the default; in conventional bond and equity markets, it is an aspiration that current regulatory and infrastructure reform is working toward.

Blockchain

A distributed ledger in which records are organized into cryptographically linked blocks and maintained across a network of computers. No single party controls the ledger; adding a fraudulent record requires rewriting every subsequent block simultaneously across the majority of the network, making this computationally prohibitive at scale. The immutability and transparency of blockchain records are the properties that make it useful as an infrastructure layer for tokenized assets, but they are also what makes errors, fraudulent inputs, and poor oracle data so difficult to correct after the fact.

Capital efficiency

The ratio of productive output, revenue, yield generation, transaction throughput, to the capital required to achieve it. Digital settlement infrastructure improves capital efficiency by eliminating the gap between trade execution and payment settlement, allowing capital held as pre-funding buffers in correspondent banking relationships to be redeployed productively. A corporate treasury holding excess cash for end-of-day settlement requirements reduces capital efficiency; real-time settlement allows the same cash to earn yields throughout the day. Enhanced capital efficiency is one of the primary economic drivers of institutional adoption of blockchain-based settlement.

Carbon credit

An instrument representing a verified reduction or removal of one metric tonne of carbon dioxide equivalent from the atmosphere, issued by a certified environmental project. Voluntary carbon credits are purchased by corporations to offset their own emissions. Regulatory carbon credits are issued under mandatory cap-and-trade schemes such as the EU

Emissions Trading System. Both categories suffer from verification and double-counting problems that blockchain-based token infrastructure has been designed to address.

CBDC (central bank digital currency)

Digital money issued directly by a central bank, the digital equivalent of a banknote, rather than a commercial bank deposit. A retail CBDC is available to the general public; a wholesale CBDC is restricted to financial institutions for interbank settlement. The crucial distinction is that a CBDC holder's claim is against the central bank, not a commercial institution, making it the safest form of digital money available, and the form over which governments retain the most direct control.

Clearing

The process by which financial claims are reconciled and prepared for final settlement. A clearing system sits between transactions and final payment, netting obligations across participants and guaranteeing that each party receives what they are owed regardless of whether any individual counterparty fails. The check-clearing system made bank notes universally redeemable at par because every issuing bank participated in the same infrastructure. The absence of any equivalent for stablecoins is the central infrastructure problem this book explores.

Commodity-backed stablecoin

A digital token pegged to the value of a physical asset, most commonly gold. The issuer holds the commodity in custody and issues tokens that represent a claim on a specified quantity of it. The advantage is real asset backing outside the fiat monetary system; the limitation is that commodity prices fluctuate, meaning the token is stable relative to the underlying asset, not necessarily in terms of purchasing power.

Conditional settlement

A payment model in which money transfers only when specified pre-conditions are verified and satisfied, a shipment is confirmed delivered, a milestone is achieved, a regulatory condition is met. Implemented through smart contract logic, conditional settlement compresses transaction time by automating verification steps that would otherwise require human review. Distinct from atomic settlement (which guarantees both sides complete or neither does) in that conditional settlement defines *when* completion occurs rather than simply *whether* it occurs. The programmability of conditional settlement is the mechanism that makes stablecoins and tokenized assets useful for complex multi-party transactions in supply chains and trade finance.

Correspondent banking

The system through which banks in different countries hold accounts at one another to facilitate cross-border payments. A transfer from Lagos to Seoul might pass through four or five correspondent banking relationships before it arrives, each adding fees, delay, and opacity. McKinsey estimated the average cost of an international remittance at 6.25 percent of the amount sent. The correspondent banking model has not been fundamentally redesigned since the 1970s, and much of the case for digital money rests on the scale of the inefficiency that accumulated during those fifty years.

Crypto-backed stablecoin

A stablecoin collateralized by other cryptocurrencies rather than fiat currency. Because cryptocurrency prices are volatile, these coins are typically over-collateralized, issuing $100 in tokens might require $150 in crypto deposited as collateral, to absorb price movements without breaking the peg. The risk is that a sufficiently sharp drop in collateral value triggers forced liquidations that outpace the over-collateralization buffer, breaking the peg despite the architecture designed to prevent it.

Cryptographic guarantee

A security property enforced by mathematics rather than by institutional trust. In Bitcoin, the cryptographic guarantee is the proof-of-work mechanism that makes historical blocks computationally irreversible. In tokenized assets, the cryptographic guarantee is the digital signature proving ownership and the smart contract enforcement that executes settlement without human discretion. Cryptographic guarantees differ fundamentally from institutional guarantees (a bank's promise to honor your deposit) in that they are self-executing and cannot be overridden by any authority. The replacement of institutional guarantees with cryptographic guarantees is the core architectural shift that blockchain infrastructure represents.

DAO (decentralized autonomous organization)

An organization whose rules are encoded in smart contracts and enforced automatically, without conventional corporate hierarchy or management. Decision-making authority is distributed to token holders, who vote on proposals; the contract executes whatever the governance process approves. DAOs have been used to govern DeFi protocols, community energy projects, carbon credit registries, and science funding pools. Their practical limitations include the concentration of effective power among the most engaged token holders and the vulnerability of their governance contracts to exploitation.

DAT (digital asset treasury)

A corporate treasury strategy in which Bitcoin, Ethereum, or other digital assets are held as reserve assets on the balance sheet, alongside or in place of conventional cash and government securities. The approach became formalized following the FASB's ASU 2023-08 fair-value accounting standard and the GENIUS Act's stablecoin regulatory framework. Proponents argue DATs provide inflation protection and potential appreciation; critics identify systemic risk if DAT strategies proliferate and digital asset prices correlate with corporate credit quality.

DeFi (decentralized finance)

Financial services, lending, borrowing, trading, yield generation, delivered through smart contracts on public blockchains rather than through banks or regulated intermediaries. DeFi protocols operate autonomously according to their code; no human approval is required to interact with them. DeFi provided the early infrastructure for tokenized on-chain assets and remains the liquidity layer through which many tokenized instruments trade and are priced.

Diem (formerly Libra)

A digital currency project announced by Facebook in 2019, initially under the name Libra, that proposed to serve the company's two billion users with the ability to send money directly to one another across a permissioned blockchain. The reaction from central banks and regulators was immediate and alarmed: if private transactions began routing outside the central banking system, the traditional levers of monetary policy would apply to a shrinking share of the economy. Diem never launched, regulatory opposition and the withdrawal of major partners killed it, but the panic it triggered did more to accelerate central bank digital currency research programs than any academic paper or policy consultation in the preceding decade.

Digital Asset Safeguarding

The practice of securely holding digital assets on behalf of clients, providing the key management, access controls, and legal structures necessary to ensure assets are protected and can be recovered. The market was estimated at $57.77 billion in 2024. Best practice involves a three-pillar framework of technology (key management architecture), process (four-eyes controls, whitelisting, incident response), and law (the choice of custody model, trustee, bailee, or contractual, and its implications for insolvency treatment).

Digital dollarization

The adoption of the US dollar as a de facto currency in an economy through digital rather than physical means. Rather than opening a US bank account or acquiring physical dollars, residents of high-inflation economies hold USDT or USDC as a dollar proxy. The consequences for domestic monetary policy can be profound: a central bank whose citizens are effectively using a foreign digital currency has limited tools for managing money supply or credit conditions. It is, as several Latin American central bankers made clear in these pages, not a hypothetical concern.

e-CNY (digital yuan)

China's central bank digital currency, issued by the People's Bank of China. Unlike most CBDC projects, which remained in pilot or design phases through 2025, the e-CNY was already in live use across dozens of Chinese cities, deployed through major state-owned banks and digital wallets. Domestically it gave the People's Bank direct visibility into transactions and a mechanism to implement monetary policy without commercial bank intermediation. Internationally, China deployed equivalent bilateral digital currency infrastructure through trade corridors across Africa, Southeast Asia, and Latin America, a patient infrastructure strategy aimed at creating dollar-independent settlement rails well before any Western equivalent existed.

ERC-20

A technical standard for fungible tokens on the Ethereum blockchain, specifying the rules that govern how tokens are created, transferred, and queried. Most tokenized real-world assets, stablecoins, and on-chain fund shares are built to the ERC-20 standard, which ensures they can be held in any compatible wallet and traded on any compatible exchange. ERC-721 is the equivalent standard for non-fungible tokens.

Eurodollar

US dollar-denominated deposits held in banks outside the United States, forming a vast pool of dollar liquidity that operates beyond the direct reach of Federal Reserve policy. The eurodollar market emerged in the 1950s and expanded rapidly as international trade settled in dollars. David Parsons, among others, framed the stablecoin market as the third chapter in the dollar's long story of offshore expansion: petrodollar, eurodollar, stablecoin, each a new mechanism for extending dollar reach into new corners of the global economy without requiring a depositor to use an American bank.

Fiat-backed stablecoin

A digital token pegged one-to-one to a national currency and backed by reserves of that currency, typically held as cash deposits and short-dated government securities. USDC, issued by Circle, and USDT, issued by Tether, are the two largest examples.

The issuer holds the reserves, publishes attestations, and redeems tokens at par on request. The quality of those reserves and the credibility of the attestation process are the critical variables, not all fiat-backed stablecoins are backed to the same standard.

Flowcarbon / KlimaDAO / Toucan Protocol

Three protocols that brought carbon credit tokenization to scale on public blockchains. Toucan built the bridge technology that moved legacy voluntary carbon credits onto the blockchain. KlimaDAO created a treasury of on-chain carbon credits and a token economy designed to drive demand for carbon retirements. Flowcarbon tokenizes credits directly from project developers, bypassing legacy registry infrastructure. Together they demonstrated the capability of on-chain carbon markets and exposed the limitations of bringing poorly-verified credits on-chain faster and more efficiently.

Fractional ownership

The division of an asset, a property, a bond, a fund, a work of art, into many small tokens, each representing a proportional share of the whole. Fractional tokenization lowers minimum investment thresholds, enables diversification across asset classes previously accessible only to institutional investors, and creates secondary market liquidity for assets that are otherwise illiquid. The legal and market infrastructure required to make fractional ownership fully liquid at small denominations remains in development in most jurisdictions.

Fractional reserve banking

The system under which commercial banks hold only a fraction of their deposits in reserve, lending the remainder to borrowers. This is the mechanism through which banks create credit, and through which most new money in a modern economy comes into existence. A bank that accepts £100 in deposits might lend out £90, with that £90 eventually redeposited and lent again, multiplying the original deposit through the economy. The system is efficient in normal conditions. Under stress, the fraction held in reserve is always insufficient to meet simultaneous withdrawal demands from all depositors, which is the definition of a bank run.

Free-banking era

A period in US monetary history, roughly from the 1830s to the Civil War, during which individual states permitted banks to issue their own notes backed by state bonds. There were at one point over eight thousand separate bank note issuers, and notes from distant or unfamiliar banks traded at discounts, sometimes substantial ones, reflecting doubt about the issuer's solvency. The National Banking Act of 1863 resolved the fragmentation by creating federally chartered banks and a uniform national currency. The episode is regularly cited as a cautionary parallel for what a stablecoin ecosystem without clearing standards might eventually resemble.

GENIUS Act (2025)

The Guiding and Establishing National Innovation for US Stablecoins Act, signed into US law in July 2025. The Act established the first comprehensive federal framework for stablecoin issuance, requiring one-to-one reserve backing, mandatory par redemption, and anti-money-laundering compliance. It created a dual regulatory pathway, federal and state, and permitted non-banking entities to issue stablecoins under regulatory approval. Its secondary consequence, creating a structurally captive buyer for US Treasury bills at a moment of significant fiscal pressure, was widely noted.

IAS 32 and IAS 7

Two international accounting standards with significant consequences for stablecoin adoption by corporations. IAS 32 (*Financial Instruments: Presentation*) currently requires stablecoins to be classified as financial instruments rather than cash, meaning they appear on balance sheets in a category that triggers capital treatment and audit scrutiny well beyond what ordinary working capital attracts. IAS 7 (*Statement of Cash Flows*) defines what qualifies as a "cash equivalent": liquid assets readily convertible to a known cash amount with insignificant value risk. Until stablecoins are reclassified to meet that definition, corporate treasurers face a structural barrier to treating them as working capital. Tony McLaughlin identified this accounting reclassification as one of two critical prerequisites, alongside clearing infrastructure, for institutional adoption at scale.

Institutional adoption trajectory

The measurable progression through which financial institutions engage with digital asset infrastructure, typically: curiosity (awareness and research), experimentation (pilots and limited production deployments), material allocation (significant capital deployed as standard business practice), and systematic integration (digital assets as a component of core operations rather than a special initiative). Understanding the institutional adoption trajectory distinguishes between temporary hype and structural market shift; adoption that reaches material allocation stage across multiple institutions simultaneously indicates genuine infrastructure change rather than speculative bubble. The trajectory is neither linear nor inevitable; institutions can pause, regress, or exit at any phase depending on regulatory, technical, or competitive factors.

Interchange fees

The fees collected by the issuing bank on every credit and debit card transaction and shared with the card network. In the United States, interchange fees totaled $187.2 billion in 2023. For large retailers, these fees represent a direct and unavoidable cost of accepting card payments, approximately two percent of transaction value on credit cards, extracted by a system in which Visa and Mastercard operated at profit margins of sixty-nine and fifty-six percent respectively. The structural incentive for large merchants to develop stablecoin-based payment alternatives, bypassing card networks entirely, follows directly from this arithmetic.

IP-NFT (intellectual property non-fungible token)

A non-fungible token representing ownership of, or rights over, a defined intellectual property asset, a research project, a drug candidate, a patent, a dataset. IP-NFTs allow early-stage research assets to be financed and traded directly, outside conventional pharmaceutical venture capital or corporate licensing channels. The Molecule platform is the primary infrastructure provider; the DeSci (decentralized science) movement has adopted IP-NFTs as its primary funding mechanism for research into neglected diseases and low-commercial-priority scientific questions.

kWh Energy Token

A blockchain-based instrument representing a unit of renewable energy generated within a defined community network. The kWh Energy Token model, proposed by the 2Tokens Foundation and aligned with EU Citizen Energy Community frameworks, enables households with solar installations to sell or trade their surplus production directly with neighbors, and households without rooftop access to purchase fractional shares in community solar parks. Smart contracts automate treasury management and revenue distribution.

KYC and AML

Know Your Customer (KYC) and Anti-Money Laundering (AML), the compliance obligations requiring financial institutions to verify customer identity and monitor transactions for signs of criminal activity. These obligations are one of the primary arguments for licensed, regulated stablecoin issuance over anonymous crypto transactions, and one of the primary cost drivers for financial institutions operating across multiple jurisdictions. The GENIUS Act's AML requirements were among its most debated provisions, with critics arguing they effectively limited stablecoin issuance to large regulated entities and entrenched incumbents.

Layer-1 / Layer-2

A layer-1 blockchain is a base-level network, Ethereum, Bitcoin, Solana, that processes and records transactions on its own native infrastructure. A layer-2 is a system built on top of a layer-1 to increase throughput and reduce transaction costs, bundling many transactions together before settling them on the layer-1. Most tokenized asset applications operate on layer-2 networks or purpose-built enterprise blockchains rather than directly on public layer-1 infrastructure, to manage cost and speed.

Legal wrapper

The legal entity or structure, typically a limited liability company, trust, or regulated vehicle, interposed between a blockchain token and the underlying asset it represents. Most jurisdictions do not recognize a blockchain token as a direct title instrument for physical assets; the legal wrapper is the mechanism that makes on-chain ownership enforceable in conventional courts. Every tokenized real estate, fund, or commodity product currently operating commercially uses a legal wrapper of some kind.

MiCA (Markets in Crypto-Assets)

The European Union's comprehensive regulatory framework for digital assets, adopted in 2023 and in full effect from 2024. MiCA establishes licensing requirements, reserve custody standards, and disclosure obligations for token issuers and crypto-asset service providers. Its treatment of stablecoins, requiring significant reserve holdings in EU commercial bank deposits, created regulatory pressure that influenced the issuance geography of major stablecoins. MiCA is widely regarded as the most developed digital asset regulatory framework among major economies.

Multi-party computation (MPC)

A cryptographic technique that distributes key material across multiple parties, such that no single party ever holds the complete private key. A transaction can be signed only when a defined threshold of parties co-operate. MPC is the primary technology underlying institutional digital asset custody, replacing earlier models where a single hardware security module held a complete key. MPC architecture means that the compromise of any one party does not expose the assets associated with the key.

Multi-signature wallet

A digital wallet that requires authorization from multiple private keys before any transaction can be executed. A 3-of-5 multi-signature wallet, for example, requires any three of five designated keyholders to co-sign, making unauthorized transfers from a single compromised key impossible. Multi-signature wallets are the primary mechanism for digital asset inheritance planning, designating future signatories in advance, and for institutional governance of shared treasury assets.

Narrow banking

A banking model in which one hundred percent of deposits are held in liquid, safe assets, at the central bank or in short-term government securities, and no fractional lending occurs. ClearBank operates this way. The most credible stablecoin issuers adopt a similar structure. The safety properties are compelling: a narrow bank cannot fail in the classic sense because it always holds its obligations in liquid form. The trade-off is that it cannot create credit, and its returns are limited to yield on the reserve assets. Whether a monetary system substantially reliant on narrow banking can generate the credit expansion that economies depend on for growth is a genuine open question.

NFT (non-fungible token)

A digital token that encodes uniqueness: no other token is identical to it, and this uniqueness is enforced by the blockchain's consensus mechanism. NFTs are most commonly associated with digital art and collectibles, but their structural properties, verifiable provenance, programmable ownership terms, resistance to forgery, are applicable across any context where a unique claim must be recorded. Cultural institutions, scientific bodies, and intellectual property registries have all deployed NFT infrastructure for provenance and rights management purposes.

Nostro and vostro accounts

The bilateral accounts banks hold at one another to facilitate cross-border payments. "Nostro" (Latin: ours) refers to an account a bank holds at a foreign correspondent bank; "vostro" (Latin: yours) refers to the corresponding account the foreign bank holds. Together they constitute the plumbing of correspondent banking. McKinsey estimated the capital tied up in pre-funded nostro and vostro accounts globally at several trillion dollars, money that sits locked in the mechanics of international settlement rather than being deployed productively.

Oracle

A system that feeds real-world data into a blockchain or smart contract. Because blockchains cannot independently observe events outside themselves, any smart contract that must respond to external conditions, a commodity price, a weather event, a delivery confirmation, a satellite image, requires an oracle to report that condition on-chain. The reliability of tokenized assets that depend on real-world data is ultimately constrained by the reliability of the oracles reporting it. Oracle manipulation was responsible for an estimated $400 million in losses in 2022.

Petrodollar

The informal system, established through agreements between the United States and Saudi Arabia in the 1970s, by which global oil exports are priced and settled in US dollars. This structural arrangement created persistent worldwide demand for dollars regardless of whether any country was trading directly with the United States, and it underpinned dollar hegemony through the second half of the twentieth century. The petrodollar arrangement has faced gradual erosion. David Parsons and others have framed dollar-backed stablecoins as the third chapter in the dollar's long story, petrodollar, eurodollar, stablecoin, each era a new mechanism for extending dollar reach through new infrastructure.

PIX and UPI

Instant payment systems operated by Brazil's central bank (PIX, launched 2020) and India's National Payments Corporation (UPI, launched 2016). Both achieved mass adoption rapidly: PIX reached one hundred and forty million users in its first year; UPI processed over ten billion transactions a month by 2024. Neither uses blockchain technology, both run on conventional central bank infrastructure, but both demonstrate that the technical prerequisites for instant, cheap, twenty-four-hour digital payments have existed for years. Their success is a rebuke to the argument that the existing financial system cannot move faster; it is a political and commercial argument, not a technical one, that has kept equivalent systems from being built in G7 economies.

Post-quantum cryptography

Cryptographic algorithms designed to remain secure against attacks from quantum computers. Current public-key cryptography, including the elliptic-curve algorithms that protect blockchain transaction signatures, is vulnerable to Shor's algorithm running on a sufficiently powerful quantum machine. The US National Institute of Standards and Technology published its first post-quantum cryptographic standards in 2024. Migration of blockchain infrastructure to post-quantum standards is a multi-year process that institutions managing long-duration digital assets should be planning for now.

Programmability

The capacity to embed self-executing code within money, to make payment conditional on verified events rather than dependent on human instruction. A smart contract can release funds only when a shipment is confirmed delivered, only when a milestone is achieved, only when a deadline passes. For corporate operations, this eliminates manual reconciliation and counterparty risk. For government disbursements, it enables precise targeting. For trade finance, it automates documentary processes currently handled by human review cycles. Programmability is not a feature of the existing banking system. It exists only in digital money built on programmable infrastructure from the ground up.

Proof of stake

A blockchain consensus mechanism in which validators are chosen to add new blocks in proportion to the amount of cryptocurrency they hold and "stake" as collateral. Validators who behave dishonestly lose their stake. Proof of stake replaced proof of work (energy-intensive mining) in most modern blockchain networks, including Ethereum, following its 2022 "Merge" upgrade, reducing Ethereum's energy consumption by more than 99 percent. Proof of stake also introduces validator risk for custodians, as staked assets can be "slashed" (partially destroyed) if the validator misbehaves.

Real-world asset (RWA)

An asset that exists in the physical or regulated financial world, a bond, a property, a commodity, a fund share, a receivable, that has been represented as a blockchain token. The term distinguishes tokenized traditional assets from crypto-native assets such as Bitcoin or ETH, which exist only on-chain. The RWA market reached approximately $24 billion in mid-2025, with projections from McKinsey ($2 trillion by 2030), BCG ($16 trillion by 2030), and Standard Chartered ($30 trillion by 2034) reflecting different assumptions about adoption pace.

Regulated Liability Network (RLN)

A shared ledger infrastructure in which regulated institutions, commercial banks, central banks, electronic money institutions, each represent their own liabilities as tokens on a common platform, enabling them to settle with one another atomically without requiring bilateral correspondent relationships. The UK's RLN proof-of-concept, involving Citi, JPMorgan, Visa, Swift, Mastercard, TD Bank, and others, tested whether tokenized commercial bank deposits could interoperate with tokenized central bank money in a regulated settlement environment.

Remittance

A transfer of money by a worker in one country to recipients, usually family members, in another. Global remittance flows represent hundreds of billions of dollars annually. The United Nations estimated the average cost of sending $200 internationally at approximately 6.25 percent, meaning $12.50 extracted by correspondent banking infrastructure before the money reaches the person it was sent to. Stablecoin transfers can settle the same transaction in minutes at a cost of under one percent. For the approximately one billion people whose primary connection to global capital is a monthly remittance from a family member working abroad, this cost differential is not a footnote. It is the difference between twelve dollars reaching them or not.

Security token offering (STO)

The issuance of a digital token that represents a regulated financial security, an equity, a debt instrument, a fund share, on a blockchain. Unlike an initial coin offering (ICO), an STO is conducted under the applicable securities law of the issuing jurisdiction and must comply with disclosure, licensing, and investor protection requirements. South Korea's STO regulatory framework, introduced in early 2023, became one of the most developed national frameworks for tokenized securities issuance.

Settlement finality

The point at which a transaction cannot be reversed, amended, or disputed, the moment a transaction becomes permanent in the ledger. In traditional banking, settlement finality is conditional and legally defined: a transaction is typically considered final for operational purposes after two business days, though in enforcement scenarios it may be subject to reversal through legal action. On a blockchain, settlement finality is cryptographic and irreversible: once a transaction achieves sufficient confirmation blocks, reversing it would require recomputing all subsequent block proof-of-work, which is economically prohibitive. The immutability of blockchain finality is a security advantage for the recipient (no transaction reversal risk) and a limitation for error correction (there is no "undo" mechanism).

Settlement infrastructure

The systems, protocols, and institutions through which financial transactions are confirmed and completed, the plumbing that moves money from payer to payee. Traditional settlement infrastructure includes SWIFT messaging, correspondent banking relationships, clearing houses, and central bank reserve accounts. Blockchain-based settlement infrastructure includes consensus mechanisms (proof-of-work, proof-of-stake) that confirm transactions, smart contracts that execute conditional logic, and distributed ledgers that maintain transparent account records. The shift from institutional settlement infrastructure (requiring human intermediaries and batch processing) to infrastructure that settles automatically through code represents the structural efficiency gain that blockchain proponents emphasize and the control-loss that incumbents resist.

Singleness of money

The foundational monetary principle that all forms of money within a system should be interchangeable at par, that a pound is a pound whether held as cash, as a bank deposit, or as a digital token. The principle requires enforcement, whether through sovereign backing or through clearing infrastructure that guarantees redemption at par regardless of issuer. Tony McLaughlin articulated it clearly: in a functioning clearing system, you are indifferent to who issued the instrument because the infrastructure guarantees you will receive par value. Extending that guarantee to the stablecoin ecosystem is the central infrastructure challenge of the current decade.

Smart contract

Self-executing code deployed on a blockchain that automatically performs defined actions when specified conditions are met, without requiring human intervention. Smart contracts are the enforcement layer of tokenized assets: they distribute yields, process redemptions, enforce transfer restrictions, and automate settlement. They do not replace legal frameworks, they operate within them, but they compress execution time and remove the human steps that currently create cost, delay, and counterparty risk in financial transactions.

Stablecoin

A digital token designed to maintain a stable value relative to a reference asset, most commonly the US dollar. Fiat-backed stablecoins hold reserves of the reference currency; commodity-backed stablecoins hold physical assets; crypto-backed stablecoins are over-collateralized with other digital assets. Stablecoins function as the settlement currency of tokenized markets: they are the medium through which tokenized assets are purchased and yields are distributed. The global stablecoin market grew from approximately $200 billion to $312 billion during 2024.

SWIFT

The Society for Worldwide Interbank Financial Telecommunication, the messaging network through which banks communicate payment instructions across borders. Founded in 1973 and headquartered in Belgium, SWIFT connects over eleven thousand financial institutions in more than two hundred countries. It does not itself move money; it transmits the instructions that prompt banks to debit and credit accounts in their nostro and vostro ledgers. Every correspondent banking delay, every multi-day international transfer, every layer of fee extraction described in this book routes through or alongside the SWIFT infrastructure. Its exclusion from geopolitical sanctions, as applied to Russia in 2022, demonstrated how central the network had become to the global financial system, and how significant its absence could be. Digital money built on shared ledgers makes SWIFT's messaging layer structurally redundant.

Token

A digital representation of a right, asset, or claim, recorded on a blockchain. A token can represent fractional ownership of a property, a unit of a bond, a carbon credit, a royalty stream, or a kilowatt-hour of energy. The word "token" is a technical descriptor of the instrument's form, not its content; the legal, economic, and contractual characteristics of what the token represents are determined by its specific structure and the jurisdiction in which it operates.

Tokenization

The process of representing the ownership rights to an asset as a digital record on a blockchain. Tokenization makes assets programmable (smart-contract logic can be attached), divisible (fractional ownership becomes technically trivial), transferable (settlement compresses from days to minutes), and transparent (the full history of ownership is permanently and publicly recorded). The costs of tokenization, the oracle infrastructure, the legal wrappers, the identity verification systems, determine whether the efficiency gains outweigh the complexity of implementation for any given asset class.

Tokenized deposits

Digital representations of traditional commercial bank deposits, recorded on a blockchain. Unlike stablecoins, tokenized deposits are issued by regulated commercial banks and carry the same depositor protections as a conventional account. Unlike conventional deposits, they are programmable, can settle in real time, and can interact with smart contracts. JPMorgan, Citibank, HSBC, and Société Générale had all developed tokenized deposit programs by 2025. They represent the banking sector's attempt to capture the efficiency properties of digital money while retaining the regulatory protections that give commercial bank money its special status.

Transfer agent

A regulated entity that maintains the official register of who owns a security, processes transfers when shares are bought or sold, distributes dividends, and handles corporate action events. In a tokenized securities market, blockchain infrastructure can automate many functions traditionally performed by transfer agents; several fund issuers have appointed regulated digital asset firms as their transfer agent of record, with the on-chain token register constituting the official ownership record.

Treasury bill (T-bill)

A short-term debt instrument issued by the US government, typically maturing in four weeks to one year. T-bills are considered the closest available equivalent to risk-free assets: they are backed by the full faith and credit of the United States, are highly liquid, and have traded without default for over two centuries. Their significance in this book is structural:

the GENIUS Act requires dollar stablecoins to hold reserves in T-bills or cash equivalents, which simultaneously makes those stablecoins among the safest instruments in the financial system and creates a captive buyer for US government debt at scale. When Citibank projected the stablecoin market reaching $3.7 trillion, that was also a projection of $3.7 trillion in potential T-bill demand, a number that commands policymaker attention in any fiscal environment.

Trust ceremony

A structured multi-party computation process in which participants collectively establish cryptographic parameters that will govern a blockchain or protocol, with none of the participants able to compromise the system individually. The ceremony typically splits secret key material across multiple parties in a way that requires a threshold number of them to cooperate to reconstruct it. Trust ceremonies are used in several zero-knowledge proof systems and in some blockchain initialization processes to ensure that no single entity possesses complete control over the system's security. The name reflects the formal, coordinated nature of the process, which requires careful security practices and often occurs as a public event with observers verifying that protocols are followed correctly.

Virtual power plant

An aggregation of distributed energy resources, rooftop solar installations, household batteries, electric vehicle charging points, flexible demand, coordinated through software to behave as a single, controllable power generation and storage asset. Virtual power plants can be dispatched by grid operators to manage supply-demand balance, and their participants can be compensated through energy tokens or fiat equivalent. The model depends on the same smart-contract settlement infrastructure as other tokenized asset communities.

Wallet

In the digital asset context, a wallet is software or hardware that holds the private keys associated with a blockchain address and enables the signing of transactions. A wallet does not hold assets in the way a physical wallet holds cash; it holds the credentials that control access to assets recorded on the blockchain. Custodial wallets are managed by a third party (an exchange or a custody provider) that controls the keys; non-custodial wallets give the holder direct control of their keys and direct responsibility for their security.

Wholesale CBDC versus retail CBDC

A wholesale CBDC is digital central bank money restricted to financial institutions, used for interbank settlement and high-value transactions between regulated entities. A retail CBDC is a digital equivalent of physical cash, available to the general public. The distinction matters because the risks and policy questions differ substantially. Wholesale CBDCs are largely uncontroversial; central banks already provide digital reserves to banks. Retail CBDCs raise questions about privacy, the potential for state surveillance, and financial disintermediation, concerns serious enough that many central banks have chosen to develop wholesale instruments first and defer the retail question to a later moment.

Yield-bearing stablecoin

A stablecoin that passes the interest earned on its reserves to its holders rather than retaining it as issuer revenue. Standard fiat-backed stablecoins invest their reserves in Treasury bills, earning yield, but in their ordinary form, that yield flows to the issuer. Yield-bearing variants, including tokenized money-market funds, distribute the underlying investment return to token holders directly, making the instrument behave more like a savings account than a pure payment vehicle. The regulatory classification of yield-bearing stablecoins, whether they constitute money, a security, or a novel category requiring new rules, remained contested across most major jurisdictions in 2025.

Appendix C: Sources and Notes

The analysis in this volume draws on three categories of source material: published research from institutional bodies (central banks, multilateral organizations, academic institutions, and commercial research arms); reporting and primary sources accessed and published through the Digital Bytes weekly newsletter and podcast; and primary statements from legislation, regulatory filings, and official communications. Where figures or findings are attributed in the text to a named individual or organization, the full source is identified below. Podcast conversations are cited by guest, date, and episode context where known.

Chapter 1: Why Reinvent Money?

Foundational Bitcoin and Satoshi Context

The Satoshi Nakamoto white paper, *Bitcoin: A Peer-to-Peer Electronic Cash System*, was published on 31 October 2008. It is available in its original form at bitcoin.org/bitcoin.pdf and is one of the most widely cited documents in the history of financial technology. The context of its release, coming at the height of the 2008 global financial crisis following the collapse of Lehman Brothers on 15 September 2008, is a matter of public record and widely discussed in financial history literature.

The cypherpunk tradition that preceded Bitcoin is documented in Timothy May's *Crypto Anarchist Manifesto* (1988), Wei Dai's b-money proposal (1998, weidai.com), Nick Szabo's Bit Gold proposal (1998, published on his personal site), and Adam Back's Hashcash white paper (1997, hashcash.org). All are available in publicly archived form.

Vitalik Buterin's Ethereum white paper, *Ethereum: A Next-Generation Smart Contract and decentralized Application Platform*, was published in late 2013 and is available at ethereum.org. The Ethereum network went live in July 2015.

The argument that the payments system is "electrified, not digitized" was made by Charles McManus on The Digital Bytes Podcast in 2025. McManus is co-founder of ClearBank and co-chair of Innovate Finance's Unicorn Fintech Council. The extended discussion of what digital money would mean for GDP draws on analysis McManus has published and presented in multiple forums.

The payments industry data, 3.4 trillion transactions, $1.8 quadrillion in total value, $2.4 trillion in revenue, and the projection to $3.1 trillion by 2028, comes from McKinsey & Company's Global Payments Report, 2023 and 2024 editions. The estimate that cash usage stands at 80% of 2019 levels and is declining at 4% annually is also from McKinsey's 2023 Global Payments Report.

The BIS analysis modeling a 1% increase in GDP from 10% digital money adoption over 2 years is from a

Bank for International Settlements working paper cited by McManus in the same Digital Bytes conversation.

The $290 trillion in cross-border payment flows projected by 2030 was cited by Sarah Breeden, Deputy Governor for Financial Stability at the Bank of England, in public remarks in 2024 and 2025.

The SVB collapse is a matter of public record; the Federal Reserve's post-mortem report, published in April 2023, provides the authoritative account.

The Facebook Libra announcement, its later renaming to Diem, and the project's eventual wind-down in 2022 are documented extensively in contemporaneous financial press coverage and in the Bank for International Settlements Annual Economic Report, 2019.

Chapter 2: The Rise of Stablecoins

Bridge Tilley's account of why stablecoins became the "killer app" of tokenization was given on The Digital Bytes Podcast in 2025. Tilley is Head of Market Development at Archax, the UK's first FCA-regulated digital broker, exchange and custodian.

The stablecoin market capitalization figure of $220 billion is from multiple sources including CoinGecko and DefiLlama market data, as of early 2025. Tether's USDT figure of approximately $140 billion and Circle's USDC figure of over $40 billion are from the published reserve attestations of both companies.

Visa's on-chain analytics figure of $5.4 trillion in stablecoin transaction volume for 2024 is from Visa's published stablecoin on-chain data dashboard. The estimate that stablecoins could represent up to 10% of US M2 and FX transactions globally is from Standard Chartered and Zodia Markets, *Digital Assets in the Mainstream*, joint research note, 2024.

BlackRock's BUIDL fund surpassing $1 billion in assets under management is documented in BlackRock's investor communications and widely reported in the financial press, 2024.

The USDP property-backed stablecoin project and the thesis about stablecoins as the third chapter in dollar expansion were set out by David Parsons in The Digital Bytes Podcast conversation in mid-2025. Parsons is entrepreneur-in-residence at the London Digital Exchange.

The critique of the UK's "cart before horse" position on stablecoins and the digital securities sandbox is from multiple Digital Bytes newsletters and podcast episodes throughout 2024-25.

Chapter 3: The Terra/Luna Collapse

The Terra/Luna collapse of May 2022 is extensively documented. The principal primary sources are: Do Kwon's public statements on Twitter/X throughout the collapse period; the Luna Foundation Guard's on-chain wallet activity (publicly verifiable); Terraform Labs's court filings in subsequent SEC litigation; and the SEC's complaint against Terraform Labs and Do Kwon, filed February 2023.

The Anchor Protocol 20% yield and the $17 billion in deposits at peak are from Anchor Protocol's own published statistics, 2022, and subsequent post-mortem analyses including Chainalysis's report on the collapse. The Luna Foundation Guard's $3.5 billion Bitcoin reserve and its deployment during the collapse are documented in LFG on-chain records.

The contagion effects on Three Arrows Capital, Celsius, Voyager Digital, BlockFi, and Genesis are matters of public insolvency record. Three Arrows Capital's liquidation was ordered by a BVI court, June 2022. Celsius filed for Chapter 11 bankruptcy, July 2022. Voyager Digital filed for Chapter 11 bankruptcy, July 2022.

The broader analysis of algorithmic stablecoins and the structural distinction between code-based and reserve-based stability draws on published Digital Bytes research and editorial analysis, 2022-23.

Chapter 4: Central Banks Enter the Race

The figure of 134 countries and currency unions exploring CBDCs is from the Atlantic Council CBDC Tracker, as of 2025. The tracker is maintained by the Atlantic Council's GeoEconomics center and is updated on an ongoing basis.

OMFIF's outlook figures, 81% of central banks formally exploring CBDCs, 47% expecting to launch within 5 years, are from OMFIF, *Annual Global Public Investor Survey*, 2025 edition.

McKinsey's estimate that broad digital finance adoption could increase emerging economy GDP by 6%, equivalent to $3.7 trillion and 95 million new jobs, is from McKinsey Global Institute, *Digital Finance for All*, 2016, updated in subsequent McKinsey Global Payments research.

The BIS working paper finding that a one percentage point increase in digital payments use was associated with a 0.10 percentage point increase in GDP per capita growth is from Bank for International Settlements, working paper series, cited in Digital Bytes research compilation 2024.

The FSB target of 75% of cross-border retail payments settled within 1 hour by 2027 is from the Financial Stability Board, *Roadmap for Enhancing Cross-border Payments*, 2020, with progress updates to 2023.

The World Bank average remittance cost of 6.35 percent on a $200 transfer is from the World Bank's Remittance Prices Worldwide database, Q3 2024.

The quote from Sheila M'Mbijjewe, former Deputy Governor of the Central Bank of Kenya, "Being scared of having your business model interrupted is not the way to go", was made at a public industry event and reported in Digital Bytes commentary.

China's e-CNY program data, deployment across dozens of cities, introduction to Hong Kong in 2024, is from People's Bank of China official communications and contemporaneous reporting.

The MIT Project Hamilton findings, including the conclusion that a distributed ledger operating under multiple actors was not required to achieve CBDC goals, are from Federal Reserve Bank of Boston and MIT Digital Currency Initiative, *Project Hamilton Phase*

1: A High Performance Payment Processing System Designed for Central Bank Digital Currencies, February 2022.

Umar Farooq's account of transaction volumes on JP Morgan's Onyx platform "exploding by factors of ten" is from public remarks made by Farooq at industry conferences in 2024, cited in Digital Bytes commentary.

Dr Jameel El-Iman's observations on privacy and the human dimension of digital money were made in conversation with Digital Bytes in 2025. El-Iman is an honorary senior fellow at Imperial College London.

Chapter 5: The Digital Currency Race

The GENIUS Act was signed into US law by President Trump on 18 July 2025, following Senate passage by 68 votes to 30, and House passage by 308 to 122. The full text of the Act is available via the Library of Congress.

MiCA (Markets in Crypto-Assets Regulation) was adopted by the European Parliament in April 2023 and entered full effect in December 2024. Its full text is published in the Official Journal of the European Union.

David Parsons's analysis of the GENIUS Act and its parallel with the petrodollar and eurodollar systems was published as a Digital Bytes article in June 2025, and developed in The Digital Bytes Podcast conversation.

The ECB's DLT interoperability trials, sixty-four market participants across nine countries, approximately €1.6 billion settled between May and November 2024, are documented in European Central

Bank, *Report on the DLT settlement trials*, November 2024.

The analysis that the ECB appeared to be "projecting the traditional bank run experience onto the very different context of stablecoins" is from John Orchard, Chairman of the OMFIF Digital Monetary Institute, and Katie-Ann Wilson, OMFIF analyst, published in OMFIF commentary, 2025.

Lewis McLellan's observation on the GENIUS Act as a financing mechanism for the US fiscal deficit is from remarks made to Digital Bytes and published in OMFIF Digital Monetary Institute commentary, 2025.

Imperial College Business School, *Mind the Gap: The UK's Stablecoin Regulatory Deficit*, 2025. The quoted passage, "Delay is not a passive choice, it is an active risk", is from the report's executive summary.

The MiCA leverage trap analysis, euro banks facing capital constraint from the 30% commercial deposit requirement, draws on analysis published by multiple Digital Bytes contributors and echoed in ECB and BIS research on stablecoin reserve requirements.

Tether's growth from $89 billion to $181 billion during the MiCA enforcement period, and Circle's growth from $24 billion to $76 billion, are from the reserve attestations of both companies and CoinGecko market data.

The JP Morgan and Reuters projection of $2 trillion in stablecoins by 2030 is from JP Morgan Markets research note, 2025, and Reuters reporting on the same.

CBDC Pilot Programs and Institutional Deployments

The European Investment Bank's €100 million digital bond, issued in April 2021 on the Ethereum public blockchain with BNP Paribas, Goldman Sachs, and Santander as joint bookrunners and settled using a Banque de France wholesale CBDC, is documented in the EIB's official press release and is widely cited in the tokenized debt literature as the first regulatory-grade tokenized bond issued on a public blockchain.

The Monetary Authority of Singapore's Project Guardian, a cross-border wholesale CBDC and tokenized asset settlement pilot involving DBS Bank, JPMorgan, and SBI Digital Asset Holdings, with cross-border Japanese Government Bond settlement conducted in 2023, is documented in MAS's published Project Guardian reports, 2022-24.

The BIS mBridge project, a multi-currency cross-border CBDC platform involving the central banks of China, Hong Kong, Thailand, and the United Arab Emirates, completed its minimum viable product phase in June 2024. BIS mBridge documentation is available from the BIS Innovation Hub's published project page. SWIFT's tokenized settlement trials, announced in 2024 as part of SWIFT's multi-year digital asset strategy, are documented in SWIFT's published communications and in Digital Bytes analysis of correspondent banking infrastructure transformation.

The Hong Kong Monetary Authority's HK$800 million tokenized green bond, issued in February 2023 as part of the HKMA's Green Bond program, and subsequently expanded in 2024, is documented in HKMA's official communications and has been reported in detail in the Asian financial press.

Chapter 6: Payments Transformed

The JP Morgan 2010 observation about accelerating a New York-London transfer by buying a plane ticket is from JP Morgan's internal and published commentary on cross-border payments infrastructure, cited in Digital Bytes analysis.

Cross-border B2B payments projections, $43 trillion by 2025, $56 trillion by 2030, are from McKinsey & Company, *Global Payments Report*, 2024. B2B e-commerce projections ($30.4 trillion in 2024 to $66.9 trillion by 2029) are from industry forecasts compiled in McKinsey's 2024 payments analysis.

Dan Feaheny's description of SWIFT as "a quite expensive email system, around twenty-five dollars a pop" was made on The Digital Bytes Podcast in April 2025. Feaheny is a payments entrepreneur specializing in cross-border infrastructure.

SWIFT's own published statistics, approximately 44 million messages per day, over 11,000 institutions, more than 200 countries, are from SWIFT's annual review, 2024.

The Russia SWIFT exclusion of 31 May 2022 is a matter of public record, announced jointly by EU member states and G10 partners.

Stablecoin transfer volumes of $27.6 trillion in 2024, surpassing Visa and Mastercard by 7.7 percent, are from on-chain settlement data compiled by multiple analytics providers including Chainalysis and Visa's own on-chain analytics.

Coinbase's figure of $30 trillion in stablecoin settlements in the prior year, representing three times year-on-year growth, is from Coinbase, *State of Crypto Report*, 2024.

Circle's annual report data, $18 trillion in USDC transactions, 50% year-on-year growth, wallet holders rising 45% to 3.9 million, $1 trillion settled in November 2024 alone, is from Circle, *Annual Report and Reserve Transparency*, 2024.

Standard Chartered's Zodia Markets minting $4 billion in USDC to streamline Asia-Pacific to US settlements is from Standard Chartered / Zodia Markets, published research and press communications, 2024.

Japan's Project Pax is documented in announcements from MUFG, SMBC, and Mizuho, alongside Progmat and Datachain's published technical communications, 2024-25.

JP Morgan Kinexys (formerly JPM Coin) processing over $1 billion daily is from JP Morgan's published institutional payments commentary and investor briefings, 2024.

The Minima-Mercury programmable bank account collaboration is documented in the published case studies of both companies, 2025.

McKinsey's finding that embedded B2B payments are a $2.5 trillion pool projected to grow to $6.5-7 trillion is from McKinsey, *The Embedded Finance Report*, 2024.

Chapter 7: Stablecoins vs CBDCs

The unnamed G7 central bank official's remark, "There is a wall of shit money coming our way", was made at an international monetary conference in late 2025 and reported to Digital Bytes by a source present.

John Orchard's assessment, "The world is bifurcating", was made in conversation with Digital Bytes, July 2025. Orchard is Chairman of the OMFIF Digital Monetary Institute.

The Bank of England's finding that USDC was processing the equivalent of 23 percent of UK GDP annually is from internal Bank of England analysis cited in Digital Bytes commentary, 2025.

SWIFT data on the dollar displacing the euro in global transactions is from SWIFT's currency reporting dashboard and BI analytics, 2024-25.

Ville Sointu's disclosure that twenty major eurozone banks were assessing the financial impact of a digital euro was made at an industry conference, 2025, and reported in Digital Bytes.

The OMFIF Global Public Investor Survey 2025 findings, zero central banks holding digital assets, 93% with no intention of doing so, 82% neither using DLT nor intending to, are from OMFIF, *Global Public Investor 2025*, published by the Official Monetary and Financial Institutions Forum.

Larry Hathaway's explanation of why reserve managers would not hold no-yield stablecoins is from

Franklin Templeton research and from Hathaway's remarks at OMFIF events, 2025.

Jan Kubíček's observation on gaining "hands-on experience" with Bitcoin is from remarks made at the OMFIF Global Public Investor event, 2025.

Daniela Klingebiel's assessment of legal and operational risks is from presentations at the IMF-World Bank Annual Meetings, 2025.

The share of sovereign wealth funds and public pension schemes holding or intending to hold digital assets (7% and 20% respectively) is from OMFIF, *Global Public Investor 2025.*

Tony McLaughlin's articulation of the singleness of money problem and the clearing gap is from multiple The Digital Bytes Podcast conversations, 2024-25, and from McLaughlin's published research on the stablecoin clearing infrastructure. McLaughlin is founder of Ubyx.

The Latin American central banker's comment on 100% monthly inflation is from a conference organized by Digital Bytes and OMFIF, 2025.

Chapter 8: The Regulatory Reckoning

The GENIUS Act's passage, Senate 68 to 30, House 308 to 122, and the concurrent Digital Asset Market Clarity Act and CBDC Anti-Surveillance State Act are matters of US Congressional record, July 2025.

US national debt exceeding $36 trillion, debt-to-GDP ratio above 120 percent as the highest since the Second World War, is from US Treasury published data and the Congressional Budget Office, 2025 update.

Wells Fargo's estimate that over $14 trillion in US debt would mature within three years is from Wells Fargo Investment Institute, *Government Debt and Refinancing Risk*, 2025.

Moody's downgrade of the US credit rating is a matter of public record, May 2025.

Scott Bessent's remarks on stablecoins generating $2 trillion in T-bill demand are from Senate testimony and Treasury press communications, 2025.

Citibank's projection of $3.7 trillion in stablecoin assets by 2030 is from Citi Global Insights, *Digital Dollars: Stablecoin Market Outlook*, 2025.

The BIS finding that stablecoin inflows reduce 3-month Treasury yields by 2-2.5 basis points within 10 days is from Bank for International Settlements, *Stablecoins and the Transmission of Monetary Policy*, working paper, 2024.

Kelly Kennedy's description of the GENIUS Act as "going backward in time to increase the stability of the US dollar" was made in conversation with Digital Bytes, 2025. Kennedy was at that point a third-year law student at UC Hastings, having worked on GENIUS Act implementation at Perkins Coie.

David Parsons's analysis of the National Banking Acts of 1863-64 as the historical parallel for the GENIUS Act was presented in a Digital Bytes article and podcast conversation, 2025. Parsons is co-founder of the London Digital Exchange.

Brian Moynihan's confirmation that Bank of America would "go into stablecoins if regulation were passed" is from public remarks at a financial industry conference, 2025, widely reported in the financial press.

Chapter 9: Tokenized Bank Deposits

The financial crime compliance cost figure, over $205 billion in 2023, broken down by region, is from LexisNexis Risk Solutions, *True Cost of Financial Crime Compliance*, 2023.

The account of the strategic response by banks to the stablecoin challenge draws on Digital Bytes research across 2024-25, including podcast conversations with executives from European and Asian financial institutions.

JPMorgan, Citibank, HSBC, and Société Générale's tokenized deposit programs are documented in their respective institutional communications, investor briefings, and regulatory filings, 2024-25.

ClearBank's narrow banking model, holding 100% of deposits at the Bank of England, is set out in ClearBank's published corporate communications and in Charles McManus's public statements, including The Digital Bytes Podcast, 2025.

McKinsey's finding that banks could lose up to $170 billion in global profits as AI agents began moving deposits from low-yield accounts, and the estimate of $23 trillion in deposits held at near-zero rates by systemic inertia, are from McKinsey & Company, *The Future of Banking in the Age of AI*, 2025.

Chapter 10: The Future of Money

The figures used in the synthesis, $6.3 trillion in stablecoin payments in the 12 months to February 2025, 15% of global retail cross-border payments, 21% annual growth, are from Chainalysis, *Crypto and Stablecoin Geography Report*, 2024-25, and cross-referenced against Digital Bytes data compilation.

The $187.2 billion in US interchange fees for 2023, and Visa and Mastercard's profit margins of 69% and 56% respectively, are from the Nilson Report, *Card Industry Statistics*, 2024.

Tony McLaughlin's articulation of a pluralistic stablecoin ecosystem, thousands of issuers, multiple currencies, unified by clearing standards, is from his published research and The Digital Bytes Podcast conversations, 2024-25.

The IMF-World Bank Annual Meetings reference is from Digital Bytes reporting on those meetings, 2025.

Chapter 11: Cross-Border Payments

The "missing piece" quotation from John Orchard is from OMFIF's published research, 2025. The BIS analysis of cross-border payment fragmentation and the role of stablecoins in bridging multiple currency systems draws on Bank for International Settlements working papers and Digital Bytes editorial analysis.

The estimate that blockchain infrastructure could reduce cross-border payment costs by 80 percent is from multiple institutional analyses including McKinsey Global Payments research and International

Remittances Corridor analysis conducted by the World Bank and academic researchers.

Ubyx's Tony McLaughlin's articulation of the clearing gap and the role that unified stablecoin clearing standards could play in resolving it draws on published research and The Digital Bytes Podcast conversations throughout 2024-25.

JP Morgan's Onyx platform processing over $1 billion in cross-border settlement daily is documented in JP Morgan institutional communications.

Chapter 12: Sanctions and Geopolitics

The Russia SWIFT exclusion, implemented on 31 May 2022, is documented in the joint announcement from EU member states and G10 partners and is widely cited in financial markets literature.

OFAC's approach to digital assets, including designations of specific wallets and platforms, is documented in Treasury Department published sanctions lists and enforcement actions.

The debate within the US government regarding the potential use of the US dollar's global reserve status as a strategic chokepoint, and the counterargument regarding the risks of de-dollarization, is drawn from academic literature, policy commentary from think tanks including the Council on Foreign Relations and Brookings Institution, and Digital Bytes editorial analysis.

The European Union's adoption of increasingly comprehensive sanctions regimes against Russia, including efforts to restrict access to crypto rails, is documented in Official Journal of the European Union publications and in academic and policy literature on sanctions effectiveness.

Chapter 13: Zero-Knowledge Proofs

The theoretical foundations of zero-knowledge proofs are documented in academic literature originating with Goldwasser, Micali, and Rackoff, *The Knowledge Complexity of Interactive Proof Systems*, Journal of the ACM, 1985. The evolution of ZKP applications to cryptographic systems and blockchain contexts is discussed in subsequent academic literature and in developer documentation from protocols including Polygon ID, Semaphore, and others.

The Privacy Pools proposal, allowing users to prove that their funds do not originate from sanctioned sources without revealing the full transaction history, was published by Vitalik Buterin and co-authors in September 2023 and is available as a preprint.

The tension between privacy-preserving financial technology and regulatory objectives, including the financial crimes and sanctions compliance framework, is discussed in multiple published sources including academic papers, regulatory commentary, and Digital Bytes ongoing analysis.

Chapter 14: What Is Tokenization?

The opening scene, Philipp Pieper presenting a gold NFT at a breakfast briefing as spot gold crossed $3,000 per troy ounce, is drawn from The Digital Bytes Podcast conversation with Pieper in 2025. Pieper is co-founder and co-CEO of Swarm, a regulated DeFi infrastructure provider. The $3,000 gold price milestone was widely reported in March and April 2025.

The BCG estimate that tokenized assets could reach $16 trillion by 2030 is from Boston Consulting Group and ADDX, *Relevance of On-chain Asset tokenization in "Crypto Winter"*, 2022, with subsequent updates. The McKinsey figure of $2 trillion in tokenized financial instruments by 2030 is from McKinsey & Company, *From Ripples to Waves: The Transformational Power of tokenizing Assets*, 2024.

The Netherlands Ministry of Economic Affairs analysis of the potential cost savings and systemic transformation from asset tokenization was published in 2023 and cited in Digital Bytes editorial commentary.

The statistic that 1.4 billion adults globally remain unbanked is from the World Bank Global Findex Database, 2021 and 2022 updates. The Sarafu and Circles projects are documented in their respective published technical and social impact literature. Sarafu is operated by Grassroots Economics in Kenya; Circles is an open protocol for unconditional basic income in the form of personal currencies.

The Robinhood after-hours trading figure and the structural context of the 24-hour settlement argument are from publicly documented features of Robinhood's retail trading platform. The claim that tokenized markets could enable near-instantaneous settlement on a 24/7 basis draws on multiple institutional analyses, including those from DTCC and the Bank for International Settlements.

The 2Tokens project and the kWh Energy Token concept are documented in the 2Tokens Foundation whitepaper, *The Power of the Many: How tokenization Can Drive the Energy Transition*, published by the Dutch foundation 2Tokens in collaboration with ABN AMRO, Alliander, and other partners. Erich Schnoeckel of the 2Tokens Foundation discussed the project's origins and architecture with Digital Bytes in a 2025 podcast conversation. Jonny Fry also participated in that recording as host and commentary contributor.

The oracle attack figure of $400 million in losses attributable to manipulated price feeds is an aggregate estimate derived from Chainalysis and Rekt.news incident databases, covering major oracle exploits from 2020 to 2024 including the bZx attack, Cream Finance, Mango Markets, and others. The figure is approximate and based on reported losses at the time of each incident.

The statistic that 88% of AI-driven crypto trading agents failed within their first year, with an average lifespan of 17 days, is from research on autonomous AI agent activity on blockchain networks published by blockchain analytics firms and academic researchers in 2024. The figure is cited in Digital Bytes editorial analysis, 2025.

The figure of thirty or more steps required to onboard an institutional client to a digital asset platform is a widely quoted industry estimate. It appears in Digital Bytes commentary and reflects the combined burden of KYC, AML, suitability assessments, counterparty documentation, and technical integration across multiple systems.

Chapter 15: NFTs: From Hype to Utility

The Christie's sale of Beeple's *Everydays: The First 5000 Days* on 11 March 2021 for $69.3 million is a matter of public auction record. Christie's published the result in a press release the same day. The work is now widely cited as a defining cultural moment in the history of digital art.

The Uffizi Gallery's decision to sell NFT reproductions of Renaissance masterworks, including Michelangelo's *Don Tondo*, was announced in 2021 and subsequently paused following Italian government concerns about the legal status of reproductions of works held in public collections. The reported halt is documented in Italian and international press coverage, 2021-22. The Vatican Apostolic Library's ongoing program to make its 180,000 manuscripts and archival documents accessible through digital means is documented on the Vatican Library website and in associated scholarly publications.

The Notre-Dame augmented reality network, providing donors and visitors with layered historical documentation of the cathedral's reconstruction, is an active project at the time of writing and has been reported in the French and international cultural press.

Fidelity's 2024 estate planning research, finding that fewer than one in four people hold digital asset documentation plans, is from the personal finance research series of Fidelity Investments. The Revised Uniform Fiduciary Access to Digital Assets Act (RUFADAA), which established the legal framework for executor and trustee access to digital accounts in the United States, was approved by the Uniform Law Commission in 2015 and has been adopted in various forms by the majority of US states. The UK's Property (Digital Assets etc) Bill, recognizing digital assets as a third category of personal property, was introduced in September 2024 and is documented in Hansard and parliamentary records.

The criticism of voluntary carbon credit verification bodies, specifically Verra and Gold Standard, was widely reported following investigative journalism published in The Guardian in January 2023, and subsequently in Bloomberg Green. The findings related to the percentage of verified credits that may not have represented genuine emission reductions in the Brazilian Amazon. Both organizations published formal responses.

The Braintrust, Gitcoin, and Mirror platforms are documented in their respective published materials and in academic literature on decentralized work and creator economies. The growth in the tokenized intangible asset market from $5.02 billion to $28.97 billion is from Digital Bytes research analysis, drawing on aggregated DeFi protocol data, 2023-24.

The University of California, Berkeley's tokenization of a Nobel Prize medal, raising approximately $50,000, was reported in the digital asset press in 2021 and is documented in Berkeley's own communications. The Molecule protocol and the IP-NFT structure for scientific intellectual property funding are described in Molecule's published technical documentation and in academic and practitioner literature on decentralized science (DeSci).

Chapter 16: Tokenizing Funds and Bonds

The Larry Fink quotation, that tokenization could democratize investing in the same way that ETFs had done, is drawn from BlackRock's 2025 Annual Chairman's Letter to Shareholders, published in March 2025 and available on BlackRock's investor relations website.

The analysis of capital markets inefficiency, three-day settlement cycles, manual reconciliation across multiple counterparties, and an estimated $10 billion in annual operational cost, draws on multiple published sources including DTCC operational research and McKinsey financial services analysis. The CashLink Frankfurt figure of 1.2 percent cost reduction, translating to $85 billion in system-wide savings, is from CashLink's published analysis of its tokenized bond operations on Ethereum.

The European Central Bank's first digital bond trial, involving the settlement of a central bank digital currency payment leg against a tokenized security, was announced in 2021 and documented in ECB official communications. The Banque de France wholesale CBDC trial series is documented in Banque de France annual reports and published pilot program summaries, 2021-23. Siemens's €60 million digital bond, issued in February 2023 using blockchain infrastructure, was announced in a Siemens investor relations release and reported in the financial press.

The Canton Network launch, backed by Goldman Sachs, BNP Paribas, and others in May 2023, is documented in Digital Asset's public communications and contemporaneous press coverage. The SWIFT live cross-border tokenized asset trials announced in 2025 are documented in SWIFT's published communications and described in Digital Bytes editorial coverage. HSBC Orion's tokenized bond platform and Securitize's role as a transfer agent for major institutional issuers are described in their respective published materials. The DTCC and Chainlink Smart NAV pilot, delivering net asset value data directly on-chain, is documented in joint communications from DTCC and Chainlink, 2023. Janus Henderson's Anemoy Liquid Treasury Fund, holding $11 million in tokenized US Treasury Bills, is documented in Janus Henderson and Anemoy investor communications, 2024.

The State Street 2024 Digital Assets Study, including the finding that private equity was seen as the most transformative asset class for tokenization and that private credit was expected to grow from $1.5 trillion to $3 trillion, is from State Street Corporation's published digital assets research, 2024. Hamilton Lane's entry into retail tokenized fund access via the Republic platform is documented in Hamilton Lane and Republic press releases.

The Calastone analysis, finding that tokenization could reduce the cost of running a fund by 23 percent, potentially saving the industry $135 billion globally, is from Calastone's published research on tokenized fund infrastructure. The UK funds industry figure of $11 trillion in assets under management is from the Investment Association Annual Survey, 2024. PwC's estimate of $145 trillion in globally managed assets is from PwC Asset and Wealth Management Revolution, 2022 and subsequent updates.

The "wrapper disruption" argument, that sufficiently advanced AI combined with fractional tokenization could eventually render traditional fund structures unnecessary as intermediaries, draws on analysis presented in The Digital Bytes Podcast conversation on fund tokenization in 2025. It represents an editorial synthesis of trends rather than a single published paper.

The 85.9 percent accuracy rate for AI assistants in generating fund fact sheet data is from an internal Digital Bytes evaluation exercise conducted in 2025, testing Gemini, Grok, and ChatGPT against Calastone fund data. The figure of $33 billion in tokenized funds as of mid-2025 is from aggregated reporting across rwa.xyz and Digital Bytes research. The stablecoin market capitalization of $312 billion is from CoinGecko data, mid-2025. The US Strategic Bitcoin Reserve was established by executive order in March 2025; its formation is documented in White House communications and contemporaneous press coverage.

The UK Dormant Assets Scheme has reclaimed approximately £745 million from a total identified pool of £1.35 billion. These figures are from the Dormant Assets Commission, whose most recent published report covers activity through 2024. The story of James Howells, the Newport engineer who discarded a hard drive containing 7,500 Bitcoin in 2013, is a matter of public record, reported extensively in the British and international press. Newport City Council's refusal to allow excavation of the landfill site has been confirmed in multiple council communications. Current estimates of the value of the discarded coins, based on Bitcoin's 2025 price, exceed $500 million.

Chapter 17: Real Estate on the Blockchain

The account of the British home buying process, typically twelve to sixteen weeks from offer acceptance to completion, reflects the standard experience conveyed in UK government consumer guidance and widely reported in personal finance commentary. The comparison with the speed of institutional tokenized settlement is editorial synthesis.

RealT's fractional real estate investment model, enabling investors to hold shares in US rental properties for as little as $50 with weekly rental income distributions in stablecoins, is documented in RealT's published investor materials. The secondary market limitation, relatively thin trading volumes on its own exchange, is acknowledged in RealT's communications and in independent analysis.

MUFG's participation in retail tokenized real estate products in Japan is documented in MUFG investor and strategic communications through 2023-24. The South Korean Financial Services Commission's STO guidelines, published in February 2023, are available in translation through the FSC's English-language communications and are cited in Digital Bytes research coverage. The aircraft engine SPV tokenization example from the South Korean pilot program is documented in Korean financial press coverage and Digital Bytes editorial analysis.

The Bali resort fractional ownership project using the Tokeny platform and CofundX is documented in CofundX's published investor materials and the Tokeny case study library.

The Honduras ZEDE (Zone for Employment and Economic Development) experiment with alternative legal frameworks and its relevance to blockchain-based registry projects draws on academic and policy literature on special economic zones and land rights. The Zambia farmland tokenization initiative, including GPS-linked production records and mobile-based investor access, is described in published materials from the relevant project operators and in Digital Bytes coverage. Both projects illustrate the tension between formal legal systems and tokenized title claims that remains under-resolved in international property law.

The Manhattan condominium settlement via Ethereum, a $30 million residential property, was reported in the US financial and digital asset press in 2021. The account in the text emphasizes that the technology compressed execution rather than preparation, a distinction made in Digital Bytes editorial commentary at the time.

Chapter 18: The RWA Boom

The account of the first AI-to-AI cryptocurrency transaction, cited by Coinbase CEO Brian Armstrong in August 2024, was reported widely in the technology and crypto press. Armstrong's remarks are available in contemporaneous reporting and his public social media posts.

The UK FinTech statistics, 134 tech unicorns, £7.8 trillion in assets under management by UK asset managers, and 3,200 FinTech companies employing 76,000 people, are from HM Treasury and the City of London Corporation's joint UK FinTech State of the Nation report, 2024.

Lloyds Banking Group's reduction of agricultural parametric insurance settlement time from 45 days to 45 minutes using smart contracts is documented in Lloyds's published case studies and reported in UK financial press coverage.

Visa's VTAP program, enabling banks to issue fiat-backed digital tokens on blockchain rails, was announced in October 2024 via Visa's developer communications, with BBVA identified as a pilot partner. The Mastercard Multi-Token Network trial with MTN Group, announced in June 2024, is documented in joint Mastercard-MTN communications. JPMorgan's Onyx platform and its intraday repo operations are described in JPMorgan institutional communications and financial press coverage.

Swarm's xGold product, a tokenized physical gold instrument, posted approximately 20 percent gains in the first quarter of 2025 against a backdrop of a 15 percent Bitcoin price decline. Swarm's published performance data and Philipp Pieper's public commentary form the basis of this comparison. The Agridex platform, enabling grain and soft commodity tokenization, is documented in Agridex's published materials. The stated interest of BRICS nations in a gold-backed alternative settlement currency is drawn from communiqués from the BRICS summit in Kazan, October 2024, and subsequent economic commentary.

The Fort Knox gold reserve figure, 147.3 million troy ounces valued at approximately $428 billion, is from the US Treasury's published monthly statement of assets and liabilities, as of early 2025.

Paul Taylor's observation, that once institutional investors, retail investors, fund managers, and regulators all accept the same rules, the dam breaks, was made in The Digital Bytes Podcast conversation in 2025. Taylor is chief executive of Multis, a company working with institutional clients on digital asset infrastructure.

MetaMask's published user figure of 30 million active monthly users is from ConsenSys, as reported in 2024.

The European Banking Authority survey finding that only 17% of 85 surveyed institutions were using crypto-assets, and the parallel finding that 85% of executives expected the sector to be mainstream within 5 years, are from EBA, *EBA Report on Crypto-asset Activities*, 2024.

The Ripple acquisitions, Metaco for $250 million in May 2023 and HiddenRoad for $1.25 billion, are documented in Ripple's press releases and widely reported in the financial and digital asset press. The claims about HiddenRoad clearing $3 trillion annually across 300+ institutional counterparties are from Ripple's acquisition announcement communications.

Polymarket and Kalshi prediction market growth statistics, including ICE's backing of the US event contracts industry growing from $2 billion to $8 billion and Kalshi's own valuation growth from $300 million to $5 billion, are drawn from regulatory filings, investor communications, and reporting in the financial press, 2024-25. Kalshi's claimed 62 percent share of regulated US event contracts volume is from the company's published market commentary.

The $24 billion figure for total tokenized real-world assets as of June 2025 is from rwa.xyz, which aggregates on-chain data across protocols and networks. The Standard Chartered and Synpulse projection of $30 trillion in tokenized assets by 2034 is from Standard Chartered's *The $30T Opportunity: Asset tokenization*, published with Synpulse, 2023. Adena Friedman's remarks about the structural shift that tokenization will bring to capital markets are drawn from her public statements as chief executive of Nasdaq. Chuck Mack's observation, that the industry is transitioning from "if" to "when", was made in The Digital Bytes Podcast conversation focused on institutional custody infrastructure and digital asset readiness, 2025. DTCC's settlement infrastructure currently processes approximately $3.8 quadrillion in transactions annually; this figure is from DTCC's published annual reports.

Chapter 19: Carbon Credits and Tokens

The Portal.Lak3 project, which tokenizes spring water rights in Switzerland, is documented in Portal.Lak3's published materials and cited in Digital Bytes research coverage. The 2005 World Bank blog post speculating that water would become a tradeable commodity comparable to oil is from the World Bank's open knowledge portal and was widely circulated in environmental economics commentary.

Verra and Gold Standard's verification credibility crisis, including allegations of double-counting and the finding that some credits may not have represented genuine carbon reductions, were reported in detail by The Guardian in January 2023 following analysis by researchers at the University of Cambridge. Both organizations published formal responses. The structural problem of manual verification in voluntary carbon markets is discussed in academic papers on carbon market design and in BIS working papers on sustainable finance infrastructure.

Tesla's cumulative revenue from carbon credit sales, approximately $10.7 billion from the time of its first credit sale through to 2024, is derived from Tesla's annual SEC 10-K filings, which separately disclose automotive regulatory credit revenue. The observation that this figure exceeds many of Tesla's other revenue streams and that the value flowed primarily from large automotive manufacturers purchasing credits rather than from individual EV or solar panel owners is editorial analysis drawing on The Digital Bytes Podcast commentary on the democratization potential of tokenized carbon accounting.

The Redbelly Network and its CarbonHood marketplace are documented in Redbelly's published infrastructure and partner communications. Toucan Protocol's role in bridging off-chain carbon credits on-chain, and the KlimaDAO controversy over the retirement or "fractionation" of credits, are documented in Toucan's published technical materials and in contemporaneous debate in the climate and DeFi press, 2021-22. Flowcarbon's Governing Nature Token structure and its Andreessen Horowitz-backed fundraise are documented in Flowcarbon's investor and project communications.

The futures market development for tokenized carbon, with settlement in pilot CBDC instruments, draws on published discussions from BIS innovation hub project documentation and climate finance research, with Digital Bytes editorial commentary.

The Australian and Californian pilot programs linking water usage to digital rights tradeable on public utility platforms are drawn from policy papers and pilot program summaries from the relevant national and state authorities. The Nigerian oil royalty blockchain pilot and the Mongolian mineral rights tokenization initiative are referred to in Digital Bytes research coverage and in the relevant country-level publications available through the World Bank and IFC. The discussion of Māori iwi co-governance and Canadian First Nations involvement in natural resource token design draws on published academic and policy literature on indigenous data sovereignty and resource rights.

Chapter 20: Art, Music and IP

The 3LAU tokenization of the *Ultraviolet* album in March 2021, raising $11.7 million in 24 hours via a royalty-sharing NFT auction, is documented in the artist's public communications and widely reported in music industry and digital asset press coverage at the time.

The global recorded music market figure of $28.6 billion in 2024 revenues is from the International

Federation of the Phonographic Industry (IFPI), *Global Music Report 2025.*

The Royal platform, co-founded by Justin Blau (3LAU) and JD Ross, is documented in its published investor materials and has been reported in music industry and technology press coverage. Audius, documenting approximately seven million active monthly users and direct revenue distribution to artists, is described in Audius's published platform statistics and white paper. Both platforms are cited in Digital Bytes coverage of the creator economy and music rights tokenization.

The Maecenas platform, enabling fractional ownership of fine art, and Artory, providing provenance registry services via blockchain, are documented in their respective published materials and discussed in art market and digital asset literature. The academic analysis of the art provenance problem, estimating a significant proportion of high-value works in circulation carry incomplete or challenged attribution documentation, is summarized in Art Basel and UBS's *Art Market Report*, published annually.

The IPwe platform for patent tokenization, backed by IBM, operates a registry of patent NFTs and is documented in IPwe's published communications. The Molecule protocol and IP-NFT architecture for funding early-stage scientific research are described in Molecule's technical documentation and in published DeSci (decentralized science) literature. The Berkeley Nobel medal NFT is cross-referenced here from Chapter

15; the figure of approximately $50,000 raised is from contemporaneous digital asset press coverage.

The commodification critique, that converting cultural and intellectual production into financialized instruments may produce new forms of economic gatekeeping, is presented as an editorial synthesis drawing on academic literature in cultural economics, platform economics, and the critical digital humanities.

Chapter 21: Fractional Ownership

The Dutch residential solar installation growth figure, 22 percent year-on-year expansion with approximately 42 percent of Dutch households carrying some solar capacity, is from the Dutch Central Bureau of Statistics (CBS) and the Netherlands Enterprise Agency (RVO), annual energy statistics, 2024. The 2Tokens kWh Energy Token proposal is documented in the 2Tokens Foundation whitepaper cited in Chapter 14 above.

The State Street 2024 Digital Assets Study is the source for all specific findings in this chapter attributed to State Street: the finding that one-third of institutional investors increased digital asset allocations in 2024, that 69 percent expected to raise them further, and that private equity was regarded as the most transformative tokenization target. The study was conducted among global institutional investors and published by State Street's institutional client services team.

The digital asset safeguarding market figure of $57.77 billion and the estimate that it serves 861 million users representing nearly 11.89 percent of the global population are from Digital Bytes research synthesis, drawing on aggregated custody and safeguarding provider data.

The Future of Finance UK survey finding, that 45 percent of respondents cited regulatory uncertainty and 26 percent cited poorly designed or inaccessible products as the primary barriers to digital asset adoption, giving a combined 61 percent figure for structural rather than attitudinal barriers, was discussed in The Digital Bytes Podcast conversation in 2025, drawing on published survey data from the Future of Finance research program.

The IMF warning about systemic fragility if financial infrastructure migrates to blockchain rails faster than regulatory and legal frameworks can keep pace is from multiple IMF Global Financial Stability Reports and working papers, 2022-24.

The UK Share Association's characterization of the current UK share registry system as an "honor system", meaning that share ownership records are maintained by transfer agents under a discretionary rather than legally enforced ledger model, is from published UK Share Association advocacy materials and cited in Digital Bytes legal commentary.

The £2 billion figure for losses attributable to cross-chain bridge exploits across 2022 and 2023 is an aggregate derived from Chainalysis, Rekt.news, and De.Fi audit firm data. Major incidents included Ronin

Bridge ($625 million), Wormhole ($320 million), Nomad ($190 million), and Harmony Horizon ($100 million).

The three-tier custody model, separating the technology layer (addresses and cryptographic keys), the process layer (operational controls and policies), and the legal or regulatory layer (statutory entitlement and protection), was described in The Digital Bytes Podcast conversation on digital asset safeguarding in 2025, drawing on the expertise of guests with direct custody infrastructure experience. The UK Property (Digital Assets etc) Bill as a legislative instrument addressing the legal tier of this model is cited from parliamentary records, September 2024.

Chapter 22: Laws and Regulations

The ByBit exchange hack, in which approximately $1.5 billion in Ethereum was stolen in February 2025, is the largest single theft in digital asset history at the time of writing. ByBit's public incident disclosures, on-chain forensic analysis published by ZachXBT and Chainalysis, and subsequent US Treasury and FBI attribution to North Korea's Lazarus Group form the primary sources. The hack involved social engineering of ByBit's multi-signature custody signers rather than a protocol vulnerability.

The history of major exchange failures cited in the chapter is a matter of public insolvency and criminal record: Mt. Gox filed for bankruptcy in February 2014 with approximately 850,000 Bitcoin missing; QuadrigaCX's CEO Gerald Cotten died in December

2018 taking the exchange's private keys with him (documented in court-appointed monitor EY's reports); Celsius Network filed for Chapter 11 in July 2022; FTX collapsed in November 2022 and its founder Sam Bankman-Fried was convicted of fraud in November 2023.

The UK Regulated Settlement Network proof-of-concept, involving Citi, JPMorgan, Visa, Swift, Mastercard, TD Bank, and SIFMA, is documented in the Financial Markets Law Committee's published pilot reports and in Bank of England supporting communications, 2023-24. Fnality International's $95 million funding round in November 2023, backed by Goldman Sachs and BNP Paribas among others, is documented in Fnality's investor communications. Ryan Rugg's observation, that the tokenization infrastructure build-out is taking "longer than many expected", was made in a public interview and cited in Digital Bytes editorial coverage. Rugg is Head of Digital Assets at Citi.

The BIS "Finternet" concept, a networked, tokenized global financial system, was articulated by BIS General Manager Agustín Carstens in a speech and working paper published in 2024 and described in Digital Bytes commentary.

The FASB Accounting Standards Update 2023-08 requires companies to measure crypto assets at fair value and report unrealized gains and losses through income, effective for fiscal years beginning after 15 December 2024. It is available in full from the Financial

Accounting Standards Board. The GENIUS Act, signed by President Trump on 18 July 2025, established a federal regulatory framework for US stablecoin issuers; the text is available via the Library of Congress.

BlackRock's BUIDL fund, launched in March 2024 as a tokenized money market fund on Ethereum, crossed $1 billion in assets under management within months of launch. Franklin Templeton's combined tokenized fund assets are cited as approximately $2 billion; both figures are from published investor communications and rwa.xyz data. JPMorgan's Onyx intraday repo product, which uses tokenization to allow institutional clients to unlock intraday collateral, is documented in JPMorgan institutional communications.

The UK Property (Digital Assets etc) Bill, introduced to Parliament in September 2024 and recognizing for the first time that digital assets constitute a distinct third category of property, is documented in Hansard, parliamentary committee records, and the associated Law Commission consultation paper, *Digital Assets: Final Report*, 2023. The UK Economic Crime and Corporate Transparency Act 2023, providing new powers to freeze and recover crypto assets, is available from legislation.gov.uk.

Ripple's acquisition of Metaco for $250 million, announced in May 2023, and the acquisition of HiddenRoad for $1.25 billion are documented in Ripple's press releases. Sagar Shah, cited in the chapter as describing Ripple's institutional ambition, is Head of

Digital Assets at Ripple; his remarks are drawn from The Digital Bytes Podcast conversation in 2025.

Elliott Hentoff's observation, that what the market is currently working through is not a crisis but an evolution, was made in The Digital Bytes Podcast conversation in 2025. Hentoff leads State Street's digital assets and fintech strategic partnerships.

Chainalysis and TRM Labs are cited as the leading blockchain forensics providers used by major exchanges and law enforcement. Both companies publish annual crime reports and have been cited in prosecutorial documents in major crypto enforcement cases.

Chapter 23: The Tokenized World

The BlackRock video circulated in late 2024 and early 2025, in which Larry Fink explained tokenization in consumer-facing terms to a mass audience, is available via BlackRock's public channels and was discussed in Digital Bytes commentary as evidence that tokenization had moved from specialist infrastructure debate into mainstream financial messaging. Fink's broader argument, that the future lies in tokenizing every financial asset, is also set out in his public shareholder letters and interviews from the same period.

Google's announcement of the Willow quantum computing chip in December 2024, and the associated benchmark comparison to classical supercomputers, is documented in Google's published technical material and the accompanying academic literature. NIST's first post-quantum cryptographic standards, FIPS 203, 204, and 205, were published in August 2024 and provide the institutional baseline for the chapter's discussion of migration risk. The "store now, decrypt later" threat model is addressed in guidance from NIST, the NSA, and GCHQ.

HSBC's quantum-safe tokenized gold trial with Quantinuum is documented in the public communications of both firms and is cited in the chapter as an example of institutional preparation for long-horizon cryptographic risk. The three-horizon framework that closes the chapter, near-term, medium-term, and long-term, is an editorial synthesis based on the institutional forecasts cited throughout this volume, including McKinsey's 2030 estimate, BCG's broader GDP framing, and Standard Chartered / Synpulse projections for the next decade.

Chapter 24: Tokenized Commodities

PAX Gold (PAXG), where each token represents one troy ounce of gold held in professional vault custody, is documented in Paxos's published product and attestation materials. Swarm's xGold product and Philipp Pieper's discussion of using tokenized gold as collateral in DeFi were covered in The Digital Bytes Podcast and in Swarm's published materials. The legal-title and custody model described in the chapter is based on those issuer documents and on the vaulting and audit frameworks of specialist commodity custodians including Brink's.

The World Gold Council's historical materials and reserve data underpin the chapter's account of gold's enduring role as monetary anchor and reserve asset. The central-bank accumulation figures, including China's continuing additions to gold reserves and the broader BRICS reserve shift, are drawn from World Gold Council reporting, central-bank disclosures, and contemporaneous financial press coverage in 2024-25. Public discussion of a live Fort Knox inspection in 2025 was widely reported in the international press and is cited in the chapter as evidence of gold's continued symbolic role in debates about trust and sovereignty.

The broader commodity-tokenization examples, including Sunified's energy-linked tokenization work, Agridex's agricultural infrastructure, Venezuela's failed Petro experiment, and Paul Taylor's Token X critical-minerals thesis, are drawn from company materials, policy coverage, and Digital Bytes reporting. HSBC's tokenized-gold work and its quantum-safe cryptography trial with Quantinuum are cited again here because they illustrate where serious institutional commodity tokenization is heading: auditable reserves, blockchain distribution, and future-proofed cryptographic controls.

Chapter 25: Decentralized Science

VitaDAO is the most widely cited operating example of a research DAO funding early-stage longevity science through token-holder governance. Its treasury activity, governance proposals, and funded research programs are documented in VitaDAO's on-chain records and public materials. Molecule's IP-NFT framework, which allows intellectual property and research rights to be represented as tokenized digital assets, is documented in Molecule's technical documentation and in the growing DeSci literature on alternative scientific funding structures.

AxonDAO's work at the intersection of AI, biometric data, and decentralized governance is drawn from its public materials and from Digital Bytes coverage of the convergence between AI and DeSci. The chapter's broader discussion of reproducibility, pre-registration, data access, and the failures of conventional incentive structures reflects a synthesis of DeSci commentary with mainstream academic concern about the reproducibility crisis and about the concentration of funding within established institutional networks.

The legal and governance challenges highlighted in the chapter, including the uncertain regulatory treatment of research DAOs, tokenized intellectual property, and privacy-sensitive data, are discussed across DeSci platform materials, legal commentary on DAOs and digital property, and academic writing on data governance. The argument that tokenization may reshape not only finance but also the economics of knowledge production is presented here as an editorial synthesis grounded in those sources and in the real-world projects now experimenting with decentralized research funding.

Key Institutional Sources

Ongoing research, databases, and publications from the following organizations were drawn upon throughout the volume:

Bank for International Settlements (BIS): *Annual Economic Report*; working paper series on digital money, stablecoins, and cross-border payments

McKinsey & Company: *Global Payments Report* (annual); *McKinsey Global Institute* research on digital finance

OMFIF (Official Monetary and Financial Institutions Forum): *Global Public Investor Survey* (annual); *Digital Monetary Institute* commentary

Atlantic Council GeoEconomics center: *CBDC Tracker*

World Bank: *Remittance Prices Worldwide* database (quarterly)

Financial Stability Board: *Cross-Border Payments Roadmap*

European Central Bank: *Digital Euro* project documentation and research papers

Bank of England: *Financial Stability Reports*; CBDC research publications

Chainalysis: *Crypto Geography Reports*; stablecoin settlement data

Circle Internet Financial: *Annual Transparency Reports*; USDC reserve attestations

Tether Operations Ltd: reserve attestations

Nilson Report: card industry statistics

Key Legislation

Guiding and Establishing National Innovation for US Stablecoins Act (GENIUS Act), United States, signed into law 18 July 2025

Digital Asset Market Clarity Act, United States, 2025

CBDC Anti-Surveillance State Act, United States, 2025

Markets in Crypto-Assets Regulation (MiCA), European Union, Official Journal of the European Union, 2023, full effect 2024

Executive Order on Strengthening American Leadership in Digital Financial Technology, White House, 23 January 2025

National Banking Act, United States, 1863; *National Currency Act*, 1864

UK Property (Digital Assets etc) Bill, 2024

Electronic Trade Documents Act, UK, 2023

About the Authors

James Tylee is a fintech and blockchain veteran with three decades of experience at the intersection of markets, media and code. Born in New York and living with Osteogenesis Imperfecta, he built a dual career in radio and Wall Street, learning to turn constraints into leverage while navigating both trading floors and studios. In 2007, he co-founded CyberFM, originally as an online radio network that later evolved to incorporate tokenization and attention-based rewards long before "listen to earn" emerged. A certified Bitcoin and Ethereum Professional and member of TeamBlockchain, James is known for combining trader realism with the ability to make complex financial systems understandable to a broad audience.

Jonny Fry spent over thirty years in financial markets before concluding that the most important story in finance wasn't being told properly. He co-founded a London Stock Exchange-listed asset management firm and served as CEO, before stepping away to build Digital Bytes. Dyslexic since childhood, Jonny learned early on that understanding something deeply enough to explain it clearly was its own form of discipline. Since 2018, that discipline has produced a weekly intelligence briefing on blockchain, digital assets, AI and programmable money, read by over 22,000 professionals across more than 170 countries. He was named Influencer of the Year in 2022. This book brings eight years of that work together in one place.

CONTINUE THE CONVERSATION

The future of money is evolving every day. Stay informed with the latest Digital Bytes articles, podcast episodes, and in-depth analysis on digital assets, stablecoins, CBDCs and the tokenized global economy.

SCAN TO VISIT

or visit us online at

teamblockchain.net

Join our global community of readers and listeners as we explore the systems shaping the future of financial infrastructure.

www.ingramcontent.com/pod-product-compliance
Lightning Source LLC
LaVergne TN
LVHW052112210926
848482LV00025B/547